WITHDRAWN

Chicken Soup for the Soul: NASCAR;
101 Stories of Family, Fortitude, and Fast Cars
by Jack Canfield, Mark Victor Hansen, Cathy Elliott
Foreword by Darrell Waltrip

Published by Chicken Soup for the Soul Publishing, LLC   www.chickensoup.com

The publisher gratefully acknowledges the many publishers and individuals who
granted Chicken Soup for the Soul permission to reprint the cited material.

Cover photo courtesy of Getty Images/ Jon Feingersh, The Image Bank. Cover illustration
courtesy of iStockPhoto.com/SilkenOne. Interior illustrations courtesy of iStockPhoto.com/
© Jake Hope (captain secret), and /© ryan burke (ULTRA_GENERIC)

Cover and Interior Design & Layout by Pneuma Books, LLC
For more info on Pneuma Books, visit www.pneumabooks.com

Distributed to the booktrade by Simon & Schuster. SAN: 200-2442

Publisher's Cataloging-in-Publication Data
(Prepared by The Donohue Group)

Chicken soup for the soul : NASCAR : 101 stories of family , fortitude, and fast
  cars / [compiled by] Jack Canfield, Mark Victor Hansen [and] Cathy Elliott ;
  foreword by Darrell Waltrip.

    p. ; cm.

  ISBN: 978-1-935096-44-3

1. NASCAR (Association)--Literary collections. 2. NASCAR (Association)--
Anecdotes. 3. Stock car drivers--Literary collections. 4. Stock car drivers--
Anecdotes. 5. Stock car racing--Literary collections. 6. Stock car racing--United
States--Anecdotes. I. Canfield, Jack, 1944- II. Hansen, Mark Victor. III. Elliott,
Cathy (Cathy M.) IV. Waltrip, Darrell, 1960- V. Title: NASCAR

PN6071.R24 C45 2009
810.80921/79672   2009942319

PRINTED IN THE UNITED STATES OF AMERICA
on acid∞free paper
17 16 15 14 13 12 11 10   01 02 03 04 05 06 07 08

101 Stories of Family, Fortitude,
and Fast Cars

Jack Canfield
Mark Victor Hansen
Cathy Elliott

Foreword by
Darrell Waltrip

Chicken Soup for the Soul Publishing, LLC
Cos Cob, CT

Contents

❶
~Lessons Learned~

❷
~Dale~

❸

~Behind, and Beyond, the Wheel~

❹

~Never Give Up~

❺

~Romance and Other Random Acts of Racing~

❻
~Behind the Billboards~

❼
~The Secrets to Success~

❽
~Heroes, Everyday and Otherwise~

❾

~The Business of Speed~

❿

~The Best Medicine~

⓫
~On (and Off) Track~

⓬
~All in the Family~

Foreword

As I look through this book and I look at all the people who have contributed to it—whether it's our current champion Jimmie Johnson or former champions like Tony Stewart, or even my brother Michael—one thing pops out at me all the way through these stories. Someone, somehow, somewhere, had an impact on all these people's lives. Someone did something kind, someone said something encouraging, or someone just walked up and just gave them a hug.

It's obvious to me that in all of our lives, there are people like that. There have been people like that in my own life, who have impacted me in a positive kind of way.

The first one was Max Helton. Max was the founding father of the Motor Racing Outreach ministry, along with me and my wife Stevie, Lake Speed and his wife Rice, and Bobby and Kim Hillin.

Max was such a great encouragement to me because of his faithfulness. That's the other thing you see as you read through these stories—how committed all these people are. They all have goals, and all they're looking for in most cases is someone to pat them on the back and tell them they're doing a good job.

In my life, that person was Max Helton.

One of the best things Max ever told me was, "D.W., good guys go to hell." That has stuck with me ever since, because in my life, up until I was saved, I thought I was a good guy. I never did anything bad; I never did anything wrong. But Max made it perfectly clear to me that good guys go to hell if they don't have that personal relationship with Jesus Christ. That saved my soul. It saved my life.

That was what Max did for me. And he didn't do it just for me; he did it for everybody. He was just that kind of guy.

Another person in my life that was a game-changer was Bill France, Jr.

Bill Jr. was a hard man, and on several occasions I witnessed to him about his salvation. Bill wasn't interested. He didn't want to hear it.

One time he said to me—and these are his words—"Let me get this straight. As long as I make my deal before they put me in the box, I'm gonna go to the same place you do, right?"

And I said, "Bill, that's exactly right, but here's the downside of that. If you wait until then, you'll never get the benefits of your salvation."

I think that impacted him. And I know, because I talked to his wife Betty Jane and some of the other people who were around him, that he gave his life to the Lord before he passed away. So that was always encouraging to me.

In fact, one of the sweetest moments of my entire career was at the NASCAR awards banquet in 2000, when Bill France gave me the Award of Excellence, the Lifetime Achievement Award. He was sitting down in the front, right in front of the stage at the Waldorf Astoria in New York. He was in a wheelchair; he had just gotten out of the hospital.

I can still see him sitting there, looking up at me. I could tell he was hurting, but he wanted to be there to see me get that award. Of all the awards I have ever gotten, of all the things I have ever accomplished, that was the greatest moment for me. You know, we had been adversaries since 1972. We started our careers at the same time, and we had bumped heads on many occasions. To see him make the effort to get there that night really impacted my heart.

Dale Earnhardt was another special person to me. People ask me all the time about Dale and whether he was a Christian. My wife in particular knows about this, because Stevie used to put Scriptures in his car every Sunday from 1994 until the day he died in 2001. Those Scriptures didn't save him, but Stevie also witnessed to Dale personally on many occasions.

My wife is a godly woman. She knows that he was saved, and she knows Dale Earnhardt went to Heaven.

Those are three of the people in my life who had a tremendous impact on me.

And I believe the people who read the stories shared in this book will be impacted in some way, too.

~Darrell Waltrip

Holding Court—
At an Early Age

I guess we can laugh now about my "infamous" impromptu press conference at Atlanta Motor Speedway in 1978. But back then, let me tell you, as far as my father Bill France, Jr. was concerned, it was no laughing matter.

Like most fathers and sons, we didn't always see eye-to-eye on things. But in this instance, a disagreement turned into a bit of a public spectacle, with the media even getting involved.

This happened at the 1978 Dixie 500. The race had been over for a good while and NASCAR officials still were uncertain about who they were going to proclaim the winner. Conflicting announcements had been made, first saying Richard Petty had won, then Donnie Allison, then Petty again. So here it was, getting dark and we still hadn't decided, once and for all, the winner, but it looked like the scorers and my father were leaning toward Petty.

Well, I knew why we were having such a hard time figuring it out. I watched the race from the scoring stand and saw a scorer miss out scoring a completed Allison lap. She missed it for two reasons: Allison passed the start-finish line on pit road that lap, and also, the scorer was too busy cheering for Richard Petty at the time.

Being the very mature and worldly age of 16, when I came down from the scoring stand and ran into a bunch of sportswriters who recognized me, I gave them the scoop.

Bad idea, as it turned out.

My mom, Betty Jane, and my sister Lesa were also at the track. In fact, my sister saw me talking to this herd of reporters. She went running to find my mom. Their exchange went something like this:

Lesa: "Brian's holding a press conference in the garage."

Betty Jane: "How can that be? They don't even know him."

Lesa: "They do now."

Well, the way it ended up, Allison was indeed the winner. That scorer's error was the problem all along.

My mom loves to tell that story but I have to admit I don't love hearing it. My dad was mad to say the least but I guess he couldn't say too much to me because I did have it right.

The footnote to this is that while my dad was mad, my grandfather, Big Bill France, thought the whole thing was great. He was always looking for publicity any way he could get it.

But looking back, I would've rather done without that publicity. A 16-year-old does not need to be holding press conferences.

~Brian France

NASCAR

Lessons
Learned

Kicking the Bike

For me, racing was something I started doing with my family when I was really young. It was a lifestyle thing. We would camp out at the race track. My dad would work on the track, and my mom would run the snack bar and help the other families with their kids. We all just had a great time growing up at the track.

My dad never pushed me to race. Of course, he wanted me to go out and do my best, but if my best was something other than winning, that was OK. He just wanted me to be out there giving it my all, applying myself, and most of all, having fun.

I was racing motorcycles in California, where I grew up, and the time was approaching for me to move up to the next class. In motorcycle racing, they group you by age, because the development level between, say, a 10-year-old and a 15-year-old is so different.

I was 8 years old. My ninth birthday was coming up, which meant I would be moving up into the 9-to-11-year-old group. I had started to become more competitive, to the point where I was riding a larger motorcycle than my age bracket. I was trying to get used to the larger bike that came with that older bracket.

One problem with that was the bike was much bigger than me and I couldn't pick it up if I fell over. But that didn't stop me from trying.

So I was out there competing in the race, and went into a turn and fell over, and sure enough, I couldn't pick the bike up.

We didn't have cell phones back then, so my dad got into the habit of always carrying a whistle. He was sitting there in the trees just kind of watching the race go on and watching me try to address this problem of picking the bike up. At this point the bike was laying on the ground and I couldn't lift it up, and I got really frustrated.

So I made a decision. I decided to kick the bike.

That's when I heard the whistle. My first thought was, "Uh oh." And I heard my dad say to me, "That bike didn't do anything to you, son. Don't kick it."

I think a lot of parents push their kids a little too hard. They might be trying to live out their own dreams, or maybe they want so badly to see their kids succeed that they take all the enjoyment out of it and it just turns into work.

I was so fortunate that my parents just wanted all of us to be safe and have fun. If I wanted to race, that was fine with them as long as I remembered that was what I was there to do, and I needed to take it seriously. It wasn't about winning or losing. It was about attitude.

Thanks to them, I have always really enjoyed racing for all the right reasons. It's what I love to do and I've always found a way to enjoy it.

It's amazing to me at times that it's turned into a job. It wasn't always this wonderful experience that it is now. There were a lot of trying times, and times when I didn't necessarily produce and I thought my job was going to go away.

Then there were times when I was producing, but didn't have the funding to move on to the next level or run the next season. But fortunately, stuff came through. So it hasn't been this blissful experience with everything going just right all the time.

I didn't finish that motorcycle race. I pushed the bike back to the little pit area they had at the track, and I wasn't allowed to ride the rest of that day because I had to sort out these issues with my dad, things that have become a very big deal throughout my career, like not conducting myself in that manner, and being a better sportsman.

It's weird how sometimes the smallest things that happen to you as a kid turn out to be the big things that can stick with you for life.

We all have those days when we get frustrated and just feel like kicking the bike.

But through it all, those early lessons and my love for this sport have kept me coming back, and it has given me so much in return.

~Jimmie Johnson

Father Knows Best

There's an old adage that is sometimes used to describe a father and his son—the apple doesn't fall far from the tree. In the case of my dad, Nelson Stewart and me, the tear-off doesn't fall far from the helmet.

I've turned out to be a lot like my dad, who raced late model stock cars across Northern Indiana in his 20s. He was tenacious, tough, determined, and above all, focused. But at the age of 44, Dad's focus changed. He sold his SCCA D Production car in favor of a go-kart for his 7-year-old son.

In addition to the go-kart, my dad gave me all of the traits that separate a good driver from a good racer. He never let me settle for second. He didn't like it when we ran second, and he knew that I didn't like it when we ran second. If he saw that I wasn't giving 100 percent, then he was on me pretty hard about it. He pushed me to be better.

He never pressured me to be the best race car driver in the world, but he did want me to be the best race car driver that I could be. He never compared me to anybody else. He expected that what I could do was what I could do. He never said that because this guy over here could do something, that I should be able to do it, too. He pushed me hard, but he was fair about it. That's probably why you see so much fire in me today, because he always wanted me to be the best that I could be.

My hometown is Columbus, Indiana, but I was living in

Rushville when I won the United States Auto Club (USAC) Triple Crown in 1995, taking the national Midget, Sprint and Silver Crown titles. That's when the 'Rushville Rocket' moniker was born. But Nelson's status as Dad trumps everybody who lays claim to me, with the exception, of course, being my mom, Pam Boas.

Both my parents supported me while I raced in the Indy Racing League in 1996, and when I won the IRL championship a year later. That paved my way into NASCAR country with Joe Gibbs Racing, where I enjoyed a lot of success before moving on to become a driver/owner in 2009 with Stewart-Haas Racing, the team I co-own with Oxnard, California-based Haas Automation.

Through it all, my dad has been there. He says that at the time when I won my first Brickyard 400 at Indianapolis Motor Speedway in 2005, he thought it had to be the biggest thing we have ever been involved with or ever seen. But when I won my first race as an owner/driver, at the Pocono Raceway in June of 2009, he said he wasn't going to put it above the first Brickyard win, but it was right up there with it.

I'm having fun now, and Dad says he likes to see me having fun. He says it's the most important thing, that with fun comes success. I love a good challenge; that's another trait I inherited from my father. And I think a big part of the reason why I have been successful is thanks to the guidance he gave me, from go-karts all the way up to the NASCAR Sprint Cup Series.

He's my dad, so obviously he's seen and done a lot of things that I haven't. He's given me some good advice over the years, but probably the best advice he ever gave me was to just remember the people who have helped me, because somewhere along the ladder you're climbing up, you're eventually going to climb back down, and you're going to meet those people again sometime.

I've watched the folks that he's dealt with in his career and in mine, and we're still friends with all the people that we've raced with in the past. We never felt like we were better than anybody else. We always kept those relationships, and we always treated those people the way they treated us. Dad told me that if you go about your business in a systematic manner, one step at a time instead of trying to make big leaps, that good things come from it. Just take your time and do it right.

I may not even have been aware of it at the time, but I think I picked up somewhere along the way that he was right, because that's the way everything has gone for me since then.

~Tony Stewart

"Son, Don't Forget to Kiss Your Race Car Goodnight"

I don't think I can remember a day when my dad hasn't been in my ear about something. He's always been advising me on my next move—in life and on the race track.

I think by now everyone has heard the story that when I was born, my dad was quite the proud papa. According to the story I've been told, he announced right then and there in the delivery room that, "We have ourselves a race car driver." I guess I was destined to be in NASCAR.

My dad, Greg Newman, had wanted to be a race car driver, but things didn't work out for him. So I guess having a son was the next best thing. Don't get me wrong—Dad didn't push me into racing or make me do it. In fact, there was a time when I was about 10 years old that he started worrying about just that. He was afraid that driving a car wasn't my dream—that it was his. So he took the racing away from me. I wasn't very happy with that decision, and I made it known. It wasn't long before Dad realized that racing was my passion.

But like I said, my dad was pretty excited to have a son that he could share his love of racing with. When I was 4½ years old, Dad bought me my first Quarter Midget and that's really where it started for us.

Back then, Dad coached me. He taught me how to drive it, and where to hit my mark in the corner of each turn. He would stick his foot out in the path of the race car, and then tell me to literally hit his foot. By repeating this time and again, Dad believed that I would be faster and sharper on the race track.

Dad worked really long hours at his auto body repair business to make money so that I could race each weekend. When he wasn't at the body shop working, he was with me at home in our garage, tinkering on the cars, getting them just right for the upcoming weekend's race. I can remember that every night before he turned off the lights in the garage, Dad would tell me: "Don't forget to kiss your race car good night."

I didn't really kiss my race car good night, although Dad will tell you I did. It was more of a figure of speech—a lesson that my dad was trying to teach me from a very early age. He was trying to teach me that if I show respect, it is returned. He wanted me to show appreciation and respect for my race car and for all the hard work that we and countless others had put into our dream.

You see, it was a dream that my whole family made sacrifices to help me achieve. My dad, my mom, my sister gave up a lot of things—time-wise and money-wise—so that I could race. Every weekend, the four of us would pack up and go to the race track. On the way, I would have to get all my homework done in the car because if the school work wasn't done, I wasn't racing.

Once we got to the track, though, the whole family pitched in. It was a team effort to get me on the track, and we had fun.

My dad has been with me every step of the way. From quarter midgets to full-size midgets to sprint cars and, now, stock cars, Dad has been my mechanic, crew chief, pit crew member and spotter. Believe me when I tell you that it hasn't always been smiling faces and high-fives. We've had our share of fights. We've given each other the silent treatment. In fact, there was even a time when I took the radio away from him because I didn't want him to talk to me during the race.

But now, I really rely on hearing that familiar voice each lap and every weekend of the NASCAR Sprint Cup Series season. Dad's been my spotter in the NASCAR Sprint Cup Series since 2006. He understands what I want to hear, and he probably knows my driving style better than I do.

We still have our moments on the radio where it's a little tense, but in the end it is worth it. We are living out our dream together. I don't think there are very many fathers and sons who can say that.

For us, there was no better moment than winning the 50th running of the Daytona 500 in 2008. When I was a kid, Dad and I had come to Daytona and sat in the grandstands. We had snuck into the garage to meet the drivers. We had talked about how one day I wanted to race at Daytona.

That evening in February 2008, I knew I had gotten a good push. I knew I was the leader coming out of Turn 4 and heading to the checkered flag. I knew I was going to win the race. But hearing my dad's voice—hearing him call me to the checkered flag—is something I will never forget. I could hear the excitement. I could hear him get choked up. I could hear his teardrops falling on the radio microphone. And when he got to Victory Lane, he about knocked me over, he gave me such a big hug.

That moment is why he had told me to kiss the race car goodnight so many times. That was our dream, come true.

~Ryan Newman

Lessons from the Raceway Grill

The 2001 spring race in Darlington was bound to be a painful one. Just a few weeks earlier, NASCAR's favorite son, Dale Earnhardt, had exited this world in spectacular, stunning fashion when his fast car hit a wall, dispatching the No. 3 driver to his heavenly reward.

Never had the world of racing faced such a void. Never had there been so many bleeding NASCAR hearts.

I was a rookie features writer at the time for the region's local daily paper, the *Morning News*, based in neighboring Florence, S.C. Though I'd lived in the area for nearly two decades, I had never gotten up close and personal with the race track known as "The Lady in Black."

At the time, there were two races annually, one in March and one on Labor Day weekend. Before I took that newspaper job, I would strategically plan to vacation out of town to avoid the crowds and all that racing camaraderie. Why, I couldn't even go out to dinner during race weekend because fans would fill the local eateries hoping to get a table near, or at least a peek at, some of those slick race car drivers as they tried to throw back some grub and sign autographs all at the same time.

I was far too refined to be impressed by, or interested in, anything NASCAR. I cared nothing for racing news, and sniffed at what

I considered the bizarre enthusiasm of race car drivers and their die-hard fans.

Such condescension would not be brooked, however, by the editors in the newsroom. When I accepted a position as a staff writer, I didn't suspect that I was in for a rude NASCAR awakening. There was an unwritten rule in the newsroom and this was it: Everybody covers the Darlington races. Everybody writes a story. Everybody.

I was enlightened that March of 2001 when my editor instructed me to head to Darlington, pick up my track credentials, and bring back a feature story about how race fans were reacting to the death of Dale Earnhardt.

Moi? Come again?

It was no mistake. I had a race assignment and a deadline. Dread set in as I maneuvered my way through the Darlington traffic. Frankly, I had little confidence in my ability to snag a good story. For one, because I wasn't a fan, I really didn't know much about the NASCAR culture. I also felt some major trepidation about approaching strangers and asking them how they felt about the demise of their beloved NASCAR warrior.

I strolled the raceway grounds, seeking out fans who openly sported the No. 3 on their jackets, hats and T-shirts, and sometimes on their bodies in the form of tattoos. Their grief seemed genuine — some even wept — and I admit I was touched by their expressions of sorrow and loss. Still, nobody offered up any particularly special memories or anecdotes, the ingredients I badly needed to give my story a compelling, personal angle.

Frustrated, I parked myself at a table in the Raceway Grill, an unassuming diner next door to the track. Beer was being served up in frosty cola glasses, and I ordered one for myself.

I'd never been in the place before, and was surprised to see that almost everyone seemed to be eating the same thing: generous patties of hamburger steak blanketed with onions, cheese and gravy. Were those hand-cut fries on the side?

"They sure are, and they go great with the hamburger steak, which, by the way, is the best in the world," said the man at the next table.

I hadn't realized I had spoken aloud.

"You should try it," he said as he forked a triangle of smothered meat into his mouth.

I ordered a plate and thanked the man for his recommendation.

"So, who are you rooting for in the race?" he asked.

"Oh, no one, not me," I laughed. "I'm not much on NASCAR."

He paused, his fork hovering in mid-air.

"Well, what are you doing here?" he asked, clearly puzzled.

I let it fly, describing my assignment and the resentment I was feeling about having to be at the track. I unabashedly confessed to my NASCAR ignorance, and my minor interest in the whole Dale Earnhardt tragedy.

"Don't get me wrong," I quantified. "It's a sad tale, but, honestly, I just don't get why everybody is so crazy for race car drivers and this whole racing thing."

He nodded, holding my eye as he slid a few spears of fried potatoes into his mouth.

"I mean, this whole Earnhardt thing—I'm never going to get a decent story," I continued, the beer opening wide the floodgates of my exasperation. "The fans loved him, but I can't find a soul among them who actually knew him. So I've got to settle for a mediocre story, and I hate mediocrity."

Again, he just nodded.

"So, why are you here?" I asked, remembering my manners.

"Well, I like racing. In fact, I used to race some back in the '70s," he said. "But don't be so hard on us fans. We're actually pretty nice people. I'll bet you end up with a really good story by day's end."

"That'll be a miracle," I sighed. "But, hey—why did you quit racing?"

"Because I found a better driver," the man said slowly, cutting another piece of meat. "His name was Dale Earnhardt."

Did I see a joke in his eyes? Maybe. Still, I wasn't taking any chances. I reached down into my purse for my notepad.

Just then, a man and woman in twin Earnhardt jackets approached, interrupting what was potentially a prize interview.

"What do you say to driving the No. 3 car around the track just once for the fans before Sunday's race?" they asked the man.

I snagged the waitress with one hand.

"Who is this guy?" I whispered, my eyes fixed on the scene before me.

"Why, that's Richard Childress," she said, "just one of the most famous NASCAR owners ever. He owned Earnhardt's car, you know?"

No, I didn't. But, everyone else seemed to. He had the attention of most everyone in the diner.

Mr. Childress smiled the saddest smile I'd ever seen, and told the couple he hoped to coordinate a memorial lap in Atlanta in the fall as an Earnhardt tribute.

"That is, if I can stand it," he said.

About that time, my hamburger steak arrived. It sure smelled good, but this interview opportunity smelled even better. No problem, though. Mr. Childress instructed the waitress to move my plate to his table, and we finished our lunches together. He talked NASCAR and Earnhardt. I wrote furiously, stopping to take a bite of hamburger steak whenever he reminded me to.

It wasn't long before he pointed out another fellow diner, a NASCAR driver by the name of Sterling Marlin. When it became obvious that I had no clue who he was, Mr. Marlin invited me to join him for a few minutes of NASCAR talk, eager to express his sorrow over the death of his competitor. He stopped periodically to sign the hats and programs of excited diners, even briefly leaving his half-eaten hamburger steak to run to his trailer for photos that he autographed and handed out to his fans, which now included *moi*. Yes, *moi*.

I returned to the newsroom that afternoon with a story that would be one of my career's best. My editor just kept smiling in disbelief. My co-workers congratulated me repeatedly on my scoop.

It's my tradition now to claim a seat at Raceway Grill each race weekend. I look forward to ordering up the best hamburger steak in the world and making new friends. Most are fans, some are major

NASCAR players, but all share a common attribute: They are among the most generous, friendliest people in the world.

And I'm proud to count myself among them.

~Libby Swope Wiersema

A Moment with a Legend

I like to think there are two types of events in life, memories and moments. Memories are something that years later, you think back on and say, "That was great." Moments are times when you KNOW you are doing something that is very special and impactful while it is happening.

I started working for NASCAR in February 1990. Shortly after I began working for the France family, the opportunity arose for me to meet Bill France, Sr., patriarch of the family and the man who created NASCAR.

I was sitting in my office and a co-worker mentioned that he was heading down to another NASCAR building where Bill, Sr. had an office. I knew with Bill, Sr.'s ailing health I wouldn't have many opportunities to meet the biggest man to live in this sport that we all love, so I offered to ride along.

Sitting in the car for that ride seemed to take hours even though it was just a short trip from Daytona International Speedway to his office. I was filled with excitement. All I could think about was the fact that I was about to walk into a moment. I was going to meet and shake hands with a man who was larger than life. Compare it to a baseball fan who had a once-in-a-lifetime chance to meet Babe Ruth. Bill France, Sr. was and still is NASCAR. Who he was, what he had done, knowing that I was about to meet the largest figure in the history of this sport—THIS was my moment.

As I walked toward the door to this legend's office, I was filled with emotions. I knocked on his door, was invited in and introduced myself. I could hardly believe I was standing in the presence of a legend. The conversation didn't last long, but Bill, Sr. did say one thing that stood out to me. It's something that NASCAR still lives by, and as a track promoter, I live by. He told me to never forget that "NASCAR is all about family."

When Big Bill mentioned family, he was talking about the race fans, our extended family.

That statement sank in as I walked out of his office. I knew I had just experienced a moment in my life I would never forget. When I think back on it today, I am grateful for the short time I was able to spend with Bill, Sr., because that ended up being the one and only opportunity I had to meet and speak with him.

Bill, Sr. prided himself on being family-oriented and he built his business on that premise. Remembering that NASCAR is about family reminds me of conversations that I have had with Brian France and Lesa France Kennedy about their grandfather. He taught them that our race fans are family, and we should always remember that and treat them the way we treat our own family.

As president of Richmond International Raceway, I try to live by Big Bill's words, making sure that our fans are treated like family. We pride ourselves on being family-friendly and realize that our youngest family members will grow up and one day become our biggest fans.

As I walk around on race weekends, I see fathers with their sons and mothers with their daughters, so excited about a chance to see their favorite driver. It takes me back to my first trip to a NASCAR race with my father. A huge race fan who spoke highly of his visits to Darlington Raceway, Dad invited me to join him at Dover International Speedway for the day. At the time it didn't have a real impact on my life, but many, many years later I had the proud opportunity to take my son, Scott, to Daytona International Speedway for his first-ever

NASCAR race. It was not until that day that I realized the impact that the first race with my dad had on me.

My father died long before I started working in NASCAR, but I know he'd be proud and excited about what I do for a living and the fact that his grandson loves NASCAR as much as he did.

That brief meeting with Bill France, Sr. is a moment in my life that I often think back on. Because of the statement he made to an up-and-coming young adult with dreams of being successful in the NASCAR business, I do everything I can to make sure our race fans feel just like family.

I'd like to hope he knows I heard his words and strive to make sure that my contribution to this sport continues to be all about treating our extended family of NASCAR fans just the way he would have wanted me to.

~Douglas S. Fritz

Just What I Needed

There were days when I wished I'd be refunded for having to page through Lee Spencer's NASCAR columns in my weekly edition of *The Sporting News*. Days when I wondered why stock car racing got so much attention. Days when I was more ignorant to the world than I am now.

I was young—really young, with no sense of identity, nothing outstanding to harp on, and few to look to for guidance except a handful of peers who all shared my same problem. Adults didn't know anything, and kids, well, they knew everything.

I was 14 years old and barely six months away from my freshman year of high school when I truly discovered NASCAR racing thanks to an early afternoon nap. When I fell asleep, TV still on and tuned to FOX, I had no idea I'd wake up to the 2004 Daytona 500—one of the greatest spectacles I've ever witnessed live from the couch in my family room.

We all know how it ended. Dale Earnhardt, Jr. crosses the finish line in front of drafting partner Tony Stewart, team rushes out to meet their driver on the infield grass, tearful celebration ensues. And I became the most unlikely member of Junior Nation since … well, I didn't know any others. Not Earnhardt, Jr. fans. Just NASCAR fans in general.

Being a NASCAR fan is like finding a wicked vacation spot in the middle of North Dakota. People just won't buy the validity (no offense, Dakotans). What's the point, or what could a person possibly gain from the painful task of watching cars go in circles for four hours every Sunday afternoon? Not many bought it.

So my NASCAR fandom became an anomaly rather than a trend, and that was for the best. Entering high school, I needed an influence, and a positive one. That was what NASCAR was for me, along with a consistent "yes" answer to the most-asked question from all eighth through 12th-grade students: "Got any plans this weekend?"

Friends were hard to come by and inconsistent while around, so early on, at least, I had nobody to count on except for 43 drivers, every Sunday, every week. While it wasn't a palpable goal, NASCAR gave me something to look forward to, something to work toward. In many ways, NASCAR was my drive for much of high school.

I read a lot about how people don't believe that their home sports team has truly "given back" until they deliver a championship-winning run—like how the Cubs and the Bears owe one to Chicago, or that it's been way too long since the Dukies have experienced the euphoria of winning an NCAA basketball title.

I'll never have to worry about that. Sure, I like to see a certain few take the checkers in front, but NASCAR has given me more than I ever would hope to get from a sport I've been following for only half a decade.

It's the Friday night out with a group of friends, a Saturday night party and a Sunday afternoon at the park rolled into one. While I found that being social and keeping up with school wasn't always an easy combination to master, NASCAR filled in the gaps throughout the longest season in all of sports. It always gave back when I needed some motivation, some willpower, or even just something to do.

It's not just that NASCAR was there, but through all that encircled it, I learned a lot about life. The drivers, the crews, even the guys working for profit on TV all seemed to spread a positive, uplifting message, one that fueled me through high school to the point where I became the "NASCAR guy."

I knew what was going on within the sport all the time. If someone watched the race the previous weekend, they let me know. If they hated it, they'd let me know. If there was a fantastic finish, they'd let me know they liked it, but probably wouldn't watch again the next week. That's just how it was within the confines of an all-boys' private school in Louisville, Kentucky.

That's how I liked it, as I did bring it upon myself. When my English teacher during my junior year requested a poem, mine revolved around stock car racing, as did my senior year research paper and eventually, online articles in my free time. It was so easy to write about something that I was so passionate about.

So as I grow and progress through college, I now hope NASCAR can give me a career. There's a point in time when a person sets in his head what he wants to do in life. For me, I'd be happiest sharing my appreciation for something that's given me so much, and that's writing, reporting, commentating on, whatever—so long as the subject matter is NASCAR and the field is communications.

In my short experience of covering races live at the track, I've discovered that the vibe doesn't start and stop at the presentation of these events. It's legit. NASCAR makes people happy. It gives them something every time the green flag flies. At that moment, worries turn to afterthoughts, stress is put on the back burner, and racing flies into the forefront.

If that were to be my life, I'd do whatever I could to contribute, to give back. Because I know how much NASCAR has already given to me.

~Jonathan Lintner

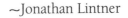

Onions 101

L ife is really a series of learning curves. Just when you think you've got something well in hand, another hand—not yours—dislodges it. One can never anticipate the next best learning moment. Often as life unfolds, lessons not planned divert every journey through time, with memorable results.

This part of my journey placed my nephew and me on a winding country road (U.S. Route 441) in rural Georgia on the way to an NHRA drag race in the Commerce area. Our next stop was NASCAR home turf in Mooresville, N.C. It was about a decade ago and we had just launched our first Internet media racing Web site. We knew to avoid the rush-hour parking lot that circles Atlanta, plus the country environment was refreshing for metropolitan Tampa, Florida, area residents. I'll get back to that point, but first let's go down the road.

The rural U.S. 441 Antebellum Trail in Georgia has few modern commercial stops, as most of the road is sparsely civilized by residential outposts in wooded turf with a handful of roadside stands. This area is Vidalia onion and pecan territory, where roadside merchants display a limited but fresh offering of the local produce.

After the race and the Mooresville stop we had plans to visit relatives in Hendersonville, N.C., so I decided to buy local Southern products on the way to share with a brother, nephews and nieces. We had traversed this same path the year before so it wasn't foreign turf, but this time we needed onions, so it was time to stop at one of the quaint stands.

We stopped at a display stand that had bags of onions hanging from makeshift roofing timbers, a roof that covered tables full of Vidalia onions in net-like bags. The onion bags had two sizes and two prices. As I studied the bags I wondered, too, about the onions—small ones in three-pound bags and large ones in five-pound bags. The price wasn't hefty for either.

A young girl, about 16 years old, sat at the stand's front as an older lady worked behind the structure, bagging onions. I pondered a bit about the produce and then asked the young girl what the difference was between the small onions and the large onions. She wasn't prepared for any inquiry and turned to her mom for an answer.

"Momma … What's the difference between the big'ns and little'ns?"

Mom wasn't swift to answer, but with a smooth Southern drawl she soon spoke in a helpful country way.

"The big'ns have been in the ground longer."

I quickly bought a bag of small onions, got in my truck and drove down the road while my nephew and I laughed for about two miles.

I've told this story many times and it almost always produces chuckles. It was only later that I wondered about the onion lady behind the stand and what she might have said to her daughter after we drove off. Something like, "These city slickers just don't understand," might have been the discussion.

It was later still in my career that I drew comparisons to that one question about onions and my work as a reporter. In time it was clear I blew that onion moment, because I wasn't specific. Was I wondering about taste, or price? Was I wondering about weight, or quantity? I didn't ask the question properly so I got a humorous and unexpected answer. This city slicker deserved that.

Don't get me wrong; I wouldn't change that moment for the world. Always as I craft questions now I suspect an onion lady is lurking, ready to give a surprise answer if I don't ask the question properly. I know I have to tweak the content of every inquiry to make sure the delivery is clear.

Our access and media credibility grew with the Internet and my chances to ask questions rose exponentially. I went from obscure motorcycle drag racing to dragsters and then open-wheel cars and stock cars, from tiny sanctions to giant NASCAR.

Many times since the onion encounter I've been privileged to ask NASCAR, IndyCar, NHRA stars and other celebrities multiple questions. As my access improved I worked harder to make my questions tough and specific. Thousands of experiences later the effort has proved productive. Sometimes my questions are even sought out by sanctioned media in press conferences.

Often my questions are unique, intense and prone to swift delivery. Sometimes they startle the drivers who expect routine journalistic inquiry. Infrequently the question is too complex and results in confusion. Occasionally I'll get very positive feedback from sanction media managers. Many times my questions invoke laughter, but not the ridiculing type. Most of the time a smile bounces back.

That's not just my observation, that's the summation of sporadic comments in an environment where verbal pats on the back are rare. At least that's my take, but what do I know?

I learned as much from an onion lady on a country road as I did in numerous writing classes.

So even when I ask a carefully crafted question of a spirited public personality like Tony Stewart who might cut me off before I can finish it, I'm ready. I'll repeat the question. I'll explain it. I'll condense it. I'll do everything but withdraw it.

I just wish I could thank the onion lady by name.

~Dwight Drum

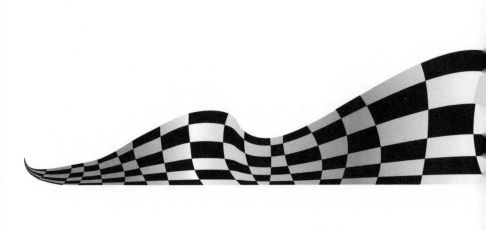

Dale

An Earnhardt Family Christmas

Like many other people, when I think of Christmas and the holiday season, I think of our families being together. Most of my family lives in North Carolina, while my wife's family lives in Virginia. So we have to divide our time and travel some, but the traveling has become more of a tradition than a hassle.

I think most of my favorite Christmas memories center on my children. It's always such fun to just sit back and watch them open their gifts from Santa Claus. I like to see their faces light up as they tear into the packages and open some things they really wanted to receive.

When the boys were growing up, they loved getting the cars, trucks, tool sets, all the things boys like to get, but it's been different having a little girl. It was a special experience when she turned two and was finally old enough to enjoy the Christmas lights, the gifts, and spending time with her cousins and other family members.

If I had to pick a couple of things that stand out in my mind as a boy growing up, it would be the time my mother, my stepfather and I would go up into the mountains in North Carolina and cut down a Christmas tree. People don't seem to do that anymore.

We would look and look and finally find our perfect tree. We would cut it down, haul it home, and let the decorating begin. There would be tinsel all over the tree, all over us, and all over the house.

Once the tree was up and decorated you would feel proud of it, and love looking at it with its lights and shiny tinsel.

After my father was back in my life, we were able to share in some great Christmas memories, as well. And I'm thankful for all of them.

Dad was an avid hunter and fisherman, and so am I. One gift he gave me was a Remington 280 rifle. I still have it and always will. Not only does it have great sentimental value, it's a great gun to hunt with. Dad and I didn't get to do a lot of big-game hunting due to time constraints, but we would go dove hunting or something and I'd always take that gun.

My oldest son was able to do a little hunting with us, too. I took him out to the farm where Dad was living and he shot his first big buck with it.

Because of that gift from Dad, I have memories not just with him alone, but with three generations together.

~Kerry Earnhardt as told to Tammy Brewington

The Neophyte
and The Intimidator

As my temperamental rental car lurched toward the outskirts of Daytona Beach, I couldn't get Dale Earnhardt out of my mind.

I had covered just two Daytona 500s, but had already earned a master's degree in Dale's Daytona Demons. His strange saga had seared its way into my psyche.

They called him "The Intimidator" because of his aggressive driving style and combative spirit, and the menacing appearance of his black car, the No. 3 GM Goodwrench Service Chevrolet Monte Carlo. But when it came to the Daytona 500, he had been more like "The Intimator." He kept hinting at victory.

None of it made any sense. He had totally dominated NASCAR, winning seven NASCAR Sprint Cup Series championships. He had won 30 races at Daytona International Speedway—nearly twice as many as anybody in history—but had gone 0-for-19 in the only one that truly mattered: the Daytona 500.

It would be like Jack Nicklaus winning 73 PGA Tour events, but never a major. Earnhardt had become a symbol of frustration, much like Greg Norman at The Masters and the Buffalo Bills in the Super Bowl.

In 1986, while leading the race, he ran out of gas with three laps left and lost to Geoffrey Bodine.

In 1990, he had the dominant car and had led for 150 laps, nearly lapping the field at one point. But on Turn 3 of the final lap, he ran over a piece of bell housing that had fallen from Bodine's car. He limped to the finish on a punctured tire while Derrike Cope — in just his third Daytona 500 — won the race. The Intimidator was so distraught that he interrupted his post-race interview with this announcement: "I have to go vomit." And even the most determined, deadline-crazed journalists parted like the Red Sea.

In 1993, Earnhardt led with two laps to go. Third-place Dale Jarrett, using a push from Bodine — notice a theme here? — slid under Jeff Gordon into second and then pulled even with Earnhardt on the final lap. After they bumped, Earnhardt's car went into a slide, allowing Jarrett to win.

In 1997, as Earnhardt and Gordon battled for second place behind Bill Elliott on Lap 189, Gordon saw an opening and slipped inside. Earnhardt's car got into the wall and was clipped by others from behind, setting off a multi-car wreck in which Earnhardt's car flipped on its roof and then back onto its wheels. As they prepared to put Earnhardt into the ambulance, he took inventory of his own body and discovered that he had the driving requisites — eyesight, along with the use of his hands and feet — and he also saw what no one else did: a car that was drivable. So he hopped in, fired up the ignition and finished the race, looking more like a U.S. Postal Service employee driving a mail truck than The Intimidator.

All of this had produced a driver who was alternately miffed, philosophical, enraged and comical.

My two favorite Earnhardt lines:

"We've won the Daytona 499 a bunch of times."

"This is the Daytona 500. I ain't supposed to win the damn thing."

But maybe 1998 would be different. Maybe this would be The Year of the Sympathetic Figure. Just three weeks earlier, John Elway had erased his own tragic-figure persona by leading the Denver Broncos past the heavily favored Green Bay Packers in Super Bowl XXXII.

Earnhardt had tried to adopt a philosophical posture during the week: *What will be, will be. My career would be complete without it.* But nobody believed it. The Intimidator's business was straight-ahead, point-A-to-point-B artistry. He was about prowling and growling, not espousing.

And on race day, he prowled relentlessly and his car growled furiously, and after passing teammate Mike Skinner on lap 140 to regain a lead he had held much of the day, it became clear that only another hideous outbreak of bad luck could deny him.

Didn't happen. On lap 199, John Andretti, Lake Speed and Jimmy Spencer tangled on the backstretch, and the caution flag came out. Earnhardt crossed the finish line out in front, with no bell housing in sight.

And then came one of the most evocative scenes in the race's history. As Earnhardt maneuvered his car to pit road and some of his crewmen wept openly, he was met by the world's longest receiving line. Nearly every member of every crew had a hand extended for Earnhardt to slap as he inched past them. They hated him when he aggressively wrecked their cars, but now they honored him in a remarkable show of appreciation.

Earnhardt finished the procession, sped into the infield grass and cut doughnuts, taking massive chunks of grass out of the painted checkered flag.

As he got out of his car, he shouted, "The Daytona 500 is ours! We won it! We won it! We won it!"

Later, he appeared in the press box high above the track and greeted the media with the countenance of a man who had purged some serious pain.

"I'm here! I'm here!" he yelled. "And I'm glad I got that damned monkey off my back!"

After I finished my stories, with darkness gathering in, I looked down and saw fans ravaging the infield for souvenirs, picking up chunks of the sod Earnhardt had torn up. Somewhere in America, someone still has a chunk in his freezer and takes it out every February, genuflecting in honor of Earnhardt's win.

As it turned out, that was the last Daytona 500 I ever covered. And it was the last Daytona 500 Earnhardt ever won.

On the final lap of the 2001 race, Earnhardt was making a move. But when his car collided with Sterling Marlin's, Earnhardt lost control and hit the outside retaining wall. It appeared to be a rather innocuous collision by NASCAR standards, but Earnhardt died of a basilar skull fracture.

As a NASCAR neophyte who didn't know the difference between a bell housing and the Liberty Bell, I hardly deserved to be there on the day Dale Earnhardt dodged his demons and finally won the Daytona 500. Sometimes you just have to take your luck and run with it.

And I'm running really fast.

~Rick Weber

A Wave and a Smile

It was January 2000 at Daytona International Speedway. I had been attending the preseason testing sessions for well over 10 years, first with my daughter who had by then grown to the point where other things interested her, and now for the first time I brought my son Jon, who was 3.

Not being a member of the motorsports media at the time, my viewing of the session, like most fans, was from the grandstands near Turn 4. I had learned a little trick, though, a couple of years before, which got me into the infield. After spending most of the morning delighting in watching my son marvel at the cars roaring by I decided it was time to move a little closer to the action.

My trick to gain access was simple. I would pay a few bucks to take the speedway's infield tour. Soon we were signed up and as the tram slowly made its way around and a recorded voice droned on, Jon seemed to be having the time of his young life.

Even at 3 years old he was already a NASCAR fan, and since I was a Dale Earnhardt fan, so was he. As the tram came up out of the tunnel and slowly lumbered past Turns 3 and 4, the familiar black No. 3 Chevy came thundering by. Jon squealed with delight and said, "There he is, Dad, there he is."

All I could do was smile.

The tram would always stop and allow everyone on board to get out, line up, and then take a picture in Victory Lane. That was my cue and as the others would be lining up I would simply disappear toward the garage area. When I was done later in the day I would come back and get in line. That day I just took Jon by the hand and off we went.

Back then there was no real security to speak of. Once you were there no one bothered you. Of course I wasn't about to take a 3-year-old into the garage area, although once he got older and I was a working member of the media he became a regular.

We went to pit road near where the cars were entering the track. They would come from the garage area, zoom past us, and head out. Jon was having a ball and I was, too, just watching him.

Four cars came out from the garage. One took off down pit road, while the other three stopped short. Jeff Gordon was first, Dale Earnhardt, Jr. was second and Dale, Sr. stopped behind them. They all shut down their engines and I heard Jon say, "There's Jeff Gordon, Dad, can I wave at him?"

I of course said, "Sure," and Jon waved as hard as a little 3-year-old can. We were close enough that I was sure the drivers could hear him and sure enough, a gloved hand appeared in front of the window net and gave a little wave. Jon laughed, and then repeated the gesture toward Earnhardt, Jr., who quickly returned it. Gordon's engine roared to life followed soon by the others. I leaned down toward Jon and I heard him shout, "There's Dale, Dad, can I wave at him too?"

I told him yes, but in my mind I was already making excuses as to why it probably wouldn't be returned. People had to earn Dale Earnhardt's respect. That's just the way he was.

From our angle I could clearly see Earnhardt's face. I could see the stone cold look and his steely eyes staring straight ahead. He revved his engine and moved forward slightly and I swear that if race cars had horns he would have been laying on it right then. Gordon began to move, followed closely by Dale, Jr.

But as Earnhardt, Sr. moved forward he stopped and did something totally unexpected. Through the gap between the window netting and the front post I saw his hand emerge and I could see his face. He looked at Jon and I could clearly see a smile break out, and he waved like only a father can at a little child. After a moment or two the car moved onto pit road, did a beautiful burnout and took off. As the smoke cleared and the noise lessened I could hear Jon squealing with delight.

We both left that day with smiles on our faces. My son has talked about that wave for years, and so have I.

That was the day I realized that no matter how big or popular Dale Earnhardt was, he was just an ordinary person and a father blessed enough to be able to do what God intended him to do.

And that one little wave and a smile can make all the difference in the world.

~Greg Engle

The Other Dale Earnhardt

My first impression of Dale Earnhardt was not exactly favorable. But, as the old adage goes, "You can't judge a book by its cover." It's a lesson I have learned with the deepest humility.

The first time I ran into "The Intimidator," I had been assigned by the *Florence Morning News* to cover the 1994 spring NASCAR Sprint Cup Series race at Darlington Raceway. I had been with the newspaper for only a couple of months, and, despite my extensive experience as a sports reporter, I had never been to a NASCAR race in my 28 years or really even given the sport much thought.

Still, I was excited over a new venture, and eager to learn what all of the hubbub surrounding NASCAR was about.

It was qualifying day for the race. After obtaining my credential and getting settled inside the track, I decided to venture into the Sprint Cup Series garage. The roar of the engines and the hustle and bustle surrounding the cars proved very intriguing. This was pretty cool.

My NASCAR familiarity was limited, and I couldn't make much of a connection between the names and the faces of the drivers and the numbers of the cars. But I knew about Dale Earnhardt. Anyone who covered sports knew of the black No. 3 Chevrolet and the man behind the mustache.

Amazingly, the first driver I came across was Earnhardt himself. "What a stroke of luck," I thought. "I'm not here 10 minutes, and I'm going to get to talk to Earnhardt and get a story for the next day's paper." So, I approached him.

One look from Earnhardt, and I knew I was in trouble. Nevertheless, I told him who I was and asked if he had a minute to talk. The answer was an abrupt, "No," and he walked away from me and into his team hauler.

Literally, I felt intimidated. No one had treated me like that professionally since Bob Knight, when I covered Indiana University basketball for *The Washington Times-Herald*. I was taken aback, to say the least. I knew nothing about the man, but was told that NASCAR drivers, compared to athletes in other sports, were very accessible. That did not jibe with what I had just experienced.

For a couple of years, I harbored a grudge against Earnhardt, but as time wore on, my perspective began to change. I investigated some things, and was told that Earnhardt didn't immediately take well to reporters with whom he wasn't familiar. It began to dawn on me that, at the time, I was some guy he had never seen before, so his reaction was natural. My feelings on the matter softened.

As I became more involved with NASCAR and found myself at the track more frequently, I made it a point to try to be in places where he held interviews, and eventually, as my face became more familiar to him, the gruffness I first experienced began to dissipate.

There were even a few instances where Earnhardt and I had brief conversations about things other than racing. He began to know my name, and I began to see the man so adored by his legions of fans. As a reporter, and as a person, you wanted this man on your side.

Soon after, something happened that would endear Dale Earnhardt to me for the rest of my life.

In 1999, I was hired by a public relations firm within the industry that handled the PR for the opening of the new NASCAR Café and Speedpark in Sevierville, Tennessee. A couple of co-workers and myself were handling the duties for the grand opening—which included a number of NASCAR drivers—so we headed up to the Smoky Mountains to do our job.

My wife Patty and I had been married for two years. With a burning desire to start a family, we had been trying to conceive a child for more than a year, and had begun fertility treatments. Nothing seemed to work. To further compound things, the night I was to be in Sevierville—2 1/2 hours away from our home in Charlotte, N.C.—happened to be our monthly "opportunity."

In the early evening, I was talking to a co-worker about the somewhat delicate subject, and feeling a bit uncomfortable. I began to sense someone slowly approaching me from behind.

I turned around to see Dale standing there. He certainly had a commanding presence.

He and my co-worker were good friends, so I figured he had come over to talk to her. Little did I know that he had been listening to our conversation, and heard my distress over the fact that I would not be able to get home that night.

What happened next shocked me beyond belief. Dale Earnhardt, one of the biggest sports icons of all time and the man whom I first disliked five years earlier, called me by my first name and offered to give me a ride with him in his helicopter back to Charlotte to make sure I would get home at a decent hour.

How many times is that going to happen in anybody's lifetime? I didn't know what to say. I was floored.

Then, I did something that, to this day, I still cannot believe. I turned Dale Earnhardt down.

I told him I could never thank him enough, but that I had a lot of work to do and couldn't leave. Twice more he asked me if I was sure about my decision; twice more I said "no," but thanked him anyway.

Who knows what could have happened on that short helicopter ride back to Charlotte? It might have changed my life forever. He and I might have formed a friendship that would have lasted until his untimely death in 2001.

I'll never know, and I'll have to live with the fact that I missed out on what could have been a defining moment in my life.

Patty and I now have two beautiful children, Rachel and Joshua, the lights of our lives.

When Dale died in 2001 at Daytona International Speedway, I grieved along with the rest of the NASCAR world. In fact, I almost quit the business, but Patty convinced me otherwise, and I'm still here.

The gamut of emotions I experienced through knowing Dale Earnhardt still amazes me. The guy I believed to be egotistical and self-serving turned out to be one of the more generous and benevolent people I've ever known. From resentment and dislike to deepest respect and admiration, Dale will always live on in my mind and heart.

And, I'll always have a great story to tell my children and grandchildren about the man they call "The Intimidator."

~Shawn A. Akers

Fatherly Advice

*T*here's no substitute for great fatherly advice.

For example, people don't intimidate me. Never have. Well, not usually. And it's all because of counsel given to me by my father, words that he probably doesn't even remember speaking.

I have been fortunate throughout my career to stand in rooms and share meals and experiences with a long list of powerful figures, from politicians to movie stars to sports legends. But no matter who or what they may be, few have rattled me, because in the back of my mind I have always heard my father's voice, echoing a little piece of advice he gave me when I was just a kid. "Relax. They're only people, just like us. They were probably up all night with a tummy ache just like you were."

However, there was one man I met during all my years of covering NASCAR that I am pretty sure never had a tummy ache because I've never been convinced he wasn't actually some sort of Greek god who chose to descend and slum with us mere mortals for a while.

I'm talking about Dale Earnhardt. The Intimidator, The Man In Black, he who could supposedly see the air and bend it to his will. He of the Pass in the Grass, the chrome horn, and a handshake more powerful than the Jaws of Life.

My relationship with Earnhardt was never warm and chummy. When I was growing up as a NASCAR fan I resented the fact that he'd unseated my favorite driver, Richard Petty, as the face of the sport.

People tend to forget this now, but there was a whole faction of Petty Blue loyalists who booed heavily when Earnhardt won his record-tying seventh championship in 1994. I was among them.

The following year I became a travelling member of the NASCAR media corps and soon developed a new problem with Earnhardt. He scared me.

Barely out of college, I was a field producer for ESPN, assigned to on-air reporters each weekend at the track to help them collect sound bites and put together feature packages for *SportsCenter* and the late, great *RPM2Night*. Most of my time was spent anonymously holding a microphone in the midst of a crowd of cameras or hiding behind my reporters, taking notes while they conducted interviews.

I wasn't out front and I didn't want to be. As a result, most of the race car drivers knew my face but very few knew my name. Looking back, I've never really been friends with the drivers. It's not that I never wanted to be; I just always felt it was my job to cover them, not hang out with them. That approach has worked extremely well for some of my colleagues over the years, but not for me. I prefer being wallpaper, gathering stories rather than being in them.

To Ironhead, that just made me a more inviting target.

He once slapped a gigantic Mac Tools decal on my back without me knowing. I walked around the garage wearing it for oh, I don't know, six hours? He would hover over me and my poor photographer as we got our equipment ready for TV interviews, shouting "Y'all should have been set up already! You're wasting my time!" as, unbeknownst to us, he winked to the people watching us scramble. He always told me that I "dressed too preppy for NASCAR," and during a test session at Charlotte he walked up and gave me the patented Earnhardt neck squeeze, smearing axle grease all over the collar and shoulders of my new Oxford shirt.

This went on for nearly four years. I guessed that he liked me because he seemed to only pick on people that he'd knew could take it. But during that time we never had a conversation that wasn't an official interview. As far as I knew he had no idea what my name was. I was just "hey boy," and that was fine by me.

But no matter how hard I tried not to show it, The Intimidator intimidated me. A lot.

Shortly after the start of the 1999 season—February 28, to be exact—my mother passed away unexpectedly from a brain aneurysm. It was the most devastating time of my life. ESPN gave me three races off to deal with my grief and be with my mourning father. They offered to let me take more time, but I chose to return to the road in late March at the Darlington Raceway, my favorite stop on the NASCAR calendar.

During the frantic action of a pre-race practice session I ducked into the restroom at the end of the raceway's old-school garage area. As I blew out of the door to return to my producing duties, Earnhardt hustled by me in the tiny hallway that led to the bathrooms. He gave me a "hey boy" and I replied with a silent "man nod" as we passed one another.

Then, for the first and only time, I heard him say my name.

"Ryan ..."

I turned on my heel to answer him, wearing with what I'm sure was a slack-jawed expression of shock. He stepped toward me and reached out with his hands, holding out his palms to assure me that this time there was no trick up his sleeve.

"You doing OK?"

My eyes instantly filled with tears, just as they had every hour of every day for nearly a month. Determined not to cry in front of The Intimidator, I chose to look to the floor as I answered.

"Not really."

"I know. I lost my daddy 25 years ago. Listen, it's never going to stop hurting, but it'll get easier to live with. I promise. You hang in there."

"Yes, sir."

He squeezed my shoulder, crouched a bit to make sure my eyes finally met his, and he winked. The Intimidator had become The Counselor.

Two years later I ran into Dale Earnhardt, Jr. in that same small hallway. Two months earlier he'd lost his father on the last lap of the

Daytona 500. I hadn't had much interaction with Junior. I figured that maybe he would recognize me from the garage, but there was no doubt in my mind that he had no idea who I was.

I called out to him as he walked by and he turned to face me with eyes exhausted from grief. I told him about my moment with his father standing in that very same spot, and I repeated what he'd said. "It's never going to stop hurting, but it'll get easier to live with. I promise. You hang in there."

Junior mustered up a polite bit of a smile and thanked me for telling him. I doubt he remembers the moment now. It's likely been washed away in the endless sea of grief that he was forced to wade through during that unbearable 2001 season.

But I like to think that maybe it helped to hear fatherly advice that once came directly from his own daddy, even if it eased his pain for only a few fleeting seconds.

~Ryan McGee

Passion

Passion. It's an overused term in the sports world. But I was witness to its true meaning through the fans of NASCAR.

In February of 2001, I had been working for MRN Radio for only six weeks or so. I was just learning about the big-time world of NASCAR and what really makes the sport speed along—its loyal and dedicated fans. At that time there were no more passionate partisans of that dedication than fans of "The Man In Black," Dale Earnhardt.

NASCAR enthusiasts, in general, are an ambitious lot to say the least. Driving halfway across the country (one way) to an event. Staying in infield tents through 105-degree Sunday afternoons or rain delayed Monday races to see their favorite drivers perform on motorsports' biggest stages is pretty routine. For them it's not a big deal, it's just what life is all about. But on that unforgettable February 18th, 2001 when NASCAR President Mike Helton uttered the tragic phrase, "We've lost Dale Earnhardt," life turned upside down for the faithful followers of The Intimidator.

I was keen to the passion of NASCAR fans as I would consider myself one of them, and that is what drew me to the sport in the first place. But I never dreamed I would see what took place in Daytona Beach, Florida in the days and weeks that followed the passing of the sport's Pied Piper. For me, it redefined fervent fandom as I knew it.

At the Daytona 500 Experience, the NASCAR-themed motor-sports attraction just outside Daytona International Speedway, a fans' memorial was organized to honor Earnhardt. My office was just steps down the hallway from where the service was held. I was on my way to a gathering of MRN employees to what was supposed to be a celebration of a successful Speedweeks which turned into a celebration of the memory of a man that many people at the network knew as a friend.

As I was about to leave the track I was compelled to stop and watch as the thousands that came to the gathering lit up the entranceway with candles, lights and love. Most had planned to be on the road or even home by then but they wouldn't have missed paying their last respects to the seven-time champion for the world. When it was all over and the people went their separate ways, what was left behind could only be described as pure passion.

As I came into work the next morning, the fountain where the ceremony took place was covered with thousands of flowers. There were other things, too. T-shirts and jackets that fierce fans of The Intimidator knew they would never wear again. Dozens upon dozens of cards with notes of condolence along with other assorted Dale memorabilia people had left as a way to express their thanks for the memories. It was a tremendous outpouring of emotion, but not an unexpected one.

What I didn't predict, though, and what affirmed my belief in the most passionate fans in sports, was that the scene played out every evening for the next two weeks! The size of the crowd varied from night to night, but they were always there.

Many Earnhardt followers who by that time had a chance to stop and think about what he meant to their lives decided to make the trek to Daytona Beach no matter where they were. It was incredible to watch the vehicles rolling through the parking lot of the speedway from all across the nation, and even provinces of Canada. It was their personal pilgrimage to say goodbye, and to say thanks.

Many poured their hearts out in long poems and left them at the fountain so others could know how the composer was feeling at their moment of sadness. Some brought guitars and played songs they had written about their hero. The sight was absolutely surreal. It wasn't unusual at all to walk through the entry area of the attraction during the day and see people with tears streaming down their faces. As a matter of fact, it was the norm.

The next Sunday, Dale Earnhardt, Incorporated driver Steve Park took the checkered flag in the Dura-Lube 400 at North Carolina Speedway in Rockingham. The win brought even more admirers of Earnhardt to the Sunshine State for another six to seven days. Two weeks later, when a young Kevin Harvick took Earnhardt's former car to Victory Lane at Atlanta Motor Speedway, it ended the mourning period and began the celebration of his life.

For a guy who was just starting out being directly involved with the sport the experience was an eye-opening reminder about the greatness of NASCAR fans. They truly embody the definition of passion.

~Marty Hough

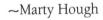

Jokers Wild

*T*here's an old line that says racing began on the day humans built the second automobile. Practical joking probably made its entry into the sport about an hour later.

And in the area of the harmless prank, one could hardly find a more focused practitioner than one Ralph Dale Earnhardt, he of the seven NASCAR Sprint Cup Series championships and the sly grin. The Intimidator was as ruthless in the garage as he was on the race track.

NASCAR veteran Kenny Schrader, no slouch himself with the verbal needle, often found himself on the receiving end of Earnhardt's pranks. Another of Dale's foils was Sterling Marlin.

"He was always doing somethin' to jack you up," Schrader recalls. "He wrecked me a lot, for starters. He could get away with it better than anybody. He'd tell my wife that I was spending a bunch of money on a racing deal, then she'd come runnin' to me. He'd tell your car owner that you were talking to another owner. It was all harmless, but he'd find a way to make you uncomfortable, then he'd laugh that silly laugh and get that spark in his eyes."

Until one day when Schrader and Marlin decided to get their revenge.

It was 1997 and the good ol' boys were in Sonoma, California for the annual race at Sears Point (now Infineon) Raceway. Earnhardt's rental car was parked Sunday morning adjacent to the transporter for Morgan-McClure Racing, Marlin's team.

Schrader and Sterling dared to tug on Superman's cape.

They tossed loose lug nuts inside the hubs of Earnhardt's rented sedan. They placed wheel weights halfway around the wheels so the car "shook terrible," Schrader recalls. They attached a fan belt to the drive shaft so the belt rattled the car's undercarriage. They spread wheel-bearing grease on the windshield and on the handle of the driver's door.

A public relations rep for Winston, the series sponsor at that time, I happened upon them as these full-grown adults giggled like schoolboys.

"Whose car?" I asked.

"Earnhardt."

Somehow I felt guilty just knowing.

At race's end, the car sat innocently as members of several teams kept an eye out for Dale. But the joke took a twist when Earnhardt, changing into his street clothes, summoned wife Teresa to fetch the vehicle. As she strode toward the car, fidgeting for the keys, I turned away. This wasn't going to be pretty.

Moments later, standing on the second level of the media center, I turned back toward the carnage. Teresa's face was contorted as she stared at her grease-laden fingers. She headed back to find Dale.

"She wasn't too amused," Schrader deadpans today.

"But Dale was really ticked. We kept our distance from the car, but we had an eye on him when he got to it. We took cover in the hauler and laughed like crazy. Dale had to drive to the San Francisco airport with that thing bumpin' and bangin'. And he could barely see to drive."

I later talked to someone who saw Earnhardt on the side of Hwy. 37, wiping goop off the windshield. Someone would have to pay.

"He got me back," Schrader says, laughing. "He threatened Henry Benfield (one of Marlin's crew members), and Henry, who had helped us in the prank, ratted out me and Sterling. I think Dale spun me out a couple of times in the next month. The next few races I was on the lookout every time he was around.

"You could never get the best of Dale. He wouldn't let ya."

~Chris Powell

How to
Treat Your Fans

I had worked in the NASCAR Sprint Cup Series as a sponsor's public relations representative for about two years, primarily with country music recording companies like Capital Nashville, when I had the opportunity to host John Anderson and his manager Bobby Roberts at the 1995 Daytona 500.

Anderson was a big Dale Earnhardt, Sr. fan and wanted to meet him, and it was my job to set it up. As it turned out, JR Rhodes, Earnhardt's publicist, was a friend of mine so that made it pretty easy.

The Daytona 500 has been a family tradition in our house since my dad first got tickets in 1979, so my parents were attending the race as well.

It was early Sunday morning and Roberts, JR, team owner Richard Childress, my parents and I were all hanging out in the garage area at the back of Earnhardt's hauler. Anderson and Earnhardt were off in the drivers' campground somewhere, just talking or doing whatever.

My mother was, as usual, trying to blend into the background and "stay out of the way," as she puts it.

After a few minutes behind the hauler, Childress invited us all inside. Earnhardt and Anderson showed up a little while later and The Intimidator headed up front to change into his uniform.

By this time, the inside of the hauler was wall-to-wall people.

This included our whole group, plus GM public relations types, some Goodwrench VIPs, a NASCAR official and smack in the middle of it all, my 5' 2"-tall schoolteacher mom, looking every bit the part in a sweater vest.

When Earnhardt came barreling out of the front lounge area, there were at least 20 people lining the sides of that hauler's hallway. And you could tell that just about every one of them was a mover and shaker of some importance.

Earnhardt proceeded to ignore every last one of us, except one. Mom was standing just outside of our group's inner circle—again trying to "stay out of the way," no doubt. She was about midway down the hall, not really paying attention to anything that was going on.

Earnhardt, gold reflective Gargoyle sunglasses and all, stopped right in front of her, stuck out his hand, and shook hers. "Hey. How you doing this morning?" he said. "Thanks for coming. Let's hope this is a good day, right?"

Mom was virtually speechless, barely managing a "Yes, thank you, and good luck."

Then as fast as he appeared, he was out the door and headed off to driver introductions. Mom was shaking as if she was 16 again, meeting Elvis. I guess in a way she had.

Earnhardt considered that small, unassuming older woman the most important person in his hauler that day. He made her weekend and gave her a great memory that she still talks about today.

This perfect lesson in "How to Treat Your Fans" has stuck with me ever since.

~Rob Fisher

Writing by Numbers

For someone who has never purchased a single lottery ticket, I have an odd obsession with numbers. In fact, I'm a writer because one of my prerequisites for employment is that "there's no math with this job."

Since childhood, my favorite number has been "3." Beyond its Biblical connotations, it is associated with one of the greatest NASCAR drivers and sports legends of all time, the late Dale Earnhardt. My dad, Bennie, who has spent a good bit of time behind the wheel and under the hoods of stock cars, passed that down to me. With his strong, often silent presence, he reminds me of Earnhardt. Growing up, I always knew there was trouble when I saw him staring at the ground, standing perfectly still except for the index finger and thumb of his right hand, which he used to pull the edge of his moustache toward his top lip.

My mom was the loud one. She was also the one who kept nearly everything except the cars running smoothly—until she lost a battle with cancer in 1989. While she was sick, I was writing a story in my head. There was a chapter with a miraculous recovery, and another in which she told other women how she had come through it. She was so strong, and we needed her so much, it couldn't be written any other way.

By the time I moved out of the house, Dad had remarried, but my stepmother would wholeheartedly agree that those first few years were trying. Although we had moved on, we were actually still in shock.

Writing was a natural career choice for me because I get to indulge in my habit of "over-thinking" everything. While the rest of the world sleeps, I'm pondering the "W" questions—not who, what and when?—but what if? Why now? And why me?

For an author, every painful event has a purpose that is ultimately revealed. But back then, nothing made sense, so I stopped writing.

Then, on February 15, 1998, something changed.

My little brother Hunter was born on the day Earnhardt got the Daytona 500 win that had taunted him for years. Hunter was a healing force in a marriage and a sign that the story wasn't over for me.

After Earnhardt's win, fans were deflated when The Intimidator didn't roll to his eighth championship. But three years later, the stars seemed to be aligned for another win that would begin an epic chapter in racing's history book. Three days after Hunter's third birthday, the green flag fell on the 2001 Daytona 500.

As the cars entered Turn 3 of the final lap, the "3" car was running in third place when it veered up the track for reasons that are still debated. The crash took Earnhardt's life, and once again, the story didn't go as I had planned.

That time, I knew I had to keep writing.

By July, I had parted ways with a comfortable job in marketing—better known as the first department to go when a CEO decides his company would look better in a smaller size. Before that, my writing career had involved an actual job as a journalist, but my new goal was independence, and to have control over my own life story. True to "Type A" form, I developed a plan that would take me from small publications to national magazines and books. By pure coincidence, I expected the plan to take three years to come to fruition.

A little over a year later, I had a weekly feature on a popular Web site devoted to racing, and was headed to Charlotte to meet with the editor of a women's magazine. It sounded fabulous, but I was struggling with some disappointment in my personal life, and the paychecks associated with independence didn't match the glory. In other words, I was feeling sorry for myself during the two-hour drive up I-85.

The balding tires on my car skated across every little pool of standing water on that grey September afternoon. It was September 3rd, to be exact, and my 3 p.m. appointment had just been canceled. I pictured myself crawling into bed — hose, shoes and all — and pulling the covers over my head.

Despite the heavy feeling that overwhelmed me, I suddenly realized I wasn't going home. The day wasn't over yet. Several publications that covered NASCAR were located nearby, and I had some great stories to pitch.

Blackberries and GPS systems were a few years away, so I relied on my crackling flip phone and its 411 service to give me street addresses for three magazines. *Stock Car Racing* seemed closest, but the part of the brain that supplies math skills is the same part that allows one to read maps.

As the rain fell and the clock ticked, I made my way to Speedway Boulevard. I was familiar with the area, but according to my calculations, the Speedway was sitting where the magazine's office building should have been. I consulted the map repeatedly. I prayed. I cried. I cursed. I prayed again and apologized for cursing. Then it dawned on me: There were offices inside that building — perhaps some that didn't belong to speedway employees.

The only person in the lobby area, a gift shop clerk, said there were plenty of offices upstairs, but he had no idea who the tenants were. I looked at my watch. It was 4:27 p.m. Thirty-three minutes left in the business day.

I stood by the elevators frantically reading the plaques between them. There was no listing for "Stock Car Racing." Yet I knew it was there. I took a deep breath and read the signs again. There, on the third floor, was a listing for "Primedia," the magazine's parent company. I jumped into the elevator and pushed "3." The third floor was as quiet as the rest of the building near 5 p.m. on a Tuesday. There was no receptionist, guard or gatekeeper. I charged down the hall and found someone in the third office.

The editor agreed to publish one of my stories in an Earnhardt tribute edition, and I headed home, elated and confused. Then, it hit me: Unexpected triumphs might be the same as tragedies. We really can't control, predict or write the details of either one.

As my brother's birthday approached in 2006, I knew something significant would happen, but I had prepared myself for the fact that it might not be good. Three days after Hunter turned six, Dale Earnhardt, Jr. claimed the Daytona 500, three years after his legendary father was killed and six years after his most awesome victory.

I still imagine perfect endings and prefer to craft them myself, but now I know I am not the author. I write every day, knowing there's no need to worry about the placement of every word in every chapter, because God has already given each one the perfect number.

~Amanda L. Capps

A Good Man to Know

Of course I knew of Dale Earnhardt before I met him in 1980, my first year covering NASCAR.

He had already earned Rookie of the Year honors and was well on his way to honing his image as The Intimidator, running roughshod over other drivers on track and walking with a convincing swagger off the racing surface.

I was no novice as a sports writer when I first met Earnhardt. My resume already included covering everything from high school to professional sports and some of the biggest events of the previous decade, including every Indianapolis 500 from 1970 through 1979.

I had met and interviewed stars from other sports like Magic Johnson, Larry Bird, Bart Starr, Mickey Mantle and Bobby Orr, along with open-wheel racing's elite: Mario Andretti, A.J. Foyt, Emerson Fittipaldi, Niki Lauda and many more. But, somehow, Earnhardt was more, yes, intimidating.

The mustachioed North Carolinian had an aura that said, "Look out! You don't want to get me mad! And that's easy to do."

So, it was with some trepidation that I first approached "The Man in Black."

Our first meeting was in January 1980, at Riverside, California, where the NASCAR season began in those days. I had just become the motorsports editor for The Associated Press and it was my first stock car race.

Walking through the garage at the sprawling road circuit, I spotted Earnhardt sitting on a stack of tires. He was alone and had a smile plastered on that craggy face.

"Why not?" I thought. "He's not doing anything."

I walked slowly up to Earnhardt and introduced myself. To my great relief, he smiled warmly and shook my hand. Then he answered all my questions.

Hey, this was easy.

The next month, at the Daytona 500, I decided to do a feature story. The Associated Press was a big deal and it opened a lot of doors, so I figured I would have no trouble getting it arranged.

I went through the proper channels, asking Earnhardt's public relations man to set up an interview. He replied, "You don't want to talk to him this week. He's getting ready for a big race and he don't want to talk."

I shrugged him off. If he wouldn't tell his boss I wanted to talk with him, I would. After all, he's a good guy, right?

Walking through the old garage area at Daytona International Speedway, I saw Earnhardt, again sitting alone on a stack of tires. But, this time, there was no welcoming smile and handshake. His eyes were hard and his mind was obviously elsewhere.

"Go away," he growled. "This ain't the right time."

I walked away, confused.

In the ensuing years, though, I learned a lot about Dale Earnhardt and his ways. I learned when to approach him and when to avoid him. And I learned that Earnhardt loved to argue a point with anybody willing to take him on.

The thing was, he could be a pussycat or he could be an angry bobcat. You just had to learn the signs. Some writers never did, and they never got along with Earnhardt.

I did learn, and some of my fondest memories are of sitting with Earnhardt away from the track or over a lunch at the track—usually at some press function—listening to him expound on things that nobody but his closest friends would expect him to know about.

He could speak eloquently on politics, current events and, particularly, marketing.

At a lunch the week before his untimely and tragic death in a crash during the 2001 Daytona 500, Earnhardt and his then business manager Don Hawk sat with me and talked about a wide range of subjects.

Everyone in racing knew Earnhardt sold more merchandise than any other driver in NASCAR, and I asked Hawk to explain their new marketing strategy to me. Hawk began to explain, but, to my surprise, Earnhardt interrupted and gave me a 10-minute lecture on marketing that would have done an economics professor proud.

Earnhardt was also noted for his little-publicized but constant charitable work and caring.

When IndyCar driver Scott Brayton was killed in a crash at Indianapolis, his widow, Becky, got a call from Earnhardt asking if there was anything she needed. Neither she nor her husband had ever met Earnhardt.

I saw an example of that humanity in person the week he was killed. I was sitting with Earnhardt when an old friend, Barbara Signore, who ran the now-defunct International Race of Champions series with her husband, Jay, was called up on stage for an honor.

As she began to leave the stage—raised several feet off the ground—Barbara stumbled a bit and Earnhardt, with those lightning reflexes honed on a thousand race tracks, leaped from his seat and, with that warm, all-encompassing smile, helped her safely to her seat.

He was tough, a little rough around the edges, and sometimes difficult to figure out. And he definitely left this earth much too soon.

But the Dale Earnhardt I like to picture in my mind is the rising young stock car star sitting on a stack of tires at Riverside, welcoming a newcomer to NASCAR with that dazzling, impish smile.

~Mike Harris

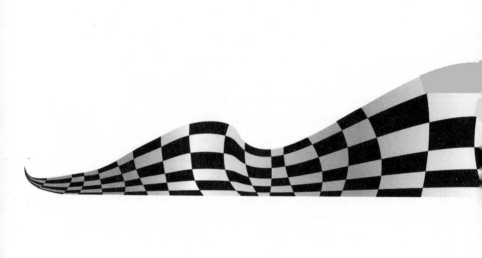

NASCAR®

Behind,
and Beyond,
the Wheel

NASCAR's
Closest Finish

I t was on a hot Sunday afternoon at Darlington Raceway, where you get to go and dance with the old "Lady in Black."
Darlington is a place where you don't race the competition. You race the race track. Your ultimate job is to protect your race car and manage to not slide up into the wall, because you have to run inches from the wall for the fastest line around that particular track.

We blew two motors during practice, so I didn't have much practice time. My crew chief and I put a car together using the setups of my teammates at the time, Mark Martin and Jeff Burton. Both of those guys ran great at Darlington.

It turned out to be a great race for us, even without a lot of practice time. We raced hard all afternoon and worked our way toward the front. The car wasn't perfect, but I just told myself to drive it like Mark Martin would, or like Jeff Burton would. What did that mean? I really didn't know. But I told myself to drive the race track and not be aggressive with the car, to drive it conservatively and not wear out any of the tires. Darlington takes patience.

Near the end of the day, I was actually able to make a three-wide pass for the lead, which doesn't really happen at Darlington. You're always racing the race track and just trying to squeak by another competitor when you can. On one of the final restarts, Jeff Gordon and Elliott Sadler were battling side by side out of Turn 2, and I saw that the two of them broke their momentum. They didn't have the speed off the corner, and I was flying through there.

I thought, "Do I check up and pass them one at a time?" Of course, my right foot said, "No. We're going to pass them both at the same time." We went three-wide down the back straightaway, and I cleared them. I was in front of them by the time we got to Turn 3, and held the lead from that point.

Now it was going through my mind, "Do I need to conserve my tires? Or do I need to stretch out my lead and then try to preserve it once the tires wear off, to find out who's going to catch me?" I felt like I just needed to run a fairly steady pace, and run pretty quick, because I didn't think my car could hold off the competitors at the end.

With only 20 laps to go, I had a pretty good lead, and it wasn't Jeff Gordon or Elliott Sadler who was running second or third behind me.

It was Ricky Craven. He was clawing away at my lead. He was only gaining little bits at a time, but I knew in the back of my mind he was going to catch me by the end.

With about 15 laps to go, I felt my power steering give up in the car. I was really wrestling the wheel. I couldn't run the lap times I had been running earlier.

Still, I felt like with 15 laps to go, this was my race. This is what a driver lives for, to have the race on the line, a few laps to go, and you're leading. You've got to bring it home for the team.

It felt like the wind went out of my sails when the power steering went away, and then I was just wrestling the car as hard as I could, and lap after lap Craven was chewing away at the lead. I knew he was going to catch me before the end of it.

But with every lap that went by, I was more determined not to make it any easier for him to pass me.

There were two laps to go when he finally caught me. I was determined not to let him pass me. I was going to do all that I could to stay in front of him for two laps. Just two more laps.

We raced down the front straightaway side by side, because he got a good run coming off of Turn 4. At Darlington, you can't race into Turn 1 side by side. There's just not enough room. I felt like it was my job to hold the lead, and if he wanted it that bad he was going to have to come and get it.

He wanted it that bad. He came and got it.

We both went into Turn and I slid up into the fence. I pounded the fence pretty hard. I realized as I was going down the front straightaway that this wasn't such a great idea, but I couldn't give up the position, because if I did, he would just walk away and win this race uncontested.

We bumped and we banged. It was intense. He slipped ahead for an instant, but he couldn't quite get his car stable underneath him. My car bounced off the fence and was ready to go. I was ready to hammer the throttle because my car would do better in Turns 1 and 2, which are wider; the Darlington track is tighter in Turns 3 and 4 and you have to have the power steering to help you through there. But my power steering was gone, and we were running out of time.

I got back to him pretty quick and thought, "Well, if you were that mean to me going into Turn 1, I'm giving some of that back to you going into Turn 2." So I bumped him out of the way to get the lead. It was a perfect bump. I just moved him up to the high side and slid by him, so I had a pretty good run coming off Turn 2 to stay ahead of him.

We raced through Turns 3 and 4, and that big lead that I had was gone again. I saw how good he was in those two turns, and I knew it was going to come down to the final corner of the last lap to see who was going to get that checkered flag.

White flag; one lap to go.

He was right on my back bumper as we raced through 1 and 2, and I stretched him about three car lengths or so and came off Turn 2 with a good run. And then, he was on me. He was the closest he'd been, right on top of our rear bumper going into Turn 3.

I thought for an instant I would just put it on the outside wall and hold the throttle all the way to the pedal. But I knew that what I needed to do was hold the car low to take away some of his momentum in the low groove, where he had been running so well. I tried as hard as I could, but without the power steering I couldn't wrestle the wheel hard enough to hold it down in Turns 3 and 4.

And then, I had one little wiggle, and that allowed him to close up and get door-to-door with us. I kept my foot in it after that wiggle and came off Turn 4, but the car was so bound up with me holding the steering wheel as far left as I could at full throttle that it kind of shot off the wall and bumped into his right-side door.

Now my left side was locked with his right side, and we were both full throttle. He had to turn back to the right to hold his car stable on the straightaway because I was fully locked to the left. I was trying not to run into him but I couldn't get the steering back soon enough.

So there we were, door-to-door. This was it. I'm looking at him like he's looking at me, through the window, and I could just tell that his nose was an inch ahead of mine. I knew it all the way from Turn 4 to the start/finish line, but our cars were literally locked together. There was nothing I could do.

I was just hoping, praying, that maybe they would say we were ahead of him, but Ricky Craven beat me to the line by two one-thousandths of a second, after a full-fledged war we waged that day at Darlington.

The best part about the war was we didn't wreck each other. We completely exhausted every idea that we had—for me to protect the lead, and for him to take it. To put that battle on created a lifelong friendship between two guys who thought the same way about how to win a race.

Still, every time I tell the story, I swear I'm going to win it one day.

~Kurt Busch

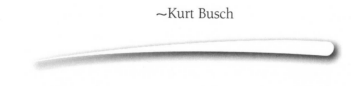

First in Line

The racing memory that stands out in my mind the most—both pertaining to NASCAR and to me personally—was when I sat on the pole for the Brickyard 400.

That one was particularly a lot of fun for me because my uncle, Rick Mears, has won at Indianapolis four times.

Every time you go into the Indianapolis Motor Speedway, there's this special feeling you get. You just know how long the place has been around, and I think that although there are several other race tracks in the sport that are very important to NASCAR, Indy is growing as one of the favorites. Even though it's really more of an IndyCar-based history, I think people just really enjoy going there. When you really understand what it's all about and how long it's been around, you realize it's really just a special place.

Every time I go there there's an extra emphasis on wanting to do well, because of the history of the track and my family history there, as well. My dad Roger has raced there, too.

During qualifying at Indy in 2004, I knew it was a pole run coming off Turn 4. The car was flying. When I came off Turn 4, took the checkers and coasted back around, you could hear over the loudspeaker, "It's a new track record." I've heard those words for years, but always as a spectator. But when I shut off the engine, I could still hear them saying it was a new track record. Jimmy Elledge, my crew chief at the time, was excited and he was telling me how fast I ran.

Indianapolis is a unique track because you're very close to the fans. The grandstands come right up against pit road, and there isn't a whole lot of room between the two, so the fans are right there. When I coasted back around, I could hear them cheering and yelling and screaming. I've never, ever, at any other time in my career, been in the race car and been able to hear the fans cheering.

It was just a very special moment. My dad was there. I was driving for Chip Ganassi at the time and he's had a lot of success at the speedway, too.

We did it kind of later in the day. It's an early morning qualifying session, and the faster times are typically run in the beginning. I had to wait a long time to see if that time was going to stand. It was stressful.

They put me on TV, because it was kind of a big deal that a Mears was on the pole at Indianapolis for the NASCAR race. They put us up in the broadcast booth and I sat with them for the remainder of qualifying. So the whole time I was on TV and they were asking me questions as other guys were qualifying, and some of those guys ran pretty quick. It was a weird feeling; I was very nervous but at the same time very confident, because the number we put down was pretty good.

Usually you qualify and you get interviewed, you talk about your run and then you go back to the motor home and find a place to kind of chill out and get away from everybody and wait to see what happens. But we were on TV the whole time, and it was a little bit of a surreal moment. I was sitting there and watching myself on a monitor while I was on TV, I'm looking over my shoulder and I'm seeing the pole times at IMS and my number is sitting there at the top of it. It was really cool when the last car finished and we knew we were on the pole.

My family has always been very supportive. My dad has raced everything. He's done all of it. He's never been partial. He's just a racer. My uncle is the same way. I think it's fun because my dad has pursued a career in off-road, my uncle did it in open wheel and now I'm doing it in stock cars.

When it came time to make the decision to come in this direction, it was pretty easy to make the choice. CART and IRL were split at the time. When I had to choose whether I was going to go CART or IRL—and I had an option in both—it was still very unclear what was going to be the right direction to go.

Then out of the blue I got an opportunity to go run in the NASCAR Nationwide Series. My dad, a year and a half before that, had already moved out to North Carolina and he was a shop foreman for Chip Ganassi. He called me every other week and was saying, "Casey, you've gotta get out here. There are race shops everywhere here. If you want to go racing, this is where you need to be." So he was already kind of pushing me in that direction.

At the time, Rick was still with team owner Roger Penske, and I went and asked him what I needed to do. And he said, "We're looking to go to IRL." But CART was my better option at the time.

And I said, "Well, I'm thinking about doing this NASCAR deal." And he said, "Do it. Go do it. Try it, and if it doesn't work out, you'll have a better idea of what you need to do."

They're the first ones to give me advice about what I need to do, and I listen to them. So far, things have worked out pretty well.

~Casey Mears

From Dumpsters to a Dream Come True

From the time I was 5 years old, I knew I wanted to be a race car driver.

I started out in racing like a lot of other guys did, in go-karts. I tried to play baseball, but I sucked at it, so I didn't like it. What I did like was driving. I guess I must be stubborn; I never really even tried anything else.

I had a go-kart when I was 5. I was always driving that thing around. It was all I wanted to do. Then my father got another go-kart that was bigger, so he could drive around with me. About a week later he moved the pedals up and I started driving that one.

It was interesting how I learned to maneuver my go-kart. After school I'd go over to my father's garbage company and drive the go-kart around. That was what I did for fun. I would just ride around avoiding the Dumpsters; well, trying to avoid the Dumpsters, at least. Then my dad and I would go out to dinner. That was my life then. I loved it.

When I was about 6, my father and I started going over to the race track for the quarter midget races. We just watched; my father was too busy with the garbage company at the time to put in a whole Saturday of playing with these quarter midgets.

That lasted about a year. Then we got a quarter midget, and started racing.

When you're a kid and going to school and everything, you always think about what you're going to be when you grow up. It has been amazing that I have been able to do exactly what I wanted. I have always had my family's support behind me. They have allowed me to follow my dream.

The time and effort and money that families have to put in to get to the level where I am now is just ridiculous. It creates a lot of stress for everybody, and I was fortunate to have my whole family behind me.

It was really awesome the day I won my first NASCAR Sprint Cup Series race, at New Hampshire Motor Speedway. My whole family was there with me. That was my goal, to be the youngest NASCAR Sprint Cup winner. It's an unbelievable moment, when that first win happens. It's really hard to win races these days and to be able to get one was amazing. I can't even really describe how it felt. That was definitely my dream, and then when it happened, it was kind of surreal. It was an unbelievable moment.

I guess what people know me best for in racing so far is just being young. The youngest driver to win a NASCAR Nationwide Series race, the youngest NASCAR Sprint Cup Series winner … all that means to me is that I have a lot of years of racing left in front of me. I plan to keep on doing this for a long, long time.

But it might not be such a good idea to tell the other guys that when I'm racing against them on the track, I just pretend they're Dumpsters. I think I'll keep that to myself.

~Joey Logano

Faster than Fear

A few years ago, I was heading out of Madrid, Spain with a friend of mine to a small village. At times, he drove the small rental car we were in at about 100 miles per hour. Other than the fact that he had to mildly correct his steering while going that fast, I didn't really feel too anxious about the fact that he was exceeding the speed limit by about 40 miles per hour!

But even this didn't prepare me for what I would be doing one spring evening in 2008, in a city roughly 25 miles northeast of Charlotte known as Concord, where the NASCAR Racing Experience provides NASCAR fans the opportunity to either drive or be a passenger in a former NASCAR stock car.

I'm never going to forget my experience of riding three laps at 170 miles per hour in one of Jeff Gordon's former stock cars around one of NASCAR's legendary tracks, Lowe's Motor Speedway. The races are so popular here that crowds in the grandstands often outnumber the population of Cabarrus County, North Carolina, where the track is located.

As I waited in line, I became more anxious. I'm a bit of a 'fraidy cat when it comes to the idea of going super fast or up and down a lot, which is why I avoid roller coasters.

Before racing, I had to sign a waiver and fill out a health questionnaire so they would know how to treat me if anything happened to me while I was in the car. I had to put on a sheet-like cover on my head under the helmet, plus a neck support apparatus before I could get into the car.

I asked the others who finished their laps if they were scared and what it felt like to go so fast. They all told me just how much fun they had and that it didn't feel that scary at all.

Still, I was unconvinced. I thought I would most likely be scared out of my wits, but I wasn't going to give in to fear, either.

Since NASCAR stock cars don't have any doors, I had to go in through the window. I was strapped in comfortably, and had plenty of leg room on the passenger's side.

Once seated, and given the signal to go, the skilled driver took off from pit road like a bat out of Hades. There was no going back. Within about five seconds, he was increasing his speed in a 2007 Chevrolet Monte Carlo numbered "24" so fast that I felt like I was being mildly crushed as the engine roared loudly.

In order to deal with this, I let out a mild scream and closed my eyes, just hoping I would survive. We made a quick turn around the oval and then another. Then came another burst of pressure on my body as the car's speed down the track increased again. I felt so creeped out, closing my eyes again because everything was coming so fast at me, like a colored blur.

But after the second turn was over, I started to get used to it and looked straight ahead. I thought several times that we were going to hit the wall of Lowe's Motor Speedway as we came toward it so quickly, but the driver always made the turns at exactly the right time. I was squinching up as much as I could though, and keeping my eyes open about half the time.

By the time I was more comfy with being in this car, my three laps were done. It only lasted a couple of minutes.

So this is what it's like to go 170 miles per hour with one's life in another's hands? Wow! One lady told me that when she looked at the speedometer, it read over 170 miles per hour. I was too busy being scared to look at the speedometer in the car I was in. Still, I would definitely do this again if given the chance, because it's fun, and I now know what to expect.

The talent that these NASCAR drivers have is incredible. It's one thing to race around the track when there is just one other car, as this riding experience is done with two cars that are close together, but not racing.

But to do this in a race with a whole bunch of other stock cars trying to pass each other while dealing with bumping, accidents, etc., for hundreds of laps at those kinds of speeds is a different experience altogether.

~Roy A. Barnes

The Divine Right of Kings

When you're born in Darlington, South Carolina, you learn at an early age the earth is not round; it's egg-shaped!

Darlington Raceway is our claim to fame. She was born in 1950, was a hippie during the '60s, and became a young lady in the '70s. She experienced growing pains in her 30s, had a facelift in her 40s, and today she stands tall as a beacon of where NASCAR came from and where it's going.

The "Lady in Black" made the word "Darlington" known to the world. Make no mistake about it; the track "Too Tough to Tame" is the Taj Mahal of auto racing. When it comes to tradition, nothing else compares—not Churchill Downs, not Indy, not Yankee Stadium. Nothing else in the world of sports compares to Darlington Raceway. She is the mac daddy and she is OURS!

Being a Darlingtonian has afforded me the opportunity to get up-front and personal with NASCAR. Being the elected County Coroner has allowed me to reach out and touch it.

Don't misunderstand; I thank the good Lord I have never had to render my professional duties at the race track. But being the Coroner puts me on the "A-list." It gives me certain benefits afforded to only a few. I am a credential-bearing, upfront-parking member of the Race Weekend Elite.

This status had afforded me the opportunity to meet rock stars, movie stars, governors, United States presidents and vice presidents, the Admiral of the United States Navy, United States senators, Congressmen, and politicians of all kinds. I shook the hands of Bill Clinton and Al Gore. I have met almost every race car driver there is at one time or another and I have rubbed shoulders with some of the most dedicated race fans in the world. I have seen it, felt it, heard it, smelled it, and wallowed in it but nothing compares to the day I met "the King."

I was returning home from my job as County Coroner early one morning on Race Weekend. Let me explain; every year you have certain holiday weekends. Some examples would be Easter Weekend, Labor Day Weekend, Memorial Day Weekend, and Clemson-Carolina Weekend. Darlington has all of the above, plus a bonus. We call it Race Weekend.

Anyway, as I was passing the track I decided to take a detour and cruise through the famous Darlington infield. Figuring all God's children would be asleep at dawn-thirty, I wanted to see what the infield looked like when it was full, but quiet.

As I made my way through this temporary sleeping city, I noticed a man sitting on the inside barrier wall, just outside of the old Turn 4 and a few feet from the end of pit road. There was not another soul around with the exception of several thousand sleeping race fans. As I approached, I nonchalantly lifted my hand to wave. When I did, the man turned toward me. He was wearing a cowboy hat with a big feather in front ... NO WAY. There was no way I had inadvertently stumbled upon THE MAN. The seven-time champion, the winningest driver in NASCAR history, "the King" himself, Richard Petty.

"Good morning, Mr. Petty," I said as I rolled up and stopped in front of him.

"Good morning," he responded. I was wearing a suit and tie, the normal dress for the Coroner. He took one look at me and I could tell he was examining my attire. I remarked that it looked like a beautiful day for racing and he said, "or preaching," as he looked at me closer. We both smiled.

Now I don't know if any of you have ever had a captive audience with a legend, but it makes for an awkward moment. I began to realize that none other than Richard Petty was fixing to give me the proverbial time of day, and I was not ready. I should have had a week to prepare.

"How is your family?" I asked, as if I had known them all my life. "Fine," he said. We exchanged niceties for a few more minutes, talking about racing, about Darlington, and about a host of other topics, and then it was over.

I did not get an autograph or ask him for anything; I figured he gets enough requests for that kind of stuff, and just maybe the reason he was sitting on the wall early in the morning was to escape the constant hounding of whatever or whoever incessantly placed demands upon his time. Who knows?

My brief encounter with the hands-down greatest driver to ever live gave me a completely new perspective of NASCAR and Richard Petty. You see, NASCAR is Richard Petty, and Richard Petty is NASCAR. The two go hand in hand. One would not exist, as they are today, without the other.

As he sat on the wall that morning talking to somebody he did not know, I wondered what he was thinking. He was probably thinking, "I wish this guy would move on!" I'm not sure, but to me it looked like the King surveying his kingdom. Everything in sight could be attributed in large part to the accomplishments of this man.

This is not to say others did not play a part, but come on, y'all. Two hundred wins, seven championships, the longest corporate sponsorship in history; this is unheard of. Richard Petty had shaped and molded the world of stock car auto racing.

But nothing comes without a price, especially success.

The success of Richard Petty seemed to be no exception. A few months prior to our impromptu encounter, the royal family of NASCAR had made the ultimate sacrifice, when Adam Petty was killed on a race track while testing his car. The youngest of the Petty drivers, the grandson of Richard and the son of Kyle, Richard's son, was now gone. It appeared, from the outside looking in, that the hopes and dreams of a racing family were shattered. Petty Enterprises cried, as did thousands who, like me, felt a sense of closeness to a family we had never met.

It seemed the family that had given so much was called upon by the Lord to give it all. This they did.

Fast-forwarding a few years, the King is still at it. Week in and week out I can glance at the television during my Sunday afternoon nap and see the Petty blue car racing her heart out with the King watching from the pit wall of some wall at some race track, somewhere.

The chances of a sighting in Victory Lane are slim. The world of big money has altered what used to be and the days of small, family-owned race teams seemed to have passed.

But this does not seem to have slowed the man who has contributed so much. The Pettys continue to shine. Whether it is Victory Lane at Darlington or Victory Junction in Randleman, N.C., you can find him still doing what he does best—making life a little better for all of us.

But really, isn't that what Kings are supposed to do?

~J. Todd Hardee

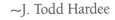

23

Chicken Soup
for the Soul

Stories with the King

Icovered my first NASCAR race on July 6, 1969. It was the first NASCAR race ever run at Dover International Speedway.

They got their first race and I had never heard about NASCAR. I knew about Daytona Beach, but the only thing I knew about that place was you could drive your car on the beach. That was unheard of at the New Jersey shore.

Richard Petty, David Pearson and Lee Roy Yarbrough were all new to me.

Dover was a new track to everyone. The inaugural race was scheduled to be run two days after the Fourth of July race at Daytona. Everyone down in Florida had less than 48 hours to get to Dover, and to make matters worse, I-95 wasn't even near completion.

On race day, drivers got a few practice laps in, qualified and ran a 300-mile race.

Petty, running his lone year in a Ford, won the race by six laps over Sonny Hutchins. I had been watching the four major sports teams in Philadelphia for over 20 years at the time — covering Phillies, Flyers, Eagles and '76ers games — and I was covering this race for the ABC Radio Network.

Petty won the race and came up to the press box. Standing next to him holding a microphone, I thought during the interview it might not be a bad idea to ask a question instead of looking like a lump on a log.

I started off by calling him, "David." Great start. I didn't have the name right and these guys are battling for the championship. I quickly corrected myself, called him "Richard," and got off a question. To his credit, he gave me a great answer.

That day, I said, "NASCAR racing is great and Richard helped sell me on the sport." But does Petty remember me calling him David?

You'd better believe he does.

•••

I got to my first race at Richmond in 1971. It was a five-hour drive and I had to cover a basketball game in Philadelphia between LaSalle and St. Joseph's the night before. I knew I had a long drive and to make matters worse, the basketball game went into overtime. Then it rained on part of the trip and I was beginning to think, "Why I am doing this? Am I making a trip for nothing?"

The answer became clear the next morning.

Three cars entered in the raced flunked inspection — Richard Petty, Benny Parsons and James Hylton. The engine in Petty's car was set back several inches, the wheel base had been altered and the fuel tank was too low. Parsons and Hylton had similar infractions.

Bobby Isaac's Dodge fuel tank was an inch and half too low. Bobby Allison's car arrived late and he missed qualifying. The cars that had been caught could start in the rear; the car had been legal the previous year, when there had been no engine placement rule.

Petty, Isaac and Allison had to run with a smaller carburetor plate. Petty started last (30th), Allison 29th and Parsons 28th. Isaac, who qualified third, was still able to start up front, but it didn't matter. Petty won by two laps over Isaac.

When the cars returned in the fall, Petty again ran away and won by a lap over Allison. During the post-race interview Chris Economaki, editor and publisher of *National Speed Sport News*, quickly got off a question. "Is this the same car you ran here in the spring?"

That got everybody's attention. How would the King answer that question?

Petty paused, cleared his throat and remarked, "We kept the hood closed this time," bringing a big laugh from everyone.

For the record, the car was legal before and after this race.

• • •

Can an 8-year-old upstage a top NASCAR driver and a top country and western singer?

Yes. It happened right before the Coca-Cola 600 at Charlotte in 1971.

I interviewed Richard Petty on a radio station in Charlotte. The broadcast originated from a big hotel. The broadcast was set up on one side of the room and there was a live audience.

Afterwards, Marty Robbins, who ran some NASCAR Sprint Cup Series races, started his show. He dedicated his first song to Petty and started to sing "Hello, Walls," which got a big laugh out of everybody, including Richard.

Before Marty could continue, a young boy of about 8 walked straight across the room past a grinning Robbins and came over for the King's autograph. After getting the autograph, he went back to the table to sit with his parents. Marty looked at the boy right to left when he crossed in front of the stage, and left to right when he returned to his seat.

The audience loved it and nobody laughed harder then Robbins, Petty … and me.

~Skip Clayton

24

The Science of Speed

While waiting for my first ride in a two-seater Richard Petty Driving Experience (RPDE) stock car with NASCAR Sprint Cup Series driver Denny Hamlin during media day at Disney World several years ago, I chatted with employees as others completed their two-lap tour at 140 mph. I was curious what most first-time ride-along participants had to say about their experience.

I was definitely on the right track, and this one wasn't asphalt. The RPDE employees all agreed the most common statement right out of the cockpit was, "I had no idea it was like that!"

One media colleague in queue for her ride commented that the cars didn't look like they were going very fast. The one-mile track at Disney limits high speeds, but hitting 130-plus was common for skilled drivers.

Before my turn came up the media colleague who thought the cars weren't going that fast got out of the car after her ride and said, "Wow!"

As I'm a photographer and reporter, I had to get out permission from the driver to take my camera with me during a ride. Hamlin had no problem with that.

After putting on a helmet and a HANS device and having seat belt straps secured around me, I quickly realized I couldn't turn my head all the way to the left, aim the camera, and snap an image of the driver at the same time. So I simply turned the camera that way, snapped a bunch of images and then checked it for the right focus.

It hadn't occurred to me that while taking the ride I would be holding onto my camera and not any solid part of the car, like a section of the tubular frame. The camera couldn't brace me for the speedy ride in and out of the corners, or the high speeds just inches from the wall on straightaways.

I remember getting out of my first ride pumping my fist. My 2006 comments: "What a thrill! You see it, hear it, feel it in every virtual way, but until you are in a race car with a pro at the wheel you can't know it."

I mentioned the impact of a ride-along to other drivers many times after that and got some curious responses. Jason Leffler noted that during ride-alongs he wasn't in the passenger seat closest to the wall, where the effect is the scariest. Jimmie Johnson doesn't like being in any fast-moving vehicle he can't control, and won't ride with jet fighter pilots. The g-forces in supersonic aircraft are renowned.

According to Wikipedia, the free encyclopedia, the g-force experienced by an object is its acceleration relative to free-fall. The term g-force is technically incorrect as it is a measure of acceleration, not force. However, it is treated as a force because the mechanical stresses it produces are always felt as a force even if they produce no physical acceleration.

Whenever the vehicle changes either direction or speed, the occupants feel lateral (side to side) or longitudinal (forward and backwards) forces produced by the mechanical push of their seats.

That's the official definition. Here's what it means in real life.

Inverted g-forces like those felt in the loops of roller coasters are the last thing one wants to feel in a stock car, as that would require flipping over on the track. Top Fuel dragsters produce 5.3 g on a straight path. Open-wheel race cars in F1 produce about 5 g during heavy braking. Normal stock cars' g-forces lie somewhere in between 1g and 4 g, depending upon the size and banking of the track and the speeds attained in a hot but successful lap. Crashes increase g-forces exponentially.

When Dale Jarrett described a ride-along incident among the many he has performed for fans, reality superseded science.

"I was doing one at Rockingham years ago and actually blew an engine going into Turn 3 there," Jarrett said. "I got into some oil and we were spinning. The guy thought I was doing that on purpose. Whenever that happens we have no control, either. If you blow a tire it doesn't matter how good you are."

Oh. So that's the reason why they have you sign several pages of waivers before you get into the seat.

Jarrett commented on fans riding along.

"It's easy to tell the ones that are really enjoying it," he said. "There are some with their eyes literally wide open. They are not sure what's going to happen. Those are the ones that are fun. You want them to appreciate what's happening. I've had ones that you could have hit the wall and they wouldn't have cared. They were looking for something exciting to happen. Others are sitting there and realizing this is a ride of a lifetime for them."

Since my first ride with Denny Hamlin I've experienced stock cars with Greg Biffle and RDPE employee drivers. In 2009, I morphed into sort of a speed junkie with a ride in an IndyCar two-seater with Davey Hamilton at the Disney track, plus a ride on the streets of St. Petersburg, and pace car rides with Brett Bodine at Darlington Raceway and NASCAR champion Jimmie Johnson on the famed Daytona International Speedway.

I took my camera on a few warm-up laps in the open-wheel cars, but at speed they wouldn't allow a camera that might easily take flight in the wind created by those aerodynamic darts on wheels.

"Gentleman Jimmie" was anything but gentle in a new Camaro at Daytona when he left the tri-oval for sliding turns in and out of the Grand-Am road course paths. This time I was in the back seat, holding onto my camera and being pushed side to side by g-forces when Johnson pulled out of the turns to go 160 mph on Daytona's high banks.

When asked later about the many ride-alongs he has done and

how he tells whether fans are thrilled or scared or both, Johnson went graphic.

"You can usually tell when you shake someone's hand after the experience. If their palms are sweaty, you did a good job and you did scare them. The other day in that Camaro there were a lot of reasons to have sweaty palms. That's a fast, fast car and I think we all had a lot of fun."

When I mentioned it was great fun that surely scared me, the gentleman smiled. "Good. Mission accomplished."

Obviously none of my rides were in race conditions, so the total real effects of racing are still not part of my resume. I've covered motorsports for nearly a decade, and knew speed and noise in many close but intangible ways before I actually got in a car and felt what driving on the edge was like. It's only in the past few years that I have been privileged to feel that speed.

I expected fast, but as for knowing it, I truly had no idea.

~Dwight Drum

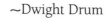

Back behind the Wheel

To race fans and television viewers, NASCAR driver Kenny Wallace is an upbeat, happy guy—even boisterous, some people say. He's at his best when he's behind the wheel of his NASCAR Nationwide Series car.

I love to talk with Kenny. Whenever I interview him, it's a fun time. His answers are always punctuated with laughter. His stories are great, and depending on whom you ask, most of them are true. He loves to tease.

But Kenny gets serious when he tells the story of how that innate happiness was almost taken away from him, in his younger days as a NASCAR competitor. It was at the New Hampshire Motor Speedway in Loudon. The year was 1991.

Kenny was the points leader in the Nationwide Series. He could actually feel that championship ring on his finger.

It was natural for him to feel that way. He has racing in his blood. His dad, Russ, was a famed dirt and asphalt race car driver. His two older brothers, Rusty and Mike, were successful drivers. In 1982, he won the first race he ever entered—in the Illinois Street Stock Championship Series. In 1986, he was the Nationwide Series Raybestos Rookie of the Year, finishing sixth in points. He was proving that he too had those winning racing genes in his body. Now he wanted that Nationwide Series championship—badly.

Chasing him in the points was Bobby Labonte. Kenny felt his championship chances were solid. He had an edge on Labonte by over 100 markers. There were only three races left in that season. His No. 36 mount, owned by Rusty's race team, performed flawlessly race after race. And then it happened …

While charging down New Hampshire Motor Speedway's backstretch, his rear suspension broke and as he entered Turn 3, his car spun out. Ultimately, he was diagnosed with "positional vertigo;" there would be no more racing for now.

A sharp fear stabbed through Kenny's heart. His championship dreams had been cruelly snatched away. But what was worse, he was just 28 years old. Would he ever be able to race again?

Kenny says that at that moment, he thought his racing was over. It was the scariest time of his life, and there were days when he caught himself crying; he had grown up as a kid wanting desperately to win a championship. Not only wanting to win, but to be the best, like Richard Petty, or David Pearson.

Over the long winter months, his injury gradually healed, much to the amazement of the doctors. Cleared to get back behind the wheel, he returned to the Nationwide Series in 1992. But was he still capable of racing competitively?

It was the second race of the year, at Richmond International Raceway. The top three in points were Labonte, Harry Gant … and Wallace. Kenny was running second, and Labonte held the lead. Kenny says he wanted to beat Labonte for that win, that it was a psychological thing with him.

He drove his car to Labonte's outside. Passed him clean. Suddenly, in a surprise move, Gant swept by them both and got the victory. Kenny finished second.

A few races later, Kenny was leading at Martinsville Speedway. To his intense pleasure, he drove his race car to victory. A new young driver, Jeff Gordon, approached him and congratulated him on a great race. Kenny says he thinks part of his recovery was not just that his brain was healing, but that he realized he could still compete.

So the fire of competition still burned in his heart. But a new uncharted territory lay ahead for him. ESPN Television tapped him to co-host a television show, *RPM Tonight*, every Monday night, which he did, until they stopped covering NASCAR.

When he was 36 years old, Kenny got another call, this time from SPEED TV. They wanted him as a color commentator for their new NASCAR Sprint Cup Series coverage. Kenny had to decline. He was racing in the Cup Series, and did not want to quit. They hired Darrell Waltrip instead.

Kenny says he told SPEED he would call them back when he was ready. And six years later, he did just that.

These days Wallace has his perfect schedule. He's competing in the Nationwide Series and does his dirt car racing. He co-hosts not one, but two, television shows for SPEED. He laughs and says he's still a competitive race car driver, and he only has to put in three hours for TV on Sundays.

He is as popular as ever with his fans. He has received the Nationwide Series Most Popular Driver three times. When his Nationwide car could not be sponsored by the U.S. Border Patrol for the race being held at the Circuit Gilles-Villeneuve in Montreal, Canada, dedicated race fans quickly raised the money, and saw their names on his car at that race.

There's still no championship ring on his finger. Kenny still has that fire, but he's now more content. He and his wife, Kim — his former high school sweetheart — have celebrated their 25th wedding anniversary, even renewing their vows.

"I'm having a very good time in my life right now," he told me, flashing that impish grin of his.

And I know for sure that he means it.

~Kay Presto

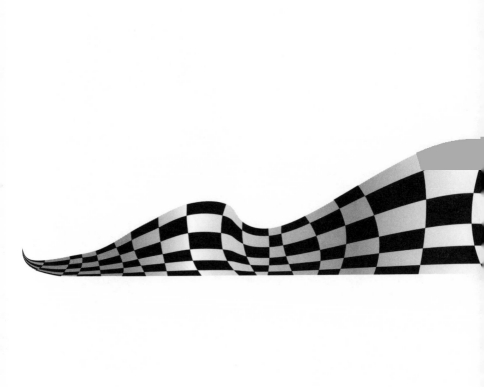

Never Give Up

Riding with Heart

My story isn't really about me. It's more about a friend of mine.

It started at Darlington in 1998. We were down there racing, and I owned my own NASCAR Nationwide Series team at the time. The week before we got here, a local bull rider, Jerome Davis, got injured in Texas in a bull riding accident. He got knocked unconscious and fell off the bull and landed on his neck. He was paralyzed from the neck down in that accident.

Jerome is younger than I am, but we went to the same high school. So I kind of knew him a little bit, and obviously I kept up with him and followed his career because he was a local guy who didn't live too far from where I lived.

We got to Darlington for the race weekend, and I decided — although I didn't tell him about it — that if I won the race, I was going to give Jerome all the winnings to help with his hospital bills and stuff. Then, lo and behold, I actually did win the race. So I was in Victory Lane and I said, "Hey, I'm going to give this to Jerome Davis." I think it was about $18,000; his mom remembers exactly how much it was, to the penny. And I made mention on TV that I was thinking about Jerome, that he was in the hospital in Texas, and I said I wanted to dedicate this win to him, and I was going to donate all the winnings to him.

It was my team and my car, so I didn't have to ask the car owner, because that was me, and I didn't have to ask the sponsor. It was for me to decide, so I decided to give him the winnings from that race. And I did that a couple more times that year.

Then I went to see him in the hospital in Charlotte when he was moved there, and I just kind of "took a heart to him," I guess you might say, more so than I did when he was riding. He was a world champion; he was somebody else to me then. I watched him, and I knew who he was, but I didn't know HIM. I didn't really get to know him until after he got hurt.

Since then I've done some TV stuff on ESPN with Jerome at his farm. He still handles bulls, still takes them to the rodeos. I went over to the coliseum to see him and his wife Tiffany one year in Las Vegas while I was out there doing an appearance, things like that. We don't see each other all the time or anything, but I see him maybe five or six times a year. Jerome is paralyzed, he's in a wheelchair—he's got mobility in his arms and somewhat in his hands—but he's still busy doing what he does.

He's just a neat guy. He's got this farm and he takes care of bulls and we're always saying we're going to do this or that together, but our schedules never seem to match up.

In 2008, around the time of my birthday, my wife Donna cooked lunch for me, and invited Jerome and his wife Tiffany over.

So I was walking over to my office and here Jerome comes in through the door and Tiffany comes in behind him, and he's in his wheelchair, and it just surprised the heck out of me. I walked over there that morning, tired, worried about everything I might run into or bump into or whatever, and he was sitting there talking about leaving to go to Jacksonville, N.C. for a bull riding thing. I just thought, "OK, do I really need to complain? About anything? What reason do I really ever have to be sour?"

One cool and kind of unusual thing that happens at Jerome's place is that at the end of the school year, kids just show up, and they don't go home until school starts again. They just come in, bring their backpacks, help out with the horses and work around the farm, and sleep on the floor or wherever. It's like their unofficial summer camp. On Tuesday nights they have something they call Cowboy Church, and about 20 kids pile in. They're the kind of people kids want to be around.

I think that if you have it, sometimes you have to give it. And so that's what I did, and it came back to me, because after Jerome got hurt, we became friends. It reminds you of a few things, like first of all the fact that we should have been friends before he got hurt. Not as if that would have changed his outlook on life, but it surely would have changed mine.

People have told me that giving those race winnings to Jerome was an impulsive thing, and maybe it was. But Jerome and Tiffany inspire me over and over again.

He doesn't mean to be inspiring to anybody. He just is who he is, and that's enough.

~Bobby Labonte

The Plan

I think it starts when you're a 10- or a 12-year-old kid. You don't really have a lot to do other than think about what you're going to do, and how you're going to go about doing it, so you start to make plans. You gather all the information that you can at that age, and you think about how a perfect template of where you're going would look. I wanted to be a race car driver.

There was an obvious route, to me, of how to do it. First you raced at your local track, and then you moved on to the next track that was bigger, with better competition, and you raced there. Then you raced a smaller division of NASCAR, and then you raced the NASCAR Nationwide Series, and then after that, you were ready for the NASCAR Sprint Cup Series. So I had all that mapped out and how it would all work.

Unfortunately for most kids, and for me, I didn't have any money. My dad worked at Pepsi and my mom was a checkout lady at the grocery store. My brother Darrell had been a really unique story. When he was a kid and my dad was young, he convinced my dad that he needed a go-kart. My dad thought it was something cool that he and my brother could do together, and my parents sacrificed a lot so Darrell could race. Darrell was good, and he became a champion.

But when I came along with the same youthful enthusiasm and the same desire to race, I was met with a whole lot of opposition. Mom and Dad basically said no way; we've been through it once, we're not going through it again. It costs way too much, and we're done with that.

So there was the first hitch in my plan. I had assumed somebody would help me. I thought my brother would help me, or my mom and dad would help me get started. But they wouldn't.

But I made my way around that. It's interesting how that worked out. I was able to go and get sponsorship and get people to help me because of what my brother had done in racing, but he wouldn't help me himself! Still, I owe him a lot for being able to get myself going, because of who he was and what he had accomplished.

At the time I was like, well, Darrell, it would be a lot easier if you would just help me. But now I think if he had done that, I wouldn't have appreciated it as much, or been as determined as I was to race.

I got to the point where I was still on track because I did get the help that I needed, and I was good at racing. I was winning. I was on my plan. I raced at the local track, and then I moved to the bigger tracks. I raced in the smaller division of NASCAR, and I won the championship there in 1983.

So the next step in my plan was to run the Nationwide Series. It was the spring of 1984, and I really didn't have any opportunities to race much. I messed around, got rides here and there in different series, but no plan. No clearly defined next step.

That fall, Richard Petty came into my world. I had gone to work at Petty Enterprises while living in North Carolina. One of my sponsors was also a sponsor of Richard's, and of course with me being Darrell's brother, Richard knew who I was and what I wanted to do. I actually lived with Richard and his wife Lynda for a while until I could get myself figured out in North Carolina.

One day Richard said to me, "What are you doing? What's your plan?" And I told him I had just won the NASCAR Goody's Dash Series championship in '83, and in '84 I was doing anything I could to be in a car, while also working at Petty Enterprises.

I said, "I need to find a Nationwide ride, that's my next step, that's what I need to do." He said, "You don't need to mess with that. If you want to race Sprint Cup, if you want to be a Sprint Cup driver, go get yourself a Sprint Cup car. If that's where you're going to wind up, you don't need to waste all your time racing in cars that aren't your ultimate goal. Go find a ride and see if you can start to make something happen."

So I did. I started in 1985 with a guy in North Carolina named Dick Bahre, who wound up being a really good friend of mine, and the man who owned my team for a while. He was just one of the sweetest people in the whole world. He didn't have the means to run a team like Richard Childress or Rick Hendrick did, but he did the best he could because he just wanted to race cars.

I brought Dick a little bit of money. I went to the speedway in Charlotte for my first race in '85 and I told the promoter there, Humpy Wheeler, that I wanted to race and he said, "Well, I appreciate your enthusiasm. I can get you a couple sets of tires to help you get started." It's funny, because he did the same thing for Dale Earnhardt and Tim Richmond and guys like that in the past.

So I took those two sets of tires and went up to Statesville, North Carolina in April of '85, and told Dick that I wanted to race. I had a little bit of sponsorship and some tires, and Dick had a car. He said, "Well, if you want to run, we'll go over there and see if we can make the race." We qualified 19th and ran competitively all day until the transmission broke late in the race.

That started what is now my 25th season of racing these cars.

I thought I had the perfect plan, but there were no resources or means to continue it. So I had to be willing to improvise. That improvisation is probably what sped up the process of how tough it is to establish yourself in NASCAR and be able to race cars for your whole life. It probably sped up my ability to get into a car, and it probably sped up my learning curve, and it might be the only way I could have been able to enjoy racing for all these years.

Looking back, there have been a lot of times when I wondered if I had spent more time racing in the smaller divisions, would I have been more prepared to go to the big division? But I look back and say if I had spent more time learning how to race down there, maybe I never would have gotten up here.

So I always try to tell people that it's important to have a plan. You have to put thought and care and love into it. You have to be passionate about your direction and how you're going to get there. If you don't have that desire and that passion to formulate a plan, then I think you probably just don't care enough.

A plan is important, but you have to be ready and willing and able to see opportunity when it comes along. Don't skip it just because it isn't on your checklist. It might be what is necessary for you to continue on down the road.

If you respect people and you listen to smart people, you're likely to get two distinctly different answers from people you think know the world about what you're asking them. But if you use your heart and your desire to trust, and you pick the right one, and you don't look back, it can pay off in the end.

It surely has paid off for me.

~Michael Waltrip

A Little Race Fan's Big Dream Comes True

The year? 2003

The city? Liberty, Missouri

It was a normal delivery day for Rich Hensley, a rep for Alternacare Infusion Pharmacy. An avid NASCAR fan, he was wearing a NASCAR racing shirt. His next stop? Medical supplies to a residence.

He rang the bell. The door opened. A friendly woman invited him in. Once inside, Rich saw a little boy wearing a ball cap, seated on the couch. He also noticed lots of Jeff Gordon memorabilia around the room. "Hi," Rich said, to the cute, round-cheeked little boy.

The medical supplies were for *him*. He was being treated for cancer.

The boy's eyes widened as he saw Hensley's shirt. "Got a NASCAR shirt," he said, with excitement. "Look, it's got a race car on it."

Impressed by this, Hensley carried on a friendly conversation with him about NASCAR and his favorite race car drivers. The boy's name? Rocky.

"My mom likes Jeff Gordon, but my favorite driver's Bobby Labonte," said Rocky, flashing a smile.

"He loves to play with his little race cars and pretend he's racing," mom Terri chimed in. She was the one who had opened the door. Rocky and Rich chatted a little more, then Hensley left for his next delivery. But he couldn't get Rocky out of his mind.

Suddenly, he had an idea. A NASCAR Sprint Cup Series race was coming up at nearby Kansas Speedway. Due to his low blood count, Rich knew Rocky would be unable to go. But what if some drivers contacted Rocky? He called Terri and told her he might be able to do something about that.

Back at Alternacare, Hensley drafted an e-mail to send to Jeff Gordon's foundation for children. He also shared his plan with co-worker Adrienne Malinowski, another ardent NASCAR fan. She had just finished reading *Chicken Soup for the NASCAR Soul*. Immediately, she planned to add to his efforts. She would write to some NASCAR reporters published in that book. That day, their fervent e-mails of appeal went out.

That's when the *Chicken Soup for the Soul* magic began.

Adrienne's e-mail reached my computer in California. It detailed her ardent wish that some NASCAR drivers could visit Rocky while in Kansas for the Sprint Cup Series race. Her message instantly touched my heart. How could I help?

Going into my NASCAR Media Guide, I forwarded her e-mail to the drivers' reps, and to Mike Zizzo, one of NASCAR's Communications Managers at the time, requesting additional help. Her plea was also being opened in other racing computers around the country.

A few days later, a package arrived at Rocky's home, addressed to him. It was a splendid 1/24 scale model No. 18 Interstate Batteries race car, personally autographed by Labonte. Bobby could not be there due to sponsor commitments, but wanted Rocky to have this car. It was sheer delight for this little 5-year-old! An autographed car from his favorite driver!

Hensley also called another *Chicken Soup for the Soul* co-author, Brad Winters, at his Indiana office. Winters quickly devised his own plan. A couple days before the Kansas race, Rocky's doorbell rang again. His mother opened the door. With pre-planning through Brad Winters, it was not a medical delivery this time, but NASCAR driver

John Andretti—in person, with his driver, Skip! Invited by Terri, Rich and Adrienne were already there.

Andretti had arrived a day early that week. Terri excitedly invited John and Skip inside. Rocky spent a happy day with John, playing NASCAR Play Station games and chatting with him about racing. Andretti had brought lots of racing mementoes, and signed Rocky's own little toy cars. He's been a friend of the family ever since, regularly staying in touch by phone and mail, sending Christmas cards with photos of his family. Brad Winters also became a steady family friend.

I continued to contact drivers. Austin Cameron, himself diagnosed with cancer, sent Rocky a handwritten letter. "Stay strong," he advised, and enclosed autographed photos of his No. 16 NAPA Auto Parts NASCAR Grand National Division West race car.

The *Chicken Soup for the Soul* miracles continued to unfold. During Rocky's next treatment at Children's Mercy Hospital, Terri told the staff about Andretti's thrilling visit. More wheels began to turn. Due to his treatments, Rocky was now strong enough to travel. Plans were soon being created through the hospital's local Make-A-Wish Foundation, a national charity that grants ill children's wishes. On a Friday morning, Rocky, Terri, dad Doug, and 12-year-old brother Nick were flown to the Sprint Cup race at Phoenix International Raceway. He would finally get to meet the rest of his NASCAR heroes after all!

At Phoenix, it became the full, wonderful dream that Rocky always had. Once checked in at their hotel, he and his family were escorted to the Hard Rock Café. Rocky was presented with a 1/24 scale model Hard Rock race car. Later, the rep at PIR invited the family into the NASCAR garages.

"All the NASCAR drivers there were so wonderful," his mom recalls. "They would raise the hoods of their race cars, and talk about their cars with my son."

And there were lots of autographs—Dale Earnhardt, Jr., Jimmie Johnson, Ryan Newman, and more.

Finally, there in person was Rocky's hero, Bobby Labonte. He introduced the tiny Missouri boy to his team, proudly saying, "This is Rocky!" Crew chief Fatback McSwain joined in. Team member Scott Zipadelli presented Rocky and family with hats, hero cards, and lug nuts from the race car. Asking permission, Labonte then picked up his little admirer and sat him on his race car—the cherished No. 18! Rocky glowed.

After they shared a meal in Labonte's hauler, Bobby dropped down on his heels, eye-to-eye with Rocky, and talked NASCAR with him to his heart's content.

The Phoenix rep then wanted to know: Was there anyone else Rocky wanted to meet?

"Of course," he said. It was his mom's favorite driver—Jeff Gordon. Rocky and Terri were soon escorted into Gordon's hauler. Smiling at the little Missouri tyke, Gordon asked, "Can I get my picture taken with *you*?" Rocky quickly obliged. Jeff signed a windbreaker and cap. Mom got her cherished autograph.

Worn out from all the excitement on Friday, Rocky slept through part of Saturday's NASCAR Nationwide Series competition, but he joyously watched all his new NASCAR friends compete in Sunday's Checker O'Reilly Auto Parts 500 presented by Pennzoil.

Then it was back to Missouri, to his PlayStation games, his little race cars and great new NASCAR mementoes, taking with him all his wonderful Phoenix gifts and never-to-be-forgotten memories.

"NASCAR people are really something; God and family are so important to them," Terri said after their trip. "This is such a circle of love. It really made an impact on our lives."

This "Chicken Soup for the Soul circle of love" had started simply, with an extremely caring pharmacy rep and a warm-hearted female NASCAR fan who loved the stories she read in *Chicken Soup for the NASCAR Soul.*

From there it mushroomed beyond all expectations to bring out the love of so many involved in NASCAR—all connecting to provide real deep-down joy to one little 5-year-old boy.

~Kay Presto

Everything You've Got

My dad's parents were born and raised in Cuba. They met there, got married there, worked there, and had a family there.

My dad and my uncle were born around the time of the beginning of the era of Castro in Cuba. My grandparents saw that things were going in a direction that they didn't really want to be a part of. They were looking at ways to get to America, so they decided to pack up and take one of the Freedom Flights that were going from Cuba to Miami in the early 1960s.

Basically what you had to do if you wanted to get on one of the flights to the U.S. was give everything you had back to the Cuban government. My grandparents had about a 40-acre farm, and they had their home, and just a lot of stuff, and they had to give it all back. They gave up everything. My grandmother even had to give up her wedding ring.

When they left Cuba to come to Miami the only thing they were allowed to bring was a spare set of underwear. Nothing else. They had the clothes on their back and that was it.

So my grandparents, my dad and his brother flew to Miami. My dad was 4 years old. When they got there, they went through Immigration and filled out all their paperwork. Then the U.S. government gave them $100, patted my grandfather on the back, and told him, "Good luck." That was part of their experience of becoming U.S. citizens.

They lived in Miami for a while and then they moved to Tampa. That's where my dad met my mom. Her family was heavily involved in racing—her father raced sprint cars and go-karts—and when my dad met my mom, he got involved in racing right along with them. My dad fell in love with it; he started going to races all the time.

After my mom and dad got married, my dad became the crew chief on my grandfather's sprint car. They spent a lot of time on the road racing and stuff, and then when I was born, I got to be a part of that.

My mom's father and my dad loved having me around the shop, and when I was a little kid I was always there, watching them work on the race cars. And I was always tinkering on something, whether it was sorting nuts and bolts or sweeping up or whatever. Anything they wanted me to do, I was happy to be a part of it.

I tried playing baseball. I tried basketball. I played every sport all the way up until I was getting ready to go to high school.

I love playing sports. I love being active; I love to be outside. But it seemed like racing was always number one for me. Racing trumped everything else. If there was a baseball game on Saturday and there was also a race on Saturday, I would always choose racing over baseball.

So when I started high school it was a big decision for me whether I was going to try out for the baseball team or for something else, because I knew that if I wanted to get serious at anything, this was the time. I needed to make a decision. I needed to choose to focus on one thing so I could do that thing really well.

I chose racing, and it paid off for me in the long run.

My dad's father passed away in 2009, but my grandmother still lives in Tampa, in the very first house she and my grandfather bought there, and she watches all the races on TV. They have always kept a scrapbook on me; they save everything. They are proud of me.

But I realize where my grandparents came from and everything they went through to start their lives completely over. They made such a sacrifice for the sake of their family. To know that I'm a part of that makes me really grateful, and really proud.

~Aric Almirola

Fighting Back

My racing story may not be the most glamorous or the easiest to tell, but it's an important one. It could help somebody.

In 2003, I was 19 years old, living in Europe and racing in the British Formula Three series. I had gotten hurt—a hand injury—but I had also been noticing something else. There was blood in my stool.

I came back to America to be treated. I got a colonoscopy and had my intestines checked and they told me I had a chronic stomach condition called Ulcerative Colitis. I had never even heard of it, but I was 19 years old so I just said, "OK, what have I got to do? Take this medicine and I should be OK? No problem."

I moved back to Europe a week later and started more therapy on my hand. And at the same time, I was on this medication for a disease that I knew nothing about.

It was about February when I was diagnosed, and by the end of that first season my bleeding had gotten so bad that I couldn't even control my own bowels. Literally, I would be walking around and looking for a bathroom and if I couldn't find one, well, let's just say it was a mess.

It got to the point where it was very embarrassing, obviously, as well as harmful for my health. My large intestine had started to shut down and I wasn't getting the nutrients that I needed, but I made it through the whole first season.

By that time it was November, and I was able to come back to America and Mom's chicken soup. I think being back home and having my mom there to take care of me instead of trying to do everything on my own took away a lot of my stress and kind of made it better.

I was still bleeding a little bit, but it seem to be under control and I was able to control myself, so we really didn't make many medical changes.

Then, when I went back to Europe the next year—I was racing for Red Bull and competing for two championships—this stuff came back, and started getting worse and worse. But I was having a really good year and I was leading the points in the two championships I was running for, so the will to dig through it was greater. I almost really hurt myself badly because my intestines had gotten to a point where they were nearly unrecoverable.

I almost lost my intestines. In mid-July of my second year in Europe, the condition got so bad and I had lost so much blood in my stool that I was actually anemic. I lost so much blood that they were talking about giving me blood transfusions.

That got my attention. It motivated me to see someone and get some more advice. Red Bull was really great about it. They sent me to one of the best doctors in Austria. But by the time I saw him my large intestine was so destroyed that he gave me only a 20 percent chance of keeping it. I would lose the intestine and have to walk around with one of those colostomy bags. That would have ended my racing career.

Thank God, that didn't happen. My doctor put me on an experimental treatment. I got some good help and some new medication, and eventually I got better.

It was a really interesting part of my life. As weird as this sounds, I think I'm very fortunate to have gone through that because it made me grow a lot and learn a lot about my body.

It also taught me to take myself lightly. Anybody who's gone through the type of situation I have gone through becomes a kid real fast, because you learn not to take yourself seriously. You realize you're a human being and there are a lot of things outside your control.

Going through this, and being a race car driver who has this disease and is not afraid to speak openly about it, caused the Colitis Foundation to approach us about being one of their spokesmen. Scott Speed Inc. is based in Scottsdale, Arizona, and it just so happens that the Colitis Foundation is located there as well, so it was a natural partnership.

Ulcerative Colitis is a disease that was super tough on me, mostly because I had just moved away from home. I was so young that things like cooking food and washing clothes were enough of a hassle, but to be dealing with this on top of all that exaggerated the whole issue for me. It was a really, really tough part of my life, and I felt that I learned a lot in the process. It made me grow a lot as a person.

Now it feels good just to be able to share my story and help other people with similar problems.

~Scott Speed

Believe

I can't say for sure when I embraced the belief that everything happens for a reason. Given a choice, I suspect we'd all prefer to skip the painful bits in our lives. But those probably teach us our most important lessons, right up there with "Remember your manners" and "Treat everyone like you want to be treated." Thanks, Mom.

My first job out of college was with SunTrust Banks. I worked my way up through the marketing department, becoming Senior Vice President of Marketing Services based in Orlando, Florida. One of the events I developed was the Rolex 24 At Daytona, which we used to promote our 24-hour banking network. For nine years I learned sports car racing "up close and personal," and loved everything about it—the people, the cars, the sponsors, the organizers and fans.

Early in 1993, I got a call from one of our marketing officers asking if I would meet with the development director of a start-up charity. A few weeks later I welcomed my visitor and asked her what they wanted to do in Florida.

Three hours later, she left my office and I had a new volunteer job—Marketing Chairman for the Hole In the Wall Gang South, a camp modeled on Paul Newman's Hole In The Wall Gang Camp in Connecticut. The Camp would serve children with chronic and life-threatening illnesses, providing traditional activities like horseback riding and fishing so they could be "just kids" for a little while, all at no cost to their families.

By the end of the year, I'd crafted the mission statement and gotten a logo designed for what was now called Camp Boggy Creek. I pulled together a core of talented people to work on the marketing and communications committee. Paul Newman and General H. Norman Schwarzkopf stepped up as co-founders. We broke ground in 1994 and welcomed our first campers in the summer of 1996.

In 1994, I made the decision to quit my job and take some time off to travel and play. During one California trip I learned that an actor friend was going to be Grand Marshal at a charity motorcycle ride in Florida. I immediately thought of Camp and asked to be introduced to the ride organizer. That's how I met Bruce Rossmeyer of Daytona Harley-Davidson. In 1995, Bruce staged his first Ride for Children, which has been an annual event to benefit Camp Boggy Creek ever since.

While planning the camp's grand opening, I started looking for a job. I'd done a consulting project for International Speedway Corporation and really enjoyed it. An offer followed to become the Director of Sales for Daytona International Speedway, a job I accepted. Within a week of starting, I was asked to also assume the General Manager position for the Daytona 500 Experience, which I also accepted.

Before I knew it, Speedweeks 1997 loomed large and I scrambled to learn as much about NASCAR as I could. Fortunately I was surrounded by employees and knowledgeable fans who had been breathing it for years.

I made it through my first Speedweeks and before I knew it we were gearing up for the Coke Zero 400. A couple weeks out, talks began with Brian Flynn, President of the Richard Petty Driving Experience, about bringing a "ride-along" experience to Daytona. The deal was made and in August, Richard Petty and I cut the ribbon.

Speedweeks 1998 began with Brian inviting me to have dinner with him, Richard, and Kyle Petty, whom I'd not yet met. At the last minute, Richard had to bow out. Kyle made Brian call me to be sure I still wanted to have dinner since it would just be him and Brian. I came to know that this self-effacing attitude was typical of Kyle. I'd already given Brian the Camp Boggy Creek story and before long Kyle, who already had his charity motorcycle ride, was asking how he could help.

Summer came and the fires raged. The July race was moved to the fall—Saturday night, October 17, 1998, to be exact. Since Kyle was in Daytona in October, Bruce Rossmeyer asked him to be Grand Marshal for the annual ride. I heard the rumble of engines and stood watching from my office window as the 4th Annual Daytona Harley-Davidson Ride For Children rolled by en route to Camp Boggy Creek, which Kyle would see for the first time.

In June 1999, the leadership of Camp Boggy Creek asked me to come to work there. It was an easy yes. In October, I headed up to North Carolina to see the Pettys. In a little shopping center, over bagels and coffee with Brian and Kyle and Pattie Petty, I asked if they'd consider having their Charity Ride Across America benefit the Hole In The Wall Camps in 2000. Pattie and Kyle exchanged a quick look and said "sure." The idea of a camp for seriously ill kids in North Carolina was already firmly on their "to do" list.

In December, Richard, Kyle, Pattie, Brian and guests from both the Charity Ride and The Richard Petty Driving Experience came to the Camp Boggy Creek holiday party to tour, spend time with the campers, meet the Board and make a generous donation.

Weeks later, both Paul Newman and Kyle Petty were driving in the Rolex 24 at Daytona and I jumped on the chance to get them face to face to talk about a new camp. During a lunch break between practice sessions, I introduced Kyle and Pattie Petty to Paul. Kyle laid out what they wanted to do. Paul encouraged them to proceed in developing their plan, and then the conversation shifted to whose car was handling how, track conditions, etc.

By mid-April work was well underway and a group of us met for a discussion at Adam Petty's (Kyle and Pattie's son) race shop. By the end of that meeting, the new camp's name was finalized. It would be called The Victory Junction Gang Camp.

In April 2000, I was on the back of a Harley-Davidson as we

launched the Ride Across America from California, a seven-day trek ending at Kyle and Pattie's farm in Trinity, N.C.

It was one of the most memorable weeks of my life. Adam was on the ride and it was obvious that the highlights for him were the stops at children's hospitals along the way.

The following Friday he had his fatal accident during practice in New Hampshire.

Pattie and Kyle asked that we temporarily put camp on hold. Officially, we did. Unofficially, we continued to quietly move things along. Then Pattie called and asked if their son Austin could come to Camp Boggy Creek for the summer. Within a week, she had him certified as a lifeguard and he came to Florida.

Lynda Petty, Richard's wife, had not yet seen Boggy Creek. On a trip down to visit her grandson she remarked that now she understood how special Camp was. A very short time later, Kyle and Pattie announced their commitment to Victory Junction, Richard and Lynda donated land and the rest, as they say, is history. The Victory Junction Gang Camp welcomed its first children on Father's Day 2004.

If you are lucky enough to live long enough I hope you'll believe, as I do … it all happens for a reason.

~Sarah Gurtis

Hope, a Bible, and a Miracle

They say everything happens for a reason.

I'd heard that expression many times, but never so much as after my 3-month-old son, Edward, died suddenly and unexpectedly in his sleep. It's called Sudden Infant Death Syndrome, and it means that after an autopsy, there is no medical explanation for the death.

It's impossible to explain the devastation I felt at the loss of my child, but it's a pain that changed who I am forever. Because of that, accepting the death of my healthy infant son was not easy. Well-meaning friends, struggling to help, told me that "everything happens for a reason." Angry and crushed by grief, I silently wondered what the "reason" could possibly be. Eighteen years later, the question remains unanswered.

Trying to move on with my life, I was blessed with two more children—a son, Hayden, and then a daughter, Hope. I chose my daughter's name in the "hope" that she would live a long life because after going through the loss of Edward, I lived in fear for the lives of ALL the people I loved. After all, I reasoned, my son had died while sleeping in the safety of his own crib. Because of that, both of my "subsequent children" (as they are referred to by grief support groups) were on portable cardio-respiratory monitors all day, every day, well past their first birthdays.

But just as my fears of SIDS were beginning to subside, a new threat emerged. It happened suddenly, when Hope was 13 months old. It was Mother's Day, a day that always brought out mixed emotions in me. I noticed that Hope didn't seem herself, and when I checked her temperature, I was struck with a deep fear. At 103 degrees, I knew it was serious.

And it was. A spinal tap revealed that my beautiful little girl had bacterial meningitis. I had heard stories of people dying very quickly from it, and I was terrified. Fortunately, Hope slowly began to recover. I remember sitting in her hospital room beside her crib, thanking God that she was alive. I listened to a doctor's caution that there could be neurological problems for my daughter in the future, but I dismissed his words, joyful that she HAD a future.

The meningitis had done its damage, however, and soon after Hope returned home from the hospital, I knew that her hearing was affected. Audiological testing revealed profound hearing loss in both ears — my beautiful little girl was deaf. But I was so grateful she had survived that I remember thinking, "Better deaf than dead." It sounds cold, but I already knew how it felt to lose a child.

I watched two NASCAR races from my daughter's hospital room as she recovered. It was May of 1995, and I watched as Jeff Gordon swept the NASCAR Sprint All-Star Race in Charlotte. I had become a fan of Gordon's two years earlier, and his victory briefly took my mind off my troubles at a very dark time in my life. A week later, I watched from the hospital room again as Gordon qualified for the pole of the Coca-Cola 600. Bobby Labonte won the race.

I owe my love for NASCAR to my father. I love racing so much, in fact, that when my marriage crumbled a few years later and I was faced with selling my house, I decided to make a very big move.

Until my son's death, I was employed as executive secretary to the CEO of a local hospital. With plenty of experience, a secretarial degree and lots of knowledge about NASCAR, I decided that it was an ideal time for me to take the big step and move to the Charlotte area, NASCAR's hub. I wanted to be a part of the excitement of NASCAR and I was confident I could find a secretarial or clerical position at one of the many race shops there.

It was no small matter to move from my home in Pennsylvania to a city 500 miles away, but with the help of my family, I managed. I rented a small house near the race track and began making arrangements for my kids.

I knew that would be a challenge as a single parent of a 5-year-old son and a 4-year-old daughter, but especially because my daughter was deaf. Although my goal had always been for Hope to learn to speak to communicate, I had been discouraged from trying to teach her because her hearing loss was so profound, even with the amplification of hearing aids. So our family had learned American Sign Language as a way to bridge the communication gap.

I knew I had to make arrangements for my daughter to receive educational intervention, as she had in Pennsylvania. Thankfully I was introduced to a great speech therapist, who talked to me at length about my daughter's situation.

Did I still have a goal of using speech to communicate with my daughter? Was I willing to be aggressive with her listening device? Would I work with her every day on speech therapy goals? Would I be willing to do it for years, not just weeks?

That speech therapist opened up my world to the possibility of a cochlear implant for Hope. I had done some research of my own about the electronic devices that are surgically placed in the skull. Man-made electrodes do the work of millions of hair cells and in many cases are successful in bringing the world of sound to the deaf. My audiologist in Pennsylvania had dismissed the implant, saying it wasn't a choice for Hope because it was "experimental."

After consulting with the staff of the Charlotte Eye Ear Nose & Throat Associates, talking with family and a lot of prayer, I made the decision to have Hope tested to determine if she was a candidate for the procedure. At 5 years old, she was considered "old" for learning to use any new sounds she might gain from the surgery. There was also the possibility that her cochlea might have filled with bony tissue due to her meningitis, which would have made the surgery impossible. In the weeks leading up to the procedure, Hope and I worked closely with the speech therapist, who taught me how to teach my daughter.

All of this meant that any job for me in NASCAR was out of the question. I was keenly aware that even the simplest job at a race shop requires a high level of commitment—and I knew that my commitment had to be to my children, no matter what opportunity might come my way in racing.

But I wasn't bitter. The gift I received as a result of relocating was even better than the dream job I had hoped for. Dr. William Roberts performed the cochlear implant surgery in May of 1999, and because of it, my daughter now is a teenager who loves to listen to rock music and talk on the telephone.

And the experience taught me something. It gave me answers.

I realized that maybe there really is a reason for everything. It's just that sometimes, perhaps understanding the reason is outside of our ability at the time. Perhaps for some things, we'll never know the reason. And for other things, perhaps we THOUGHT we knew the reason, and then we later realize the reason was completely different.

I thought the "reason" I moved to the Charlotte area was to pursue my dream job in NASCAR and live happily ever after. Because of my daughter's special needs, that didn't happen. However, as a result, something even better did. My daughter had successful cochlear implant surgery, something that I know would not have happened had we not relocated when—and where—we did.

It is clear to me now that there WAS a real "reason" for me to move—so my daughter could hear again. It seems obvious, and it's impossible to deny, especially when you consider this: my daughter's name is Hope; her audiologist was Judith Bible; and her speech therapist was Margaret Miracle.

It's very meaningful to me and still gives me goose bumps when I think about it. With Hope, a Bible and a Miracle, I knew we were on the right path. Clearly, this was meant to be.

~Ellen S. Siska

Racing on a Shoestring

Most people are familiar with the old saying, "Been there, done that, got the T-shirt." In the NASCAR fan circle, bragging rights are given to those whose track T-shirts and stories are too numerous to count. But for some racing enthusiasts, like my husband and his friends, race tracks are where dreams come true.

It started out as a family project. Miller Racing (no relation to the popular malt beverage) consisted of a driver/team owner, crew chief (the driver's father), spotter (the driver's brother) and, behind the scenes and keeping the family together, a second team owner, the driver's wife.

It was a simple task; build a race car and enter it into the Goody's Dash Touring Series of races sanctioned by NASCAR.

The former NASCAR Goody's Dash Series became part of NASCAR's touring circuit in 1975. It was a grassroots motorsports event where 4- or 6-cylinder engine vehicles competed on sanctioned tracks with the older Grand National Series (now the NASCAR Nationwide Series) chassis and little or no sponsorship dollars. The sweat of your brow and the kindness of your buddies and family's hearts pretty much paid your way in.

Racing had been in the Miller family for quite some time. The crew chief raced modified cars at local tracks, and both the driver and spotter raced at the local county speedways of Ohio.

Yes, I said Ohio, which made the task even more of a challenge, as most "good ol' boy racing" happens down south, not in the Midwest.

In fact, the motors that were used were rented from a shop in North Carolina. The body, suspension and all other non-engine parts were worked on by the crew in Ohio and then someone would "fetch" the engine when enough pennies had been scraped together.

My husband found out about this whole project and decided to pitch in and help. He has been watching and attending NASCAR races for over 20 years and has always dreamed of becoming part of the action. He is a natural with a wrench and is quick to be the guy to count on for any project that needs doing. This included being the "body double" for the driver, as he is built much the same and could sit in when needed.

So that made one "over the wall" crew member; they just needed a few more. With minimal persuasion, the rest of the crew was formed and in 2001, Miller Racing was signed up for its first NASCAR-sanctioned race. The crew chief assigned tasks and everyone pitched in to buy tires, fire suits and other safety equipment. They also took a few days off work and paid their own way down and back from the first venue, which would be Orange County Speedway near Rougemont, North Carolina.

I dubbed myself the public relations crew member, and took along my camera and a notepad to document the event. When we finally made it to the track and down into the pits, it was something else to see these guys work so passionately. It was as if they were pouring their heart and soul into each turn of a wrench or tightening of a lug nut.

As I looked around, I could see other teams getting their cars ready and sweating under the incredible heat that made your tennis shoes stick to the asphalt. You could tell who had the big-time sponsors and who didn't, but that didn't seem to make a difference to Miller Racing. We were a shoestring operation from Ohio, and if there was anyone who wanted to make a mark on this sport, it was us. We had a driver who had dreamed of this moment for a long time and some hard-working guys who would do anything to achieve that goal for him. I think racing on the NASCAR circuit was starting to become their dream, too.

I watched as my husband maneuvered the cumbersome gas can onto his shoulder and punched it into the gas tank. It was almost race time. The crew lined up outside their pit area for the singing of the national anthem and, wiping away a tear, I focused my camera to capture the moment. The call to start the engines was made and, with a last minute handshake from the crew chief dad, the Miller race car merged onto pit road and took off down the track.

Sitting with the driver's wife up in the grandstands, I could see the excitement on her face slowly fade into worry as she listened in on the driver-to-crew conversation through her headphones. That she was delighting in her husband's dream come true, yet agonizing over watching him maneuver his car at top speeds and inches away from his opponents, seemed paradoxical to me.

We watched as the bumping, grinding and spinning out of cars continued and, after 150 laps, the Miller race team picked up a 20th place finish. It was the first of three races that year.

The following year, the team placed 13th at Kentucky Motor Speedway and, in 2003, they had the ultimate dream of racing at premier NASCAR venues such as Daytona International Speedway and Lowe's Motor Speedway in Charlotte. They finished in 13th and 21st place, respectively. Later that same year, they scrapped the car and ended their illustrious careers.

The Goody's Dash Series was aptly nicknamed, "The Poor Man's Series," for its grassroots beginnings. However, for the Miller Race Team and all the other guys who were racing on a shoestring, it was an opportunity to chase your dream.

~Cathryn Hasek

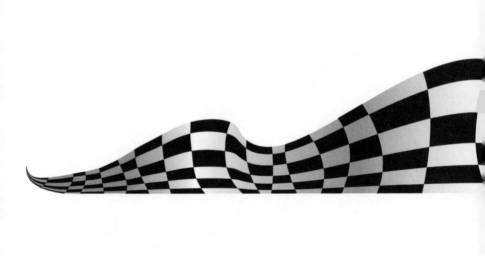

NASCAR®

Romance
and Other
Random Acts
of Racing

Scott on a Stick

May 1st found me, my sister, and two of our friends at the NASCAR race in Richmond, Virginia. Not because we are huge fans. Rather, because my husband, Scott, was a big fan.

Sundays would find Scott in front of the TV watching the race. Frequently I would hear a groan or a whoop; other times it would be, "You've got to come and see this crash." And while he was not a rabid NASCAR fan, he could name all the stats of the drivers. More often than not, Scott would get the eye roll from me as he was regaling me with information.

Scott never made it to a race. After a long battle with cancer, he died on May 1, 2008.

We often talked about the things we wanted to do. He knew about my "things to do before I die" list. Well, Scott had kept a list, too. While going through some of his personal belongings, I found it.

It was a short list, consisting of only four items. One was to ride in a real NASCAR race car. I decided that, since Scott wasn't able to complete his list, I would do it for him.

We had many amazing friends in our life. One day I received four tickets to the Richmond race, arranged by a friend. The day before the race I was told that another set of friends had arranged for me to ride in an authentic stock car. So off to Richmond we went.

As it happened, the race was on the one-year anniversary of

Scott's death. Because we were doing this in honor of Scott, he had to come along. Hence, Scott on a Stick joined us for the festivities.

We printed out an 8x10 photo of Scott and adhered it to a paint stick. Let me tell you, he had a busy day. He had his picture taken in a police car, on a motorcycle, drinking beer, trying on T-shirts, with the group of our friends, and of course, in a race car. By day's end he was exhausted.

On a day that could have been so sad, we celebrated Scott's life. The number of people that came up to us at the race to comment on Scott on a Stick was incredible. And he thoroughly enjoyed screaming around the track at 150 miles per hour. It truly was an amazing day with the loveliest of friends.

Scott has now taken a cruise and ridden in a NASCAR stock car. The remaining items on the list are to play golf at Pebble Beach, and at St Andrews in Scotland. Scott on a Stick is going to be well-traveled. His passions, and his smiling face, are showing me the world.

~Melissa Sorensen

Miss Rose by Any Other Name

I've thought of her often, the smallish, gray-haired lady who made a brief but lasting impression on me. Her name wasn't "Miss Rose," but maybe it should have been. She looked like a Miss Rose.

"Mind if I sit with you?" she said that Monday morning as she set down her cup of coffee at the table I was hogging.

It was I who was the trespasser, so I told her that I'd be proud to have her join me. I gathered that the big table for six I'd plopped down at was a sort of community table, anyhow. Being the first one there didn't preclude having company and, being the stranger, I wanted some.

I didn't ask her name, nor she mine, but I gathered she was likely the owner of the small restaurant sitting on the historic square of Madison, Georgia, some 60 miles east of Atlanta.

Madison was a frequent stopping spot on my way back to Columbia from the races at Talladega Superspeedway—a place where I both literally and figuratively ran out of gas.

"Sure is gonna be a pretty day, idn't it," she said as she settled in, adjusting her tiny half-frame reading glasses to get a better look at the interloper. "A little cooler, and they say it's gonna be even cooler on Wednesday."

You know, a quarter of a century of covering NASCAR racing

leaves a man with a backlog of memories so thick that he doesn't have to dig very deeply to find one.

I can pull up a story I've written from a certain race, or maybe a driver interview I once did, and linger over the remembrance of it like a fine cigar. Or pick and choose vignettes from all over and sample them like a box of chocolates.

But as I get further away from racing—and a decade after meeting Miss Rose—I find that my fondest memories are as much of the people who had very little to do with drivers and race tracks as the ones I was sent to write about.

The things that surface now are of people and places that were linked to auto racing only by geography.

Eric Williams, for instance, may have been one of the finest guitar pickers I've heard anywhere, but I only heard him play outside the front office of the Williams Motel in North Wilkesboro, North Carolina, when the big boys of NASCAR made their twice-annual stops in the little town.

I can't remember Diana's last name, but she was the head clerk at the motel in Griffin, Georgia, that a bunch of us called home during Atlanta races. After a few years, if you forgot to call Diana for a reservation, she'd call you, just to make sure you were coming. Checking in and checking out always included a hug.

Miss Rose absently stirred at her cup of black coffee. Carefully creasing the pages of an *Atlanta Journal-Constitution* so that it showed only the crossword puzzle, she said, "I like the cold weather better, don't you?"

I told her that I was from Columbia and mentioned that since Columbia, South Carolina was the hottest place north of the equator, I wouldn't mind a little cool weather myself. "Oh, you don't have to tell me about Columbia," she said. "I lived there from 1969 to 1971, when my husband retired from the Army. I know it's hot."

Monday mornings always found me ravenous and usually with enough time to enjoy a leisurely breakfast before I had to be back in Columbia.

That Sunday had been a long day. I got trapped in the infield before the start of the race and had to walk half the distance around the gigantic track to get to the press box. I was never so impressed with the size of the place before, but my hike also gave me an appreciation for something else.

Sure, in the press box I'd have gotten a better look at one of those patented Dale Earnhardt charges to the front in the first 10 laps, but I'd have never heard it as well.

Walking along the mezzanine behind the frontstretch grandstands, I'd stop at every other set of steps and squeeze my way into the aisle. Earnhardt, a notoriously poor qualifier, was coming, and everybody knew it.

Frankly, I'd never seen anything quite like it. No one was sitting, and two-thirds of the fans in the stands were screaming at the top of their lungs, holding up three fingers and shouting, "Threeeee!! Threeeee!!" as Earnhardt and his ominous-looking black No. 3 Chevy roared past.

At the end of the afternoon, when Earnhardt blew by Dale Jarrett to complete a sweep of both of that season's races at a track where he was an absolute master, you'd think those same fans would have had enough thrills for one day. Fully an hour later, when Earnhardt finally got to the press box, maybe 300 were still hanging around to get a glimpse of their hero. The word "Threee!!" rang in my ears until past bedtime.

One state to the right of Alabama, Earnhardt's triumph may have gotten some cheers, but the plight of the Atlanta Braves was being felt in even the far reaches of Georgia.

Locked in a fierce pennant duel with the New York Mets in 1999, the Braves had sent the National League series to a seventh game with a 10-9 loss in 15 innings in New York. Atlanta's Kevin McGlinchy gave up a game-winning grand slam home run to Robin Ventura to send the teams back to Atlanta.

"You know, I heard on the radio this morning that (Braves manager) Bobby Cox left that young boy in there just so Atlanta would lose," Miss Rose said, indignantly. "They said he wanted to play all seven games so he could make more money."

I was too polite and, for once, maybe wise enough not to mention that Mr. Cox would have made more money if he'd have gone ahead and gotten his team into the World Series.

She was too polite, too, to ask what a stranger was doing in her restaurant on the finest morning of the fall, but I let it drop that I had been in Talladega for the races.

"Oh, I don't like that racing much," she said. "Too loud. I've got a niece and her husband who race. They go to all the big ones, but I never did care much for it.

"Now, when I was a young girl, I did like that—what do they call it—powderpuff?"

We chatted for a few more minutes about the vicissitudes of baseball and racing until the young waitress who had been standing by with the coffee pot spoke up. "Why don't you tell him what you really want to do?" the young girl said.

"You know what I've always wanted to do?" she said. "I've always wanted to try that demolition derby. I bet I'd be pretty good at that."

I bet you would, Miss Rose. I bet you would.

~Jim McLaurin

The City Girl and the Country Boy

As much as I loved growing up in the South, I wanted a totally new experience when I went off to college, so I ended up at the State University of New York in Albany. Ginny, a native New Yorker, became my best friend and closest confidante. She patiently listened for hours on end while I extolled the virtues of the South, especially our passion for NASCAR.

The biggest thrill in Ginny's life had been when the high school football star took her to the senior prom. The best day of my life had been when my daddy took me to Martinsville, Va. when I was 12 to see my first NASCAR race.

Ginny thought all NASCAR fans were "good ol' boy" types, complete with pickup trucks and cowboy boots. "Come on," I once said to her. "Haven't you even glanced at the television for a few seconds when NASCAR was on? Surely you know better than that."

"I never really watched it long enough to find out," she replied.

During the four years we spent together in college, we teased one another good-naturedly about the North versus the South. When we graduated, Ginny promised that one day she would visit me so she could sit on my veranda and drink mint juleps.

"I don't have a veranda," I said, "and I've never had a mint julep. But we can do better than that. We can go to Martinsville and see a race. That will be a much better Southern experience for you to talk about when you get back home."

"Don't threaten me like that," Ginny laughed, "or I'll never dare go south."

After college Ginny and I kept in touch. She went to work for a fashion designer. I taught third grade. The years passed. She got promoted. I got married. Life kept both of us busy and that promised visit was put off time and again.

Then I got an e-mail from Ginny. "It's been four years," she said. "I said I'd come down South and visit you and your family and darn it, I'm gonna do it."

I excitedly showed my husband, Jack, Ginny's e-mail. "The Goody's Fast Pain Relief 500 will be in Martinsville while Ginny is here. We have to get tickets," I told him.

Jack's face lit up. His family members were even bigger NASCAR fans than mine. For Jack, going to the big race at Martinsville would be like a family reunion.

He patted my stomach. "It'll be our son's first NASCAR race," he said. "You know, I've heard that infants in the womb can hear things like music. So he should be able to hear the noise at the speedway."

"Well, we don't want to traumatize him," I said.

Jack eyed my huge belly. "I think there is enough cushion there to muffle the sound. Besides, he has too much NASCAR in his blood to be traumatized by a little bit of noise," he said.

When we picked Ginny up at the airport she took one look at my bulging belly and squealed, "You didn't tell me!"

"I wanted to surprise you," I said.

When I showed her the NASCAR tickets, she squealed again. "You didn't tell me!"

"I wanted to surprise you," I said. "Besides, you might not have come if I had warned you."

In spite of her misgivings, on the day of the race Ginny got into the spirit of things. "Should I go into town and buy a baseball cap?" she teased.

"I have plenty of baseball caps," Jack teased back. "And if you keep on talking, I can knock out a couple of your teeth and you can be authentic."

Ginny had kept her slim figure and she looked adorable in matching black and white shorts and a cropped shirt. Jack grinned at her. "You're gonna drive all the hot-blooded NASCAR boys wild today, Ginny girl."

"You'll protect me from them, won't you Jack?" Ginny said, pulling her long, blond hair into a ponytail.

"I'll do my best," Jack said solemnly. "But it won't be easy."

When we got to the speedway, Ginny thoroughly enjoyed people-watching.

"Who do you want to win?" she asked Jack. "You're not wearing a T-shirt with your man's name on it. Isn't that disloyal?"

"Oh, I don't care who wins," Jack said, "as long as he doesn't have a funny name. We're gonna name our kid after the winner, because this is his first NASCAR race."

Ginny's mouth dropped wide open. "Only a hardcore NASCAR fan would do that. You can't be serious," she said.

Jack tried to keep a straight face, but he couldn't. "I'm just trying to show you how silly your preconceived notions about NASCAR fans are," he said, laughing.

Just then Ginny nudged me. "Two rows down, on the right, there is a gorgeous guy in a UNC Tarheels T-shirt who keeps staring at you," she said.

"Where?" I asked, looking in the direction she had indicated. I immediately saw the guy she was talking about, and he gave me a big smile and a wave. I burst out laughing. "Ginny, I think he has been staring at you, not me."

"Why do you say that?" Ginny asked. "Didn't he just wave at you when he caught your attention?"

"He sure did," I replied. "He probably wants me to introduce you to him. That gorgeous guy is my cousin, Damon. Shall I call him over?"

"Why not? It might make the rest of my vacation quite memorable," she said, giving me a little wink. I motioned for Damon to come over, and as he walked toward us, Ginny gave me a mischievous grin. "I just might learn to like NASCAR after all."

Damon took up a lot of Ginny's time for the rest of the week she stayed with me. I didn't mind, because when I saw the way they looked at one another, I had a feeling that I would be seeing more of her very soon.

I was right. Now that she has moved south, and she and Damon are married, I see her quite often. Jack and I get together with Damon and Ginny frequently, especially at NASCAR events.

Ginny, you see, has become a most loyal fan. When her NASCAR misconceptions flew out the window, love walked right through the door, in more ways than one.

~Elizabeth Atwater

Confessions of a NASCAR Convert

*T*o be honest, NASCAR wasn't my first choice of an activity to discover with my family. I always thought it was just a bunch of cars driving in circles. Don't they get dizzy? (They don't.)

But I married a man who was a NASCAR fan. He watched faithfully every weekend between February and November. He knew all the names of the drivers. He knew their teammates, car owners, crew chiefs, and strategies. He had his favorite drivers, and he had his least favorite. It took a lot of years of watching him watch NASCAR before I began to take an interest with him.

Truthfully, my interest in NASCAR came only out of wanting to spend time with my husband. I was really tired of being alone on Sunday afternoons, and my complaining about his passion was not working. "I'll try something else," I thought. "But what? I couldn't possibly find myself interested in these races, could I?"

It was worth a shot.

Having made the decision to give NASCAR a try, I began to sit beside my husband on Sunday afternoons as he watched. At first, honestly, I got bored about a quarter of the way through the race. Sometimes I would fall asleep. Other times I would read, or leave. This wasn't working. I decided I would be much better off if I actually learned something about what I was watching.

I began asking my husband about what was happening. I had to be careful not to interfere with his viewing, and not to take it personally if he yelled his answer when the race was getting tense. But it was starting to work. I could understand bits and pieces of the commentary. I started hearing names and recognizing car numbers and paint schemes. Next I started to understand who the owners were, which cars belonged to them, and that teammates would often work together, at least off the track.

I had made a breakthrough. I understood this foreign NASCAR language, and actually began to enjoy it. Time for the next step.

My husband had a birthday coming up, and we lived only a few hours from Texas Motor Speedway. NASCAR tickets would be something he would never expect, and he would absolutely love to go to a race live. I bought the tickets and surprised him. Not only did I buy him tickets, I went with him to the race.

When we arrived, I felt as if I had entered an alternate universe. Everything was NASCAR. People camped on the grounds of the track. They literally lived this stuff. I was soaking it all in, and I was learning more about the NASCAR culture.

Early in the day, we located our seats and returned to the midway where we strolled up and down the long rows of souvenir trailers promoting drivers, NASCAR, and other race-related vendors. We operated simulators and discovered there is a reason why we are not part of a NASCAR team. We visited the trailers of our favorite drivers to purchase hats and T-shirts.

The time for the pre-race activities came, and we returned to our seats. The couple next to us had a pad of paper and a Sharpie; we didn't think anything much about it at the time. We watched in awe as the drivers we had seen on television paraded in front of us. We photographed as many drivers as we could keep up with.

The excitement was building as the drivers finished their introductory parade lap in the beds of the pickup trucks. The crews lined up in their pit boxes, and goose bumps went up and down our spines as "The Star Spangled Banner" was sung and the fighter jet flyover ripped through the air.

The drivers entered their cars and the most famous words in motorsports were finally shouted over the loudspeaker: "GENTLEMEN, START YOUR ENGINES!" The crowd erupted into cheers, and the engines began to roar. So this is what it feels like to be a NASCAR fan.

I realized later that this was just the beginning. Our seats were only six rows from the fence. We had a perfect view of the cars as they rounded Turn 4, heading for the start/finish line. As the pace car pulled off the track, I could hear the increasing roar of the engines of 43 cars as they came blazing around Turn 4, anticipating the green flag. As it waved and the drivers hit the gas, the roar was so loud I thought my ears were going to burst. It was the most exciting auditory experience of my life. The pain indicated I really ought to use my earplugs, but the rush of that sound was too exciting.

I could see the people around me shouting and jumping and screaming, and I was pretty sure there was sound coming out of their mouths, but I couldn't hear them for the roar of the engines. What a rush!

A few laps into the race, the crowd settled back into their seats and we watched as the cars continued in their quest to be the first to complete the 500-mile race. I noticed the couple next to us passing notes. Aha! That's why they brought paper and a pen. I made a mental note and put in my earplugs.

That particular race was relatively uneventful. There were no wrecks, which actually disappointed me. I don't really want to see people get hurt, but the screeching of tires and twisted metal as two cars collide was something I had been looking forward to. There were a couple spinouts, though, both of which happened right in front of us.

I did learn that I really hate the smell of burning rubber. I had to breathe through a layer of clothing for a lap or two, but it was the closest I would come to seeing a wreck that weekend, so I took it.

That weekend I finally understood why my husband really loved NASCAR. I had discovered a new hobby, and we began to really enjoy the Sunday afternoons at home.

Since that first visit to Texas Motor Speedway, we have returned with our kids to teach them the importance of learning to share each other's passions. They had as much fun as we had the first time, and it has become something we do every so often as a family. The kids ask us to take them back, and they love to tell their friends about their experiences at the track.

In today's society, connecting with the whole family and sharing experiences together is getting more and more rare. But NASCAR has given my family a common interest. We share a little part of each other's lives every time we go to the races.

~Betty Hanks

Static

I'll never forget the first race I was truly invested in. I was driving back to Florida, and couldn't listen to another song. I wanted to hear people talking. So, I turned the radio to a country station that was broadcasting the race. The announcers on MRN were exciting. They could make a simple pass in Turn 4 seem so dramatic.

I loved it.

I kept driving, not noticing as I exited one state and entered the next. Miles whizzing by, I'd lose one station broadcasting the race, and with angst switch it to another. Both hands on the wheel, I leaned forward, my face almost kissing the windshield, getting closer and closer to home. There were about 20 laps left; the race was on full blast in my car. I sat on the edge of my driver's seat ready to cheer.

Static.

In a panic, I scanned and scanned. With one hand on the wheel and the other on the radio knob, I switched stations, not missing one. I tried AM, then back to FM.

Nothing. No race. No country music. No MRN. Oh. My. God.

I called Justin immediately. "Babe, I've been listening to the race since South Carolina and I can't find MRN." I was freaking out. "Who's leading?"

For the last 10 laps, as I approached my exit, Justin announced the race to me over the phone. I was relieved. I was not about to invest four hours in a race and not know the outcome.

What was happening to me? Had Justin turned on some switch? Did I have NASCAR fever? It sure felt that way.

It wasn't always like this. I wasn't always interested in NASCAR. In fact, I was quite resistant at first.

When I met Justin, who is currently a tire changer in the NASCAR Nationwide Series, I will admit I hated NASCAR. I hated everything about it. I hated that it was on 10 months out of the year, that every weekend if your cable package included SPEED TV you could watch at least three races in one weekend. THREE RACES. It was overwhelming. I didn't want to watch cars going around in a circle.

When Justin graduated, he moved to Charlotte and began training to be a tire changer in a pit crew; I stayed behind to finish my degree. He was traveling every weekend, making it difficult for us to plan a visit, and for the longest time I blamed NASCAR and what I considered their ridiculous scheduling, their lack of care for the family, for Justin's horrible schedule. It was just one more reason for me to dislike such a horrible sport.

There was one issue: Justin loved it. He loved the traveling, the people, the adrenaline rush when jumping over the wall, everything. He'd go racing every weekend if they'd let him.

Before Justin, I had never watched a race on TV, let alone been to one, but because of his schedule there were weekends when I tagged along with him and his team. There I was standing in the infield, seeing what went on backstage, and being less than 10 feet from the pit stops. I was in a sacred place, according to Justin.

He explained, "People would pay lots of money, thousands of dollars, to watch the race from where you're standing."

What the heck was the big deal? The first few races I watched from the infield I didn't understand what the hype was about. The infield was crowded, men working, rushing to get parts, tools, change into firesuits, and eat before the race. It was no place for just anyone to be walking around. I was perpetually in the way of people working, or of teams trying to win a race. The first few events I attended, I remember the race ended and I hadn't noticed. I turned to Justin saying, "That's it? It's over?" I just didn't get it.

Some time has passed since the MRN incident, and since then I've found a kind of transformation has occurred. I've been infected with some kind of fever for sure. I find myself using phrases like "clear," "tight," "loose," and "get up on the wheel." These are words that have infiltrated my vernacular, in part, transforming me into a NASCAR fan.

I now look forward to every race that I can attend. It was easy to become a racing fan because the people involved in NASCAR are truly a family, and a broad community of wonderful people who welcome everyone and anyone with open arms.

It is a community that I'm proud to say, thanks to Justin, I have been exposed to, and am now a part of.

~Gloria Panzera

Behind
the Billboards

Kevin Harvick's Gift of Caring

After a year of suffering on dialysis, my husband, Joe, underwent his first kidney transplant at the age of 32.

When the transplant date was set in stone, I set out to find something special to give him as a get-well gift. Since both of us are diehard NASCAR fans, I considered purchasing a special addition for our collection. However, I wanted something more personal than just another die-cast car or T-shirt.

On a whim, I e-mailed our favorite NASCAR drivers' fan clubs, asking them to send Joe something—a note, a card, or even an e-mail—encouraging him to get well after his surgery.

Within a week, a large manila envelope arrived from Kernersville, North Carolina. I gasped when I read the name on the return address—KHI. Kevin Harvick Incorporated!

Bursting with excitement, I tore the envelope open and pulled out an oversized postcard featuring the famous No. 29 Chevrolet and its driver, with a personalized note saying, "Get Well Soon. Kevin Harvick."

My heart swelled with awe, appreciation, and joy. I had expected a form letter from the fan club wishing my husband well, and instead I had received a personalized note from the superstar driver. The sentiment meant more than words could express. It was a dream come true!

Impatient by nature, I yearned to give the postcard to my husband immediately. However, I knew it would be a treasured gift for him after the transplant. I shared the card with family members, swearing them to secrecy. Then I hid it, planning to present it to Joe when he arrived home from the hospital.

On March 29, 2004, Joe received a kidney from his younger brother, Jason. The procedure went as expected, and within hours of the surgery, the kidney was working and Joe's skin tone transformed from a yellowish hue to a warm pink. It was a miracle! Joe was going to start a new life, free of dialysis.

Jason struggled with the painkillers during the first 24 hours of his recovery. However, Joe's recovery began in a typical fashion until three days later, when he hit a roadblock. He had contracted a staph infection during surgery.

What transpired next was worse than the transplant.

Joe endured a more painful surgery than the transplant. After the procedure, his mood became glummer due to lack of relief from the excruciating pain.

To make matters worse, we were informed that he couldn't go home when he'd originally planned. More than anything, Joe wanted to continue his recovery in our bed, surrounded by our family, including our 3-year-old son, our spoiled rotten cats, and me.

When I heard the news that Joe wasn't coming home for at least another week, I knew I needed to do something to cheer him up. Before I left for the hospital that day, I grabbed the large manila envelope containing the precious postcard.

Upon my arrival at the hospital, I found Joe propped up in a chair, frowning. His eyes reflected the depression that had settled into his soul due to his pain level, and not being able to pack up and come home with me. I pulled the envelope from my bag and handed it to him, telling him it was a special surprise.

I'll never forget his expression when he pulled out that card. Not only did his eyes widen in shock, but they also filled with tears.

Joe asked me how on earth I'd gotten Kevin Harvick to send him a card, and I grinned, stating that I owed it all to Kevin's wife, DeLana, since I'd e-mailed her, along with Kevin's webmaster and fan club president. I explained my plan to find him a very special get-well gift and that Kevin took the gift to the next level—a precious treasure we'd always cherish.

Shaking his head, Joe was stunned and overwhelmed. He couldn't believe someone as famous as Kevin Harvick would take the time to send him a card. Holding that card in his hand gave Joe a renewed sense of hope that everything would be OK.

The staph infection lengthened Joe's hospital stay by 10 days and added a team of infectious disease doctors to the white coats marching in and out of his room.

Joe's recovery at home was also extended due to the infection. An in-home care nurse tended to his incision for several weeks, and he was unable to work for a few months. However, he made a full recovery. With his new kidney, he was strong and healthy.

Joe was back to his old self, and we enjoyed traveling to many NASCAR races. We frequented Dover International Speedway and Richmond International Raceway. Our admiration for Kevin Harvick grew, and his signed postcard hung framed with our collection of NASCAR die-casts.

Our lives have changed since Joe received his kidney from his brother in 2004. We welcomed a second baby boy into our family in March 2005, and we moved from Virginia to North Carolina in 2006. The postcard from Kevin Harvick is still framed and displayed in a place of honor between two of our NASCAR die-cast collectible cases in our boys' playroom.

In 2008, we discovered that Joe's transplanted kidney had failed. His health deteriorated quickly, and he is back on dialysis and awaiting a second transplant.

While our lives took an unexpected turn with Joe's health, I do know one thing for sure—there are special people in this world, like Kevin Harvick, who will go that extra mile and take a few minutes to brighten someone's day.

Each time I see Kevin Harvick in an interview on television, on the Internet, or in a magazine, I smile and remember how his simple postcard took my husband from dark, suffocating despair to a bright glimmer of hope. Someday I'll get a chance to meet him and thank him for giving my husband hope during one of the darkest moments of his life.

Until that day comes, I'll continue to root for Kevin from afar.

~Amy Clipston

The Price of Fame

I have a few confessions to make.

"Billie Jean" is not my lover. I don't come remotely close to being "Bad," unless we're talking about golf. Or math. And if I embraced the "Don't Stop Til You Get Enough" philosophy, I would weigh roughly the same as one of the stock cars currently racing in the NASCAR Sprint Cup Series.

And I was a big—no, make that a HUGE—fan of Michael Jackson.

Following his death in 2009, there was an awful lot of criticism about what was called the worldwide "deification" of Jackson. I'm not quite sure what all the fuss was about. We do this all the time, not only with musicians, but with artists, athletes, actors, authors and those mysteriously famous others who defy any categorization or rational thought.

If every successful businessperson in this country was set up on a pedestal the same way our NASCAR heroes are, chiropractors would never have another care in the world, because America would have a permanent crick in its neck. So many people have made so much money that looking up at them has almost become a full-time job.

I guess deep down we know—or at least we think we know—that NASCAR superstars put their flame-retardant racing suits on one leg at a time, just like the rest of us.

But it is kind of cool to imagine them doing stuff like descending into the depths of stately Johnson Manor, where their "work clothes" wait in somber splendor under a spotlight, before roaring out of a cave in the jaw-droppingly fast Lowes-mobile. Or watching a relatively nondescript middle-aged man duck into a phone booth only to emerge seconds later in full Kellogg's splendor before taking flight, faster than a speeding bullet. SuperMark, we might call him.

Granted, you might need a special sort of superpower to even find a normal phone booth in this day and age, but you get my drift.

The entertainment media would largely be plunged into bankruptcy if we didn't have an avid interest in our icons, heroes and yes, even our villains. It sometimes seems that when someone earns a big pile of money, they garner respect at the same time and in the same proportion, and we, in turn, look up to them. We admire them. They seem to be set apart from us, to be different somehow.

But are they really? Does a man's net worth necessarily equal his net measure of success in life, or define his value as a person? I can tell you from personal experience that, in NASCAR terms at least, the answer is an unqualified "no."

For seven sometimes fulfilling but always educational years, I was the director of public relations for Darlington Raceway in Darlington, South Carolina. One of the very best things about having a public relations job in NASCAR is the opportunity to have kind of a "backstage pass" with the drivers. They often come to race tracks to participate in media events and such, and you spend time with them and get to know them and have conversations with them that most folks just never get the chance to have. Preconceptions fly out the window faster than kids fly out the door on the last day of school.

But like those students eager for the start of summer, lessons can find you and teach you something when you least expect it. You see things in a different light. You learn the difference between a person and a persona.

The first example of this came courtesy of Professor Carl Edwards. I was driving Edwards back to the driver motorhome lot from an appearance on the SPEED stage one night after qualifying when he asked if we could make a detour and go up into the grandstands.

I wasn't really sure what Carl wanted to do up there. I probably thought at the time that he might be feeling a tad insecure and just needed a little love from the fans.

Wrong. He asked me to stop the golf cart in a largely deserted area of the frontstretch grandstand, no fans in sight. Then he got out and for a very long moment, just stared out at the track, which looked misty and mysterious under its newly-installed lighting system.

"Wow," he said. "I've never seen it like this before. Wow." For just a moment, a star was starstruck.

Lesson learned? We are never too impressive to be impressed.

A couple years later, I had the opportunity to judge a national anthem singing contest with Professor Kasey Kahne. A field of hopeful NASCAR Idols from all over the country had been winnowed down to three, and they participated in a sing-off in front of a semi-big crowd and an extremely big name.

Any of the three would have been worthy of the win, so there really was no wrong choice. But when the moment of truth arrived and the final decision had to be made, Kasey leaned over to me and whispered, "I can't decide. I can't choose. I don't want to hurt anyone's feelings."

Lesson learned? A hero's feelings are not more important than the feelings of his fans.

Professor Tony Stewart was addressing a motorsports marketing class at the University of South Carolina one year when the question came up, "When did you know you were famous?"

The answer, which I'm paraphrasing, stands out in my mind as one of the coolest stories I have ever heard a driver tell.

When Stewart was a kid growing up in Indiana, doing all the things normal kids do, it became his habit to visit the same Coke machine after school every day for a soda. So after he was all grown up and a NASCAR Sprint Cup Series champion and generally acknowledged as one of the greatest race car drivers in history, he visited the old neighborhood one day and went around the corner for old times' sake to get himself something cold to drink out of that same Coke machine.

But the Coke machine had changed … he was on the front of it. A life-sized, two-dimensional Tony Stewart stared back at his flesh and blood counterpart. Talk about coming face to face with your own reality. A man who deals with millionaires every day was stopped in his tracks by a one-dollar Coke machine.

Lesson learned? It is often a good thing to catch a glimpse of yourself from a different perspective.

NASCAR experiences like these have taught me something very important—the true price of fame may be a whole lot less than you imagined, but worth a whole lot more than you think.

~Cathy Elliott

A Renewed Life

*T*he day of the 2001 Daytona 500, I hurried into my house and turned on the race. I'd just finished walking the perimeter of my neighborhood as part of my recovery from open-heart surgery. I needed a diversion to boost my spirits. I'd been told that many men became depressed after the procedure.

Although I wasn't depressed, I was angry. I'd been the model patient. I'd done everything right, so it was a bitter pill for someone as dedicated to daily exercise and healthy eating as I was to still need surgery. Watching the Daytona 500 was just the remedy I needed to feel better about my situation.

I had enjoyed following Cale Yarborough and Harry Gant in years past. But in the mid 1990s, for some unknown reason, I lost interest in the sport. For me, the fun of watching the races is cheering for my favorite driver, but I no longer had one.

With my feet up on the sofa, I watched the driver introductions. I'd been a Dodge owner for years, and Dodge had reentered NASCAR in 2001. So I figured I'd pick a Dodge driver. Sterling Marlin fit my profile: an older driver approaching the end of a career like I was approaching the end of mine.

As the race entered the final laps, Dale Earnhardt, Sr. blocked the pack, allowing his DEI teammates to take the lead. Marlin was right behind him with nowhere to go. He got underneath Earnhardt's Chevy, which ultimately wound up hitting the wall. The horrible impact changed racing forever. That day, NASCAR lost a true champion.

Dale Earnhardt, Sr. would have said, "Hey boys, that's just racin'."

Over the next few weeks, I watched how Marlin went on with business. His courage touched me deeply. I had doubts about myself back then, and I wondered if I could ever fully recover from my surgery. I'm sure Marlin had doubts, too. But he didn't let that stop him, and I didn't let my surgery stop me.

As I continued to watch the races, my wife got hooked on NASCAR as well. She became a Dale Jr. fan, and we bought the stuff—T-shirts, caps, and jackets. We also purchased season tickets to the races at the Kansas Speedway, so we could experience the full impact live.

I was awestruck as we emerged from under the stadium and walked up to our seats. The mass of humanity in the stands and on the infield surpassed any football game I'd ever attended. I counted about 12 fans brave enough to wear the Marlin No. 40 T-shirts, compared with thousands of fans wearing Dale Jr. and Dale Sr. gear.

The sun shone brightly, and I realized I hadn't thought about my open-heart surgery in months. The diversity of people surrounding us was amazing. A farmer from Iowa and his wife sat next to me. They'd driven 300 miles to be here. The three fellows directly in front of us were shirtless, and one had a No. 3 shaved in the hair on his back, mimicking a commercial I'd seen on television.

On the other side of my wife sat a family of four. The kids were maybe 10 and 12 and all cleaned up with Jeff Gordon outfits on. They snacked on those big pretzels with gobs of yellow mustard.

During the driver introductions, many of the Earnhardt fans booed Marlin. But then a preacher stepped to the microphone, and we all stood and bowed our heads in prayer. Afterwards, a shiver of unity rippled through the stands when the national anthem was sung. With September 11 still etched in our memories, some people actually wept. From off to the east a rumbling could be heard, as a stealth bomber dropped low and thundered over the track. The vibration rocked the stands and a deafening roar erupted from the crowd. The feeling of national pride was overwhelming and sent chills down my spine.

The next three hours were magical. Marlin had a good day, placing fifth. Dale Jr. didn't do as well, but that didn't dampen my wife's enthusiasm for him. At the end of the day, we both agreed that we were avid racing fans.

We were at the Kansas Speedway in 2002 when Marlin crashed, ending his bid for the NASCAR Sprint Cup Series championship. I admired his courage during and after his recovery from a cracked vertebra in his neck. Seeing him get back into a race car and drive inspired me to get back into an exercise program.

We took a cruise after the 2003 racing season with other Sterling Marlin supporters, and Sterling thrilled us by spending time with his fans. He answered our questions and told tales about the pranks he'd played over the years on fellow competitors and crew members.

After Marlin went into semi-retirement, I took some time finding another driver to support. Finally, I joined the Ryan Newman fan club. Of course, that meant buying more stuff. When Newman won the 2008 Daytona 500, I wore my T-shirt proudly to work the next Monday.

My wife and I have traveled to the races at Atlanta, Texas, and Las Vegas speedways. Every track we go to is a unique experience. I value each day as a gift from God. We now combine vacations with races and take time to visit relatives and friends while enjoying the sport we love. Our next adventure is still to be planned. I'm thinking Bristol!

So come 2010, look into the stands when the broadcasters scan the crowds at Bristol. Sitting just right of the start-finish line about 40 rows up will be yours truly and his wife. We'll wave at you and smile, because we'll be there, and you'll be missing all the fun.

My love for NASCAR, and one "Sterling" example of courage, have helped renew my life.

~Bill Wetterman

Fast Enough

The grumble of motors revved at the Texas Motor Speedway at a practice session. I worked for a driving school, unaffiliated with NASCAR, but we had offices with an unobstructed view of the glory. Blue skies, banked track, and the whir of fast cars meant it was race week in Justin, Texas, north of Fort Worth.

This is a NASCAR story with no cars, but there is a motorized vehicle involved; no helmets, but earplugs were needed; and excellent reaction times were required, although no one touched a steering wheel.

Not everything during race week took place at the track. There were a lot of events to keep drivers out of their cars and in the public eye.

I learned about the behind-the-scenes generosity of NASCAR drivers when I volunteered to help at one such event, a clay pigeon shoot-out. It was a typical Texas April morning, blustery and cool with an equal chance of showers or 90-degree temperatures. Ready for anything, I dressed in layers and drove to a lovely little ranch not far from the speedway. White fences lined the property, and lazy longhorns bobbed their big horns as they moseyed and then stopped to graze. I found the volunteer parking lot and set off to sign in.

"Welcome to the Speedway Children's Charities BBQ and Shoot-Out. You're assigned to post seven to mark chits as a spotter," said a perky woman dressed in cowgirl regalia. "Here's your name tag. Hop aboard a pickup truck and climb out at seven."

"OK, thanks. Will someone at that post tell me what I'm spotting?" I asked.

"Don't worry, hon, you'll do fine, and these young fellas are real nice." She turned to greet the next person in line.

I wandered over and talked to others waiting for the truck. I was there on behalf of the MS Society, while others represented the American Heart Association, and there were a slew of groups all benefiting from the larger Speedway Children's Charities group, which thanks to generous NASCAR fans, drivers, and corporate donors doled out money to help needy children.

We finally climbed aboard a black pickup and rumbled our way over pastureland, around a slight hill, and up a small incline to a plateau. Scrubby mesquite offered shade and tents dotted the area. "Wow, this is so open," I exclaimed, and others chimed in, too.

Now at our respective posts, we were briefed on the day ahead. NASCAR drivers (both current and past) would be leading their teams through 10 sites. There, each person received five clay shot opportunities and I was one of those keeping track of hits or misses.

"One, two, three, fire," said the actual operator of the machinery. I heard something fly, but had no idea where the clay had flown. The wind increased and branches waved as if fending off real pigeons, not clay discs. "Yikes," I said to myself. "I've got to concentrate." I squinted and followed the next one, fortunately seeing the whiff of yellow from the shot as it splintered the target.

We had a few more practice rounds to watch and then awaited the clients. Laughter drifted up the hill as teams wended their way from point to point. By the time they reached pit stop seven, everyone was best buddies and in a rhythm. I could tell who the real NASCAR drivers were. They were lean and fit and had an assurance about them. Easy drawls joked about shots, but Bam! Bam! Bam!—the drivers did not miss. I didn't even have time to blink in order to keep up with the speed of the sight and shots. As fast as the clays released, those drivers whipped the guns into motion and fired instantaneously. No helmets for this sport, but earplugs muffled the echoing kerpows.

The drivers' reaction times behind a steering wheel at over 180 miles per hour served them well in the shoot-out. "You ever see anything like this?" commented the mayor of Fort Worth, Texas. In his group, the NASCAR driver aced every shot.

Busy with the scorecards, I answered, "Nope, these guys are amazing. Yet they'd have to have good hand-eye coordination and cat-like reflexes to do what they do." I marked another bulls-eye.

"Thanks for volunteering today, young lady." The mayor shook my hand, left me dutifully impressed, and clapped a driver on the back as they walked to hill eight. I overheard the mayor laugh and ask, "Will you shoot for me? I could use at least one winner." That was the tone of the day—cheerful repartee, good sportsmanship, and impressive displays of skill.

Pit stop seven was declared finished, and our little team of three volunteers cleaned up our area and dispersed. I decided that rather than wait for the pickup truck I'd walk back to the parking area. Despite the wind, the day was gorgeous and I needed the exercise. I wandered down a hill and meandered onto the gravel path leading back to the main ranch house. I strolled easily, admiring wildflowers and reflecting on the day's events. Hearing gravel crunch behind me, I turned, and saw a golf cart approaching. I stepped back, stopped, and stuck my thumb out, in jest, to hitch a ride.

To my surprise, the golf cart halted and a familiar face smiled and said, "Climb aboard." NASCAR's "The King," Mr. Richard Petty, tilted back his hat, told me to buckle my seat belt, and asked, "Where to?"

I bumbled a bit, shocked that this man was driving himself, but then again, that summed up the unassuming modesty I'd seen all day. "Um, volunteer parking lot if you're going that far, or really anywhere you want to drop me. I don't mind walking."

He introduced himself, as if I didn't know who he was, and chatted about the day. "Certainly been an excellent event. Folks with TMS know how to entertain. I tell ya, I need to practice shooting. Darn near embarrassed myself at the first stop."

I wished him luck for his Sunday race team and he thanked me. We tootled along and if there was such a thing, this was the smoothest golf cart ride in the world. He put me at ease and I finally got up the nerve to ask, "So, how fast will this cart go?"

He grinned, shifted, and said, "Never fast enough."

~Joanne Faries

Bobby Allison: Superstar

In 2003, I was honored to have my first book published with — and about — one of my heroes, Bobby Allison. This man was a hero to me and to my racing family in Buffalo, N.Y. and is now one of my heroes in life, as well.

Bobby Allison: A Racer's Racer led to a lot of time spent together in its creation and then via book signings and tours along the NASCAR circuit.

I already knew what a legend, inspiration and hero Bobby was to many people before the book. What I didn't know until we did signings and appearances is what it meant to hang out with "Bobby Allison: Superstar."

During the first at-track signings, people would basically lose their minds upon seeing Bobby. Women would cry, grown men couldn't speak, while others would say, "Oh my ... that's Bobby Allison!" and just stop in their tracks.

From the sobbing woman at Kansas Speedway to the trembling man at a signing in New Jersey to the adoring crowds he drew on the Bristol Motor Speedway midway, the affection and reaction people have for Bobby never ceases to amaze me. And he deserves every ounce of adulation, emotion and praise bestowed upon him.

What I didn't know was how Bobby Allison could motivate a small town to action until we showed up unannounced—I thought—on a Saturday afternoon in my hometown of Akron, N.Y.

While en route to Talladega Superspeedway on the weekend the book came out, I asked Bobby for one favor. Could we do a swing through the Buffalo area to sell books and raise money for my club, the FOAR (Friends of Auto Racing) Score? He said we could, and I put the tour together with the publisher and called my Buffalo media friends.

We did radio and television station visits over the course of three days. To use the word "whirlwind" would be an understatement.

On Saturday we had a signing in Rochester early in the day and one later in the afternoon just outside Buffalo. The two signings were an hour's driving distance apart with time for a lunch stop along the way.

My favorite moments with Bobby are riding along and listening to him tell stories. Whether it involves racing, his family or life, I have the world's best one-on-one going, and I learn and love every minute of it.

Leading up to the Buffalo trip, I told my dad our schedule and he attended two signings and the fundraiser on Saturday night. However, his involvement spurred one of the best moments of the trip and one of my most memorable times with Bobby.

Akron is where my family has lived since Civil War days and I spent a major part of my youth strolling up and down Main Street. Back in the day, one of my grandfathers would be doing his magic act on the main stage and the other one would be working the dime pitch during Fourth of July festivities in the park. Akron is small-town Americana at its best, where everyone knows what and where things are going on by simple word of mouth.

I told my dad it might be fun to stop at one of his favorite watering holes—the Filling Station—between the Rochester and Buffalo signings. He asked what time, and I gave him a rough estimate of when we should be there.

When he called AGAIN to ask about when we'd be there, I answered the same as before. Being a writer, you get a feeling when something is up, but don't ask because you want to see how things play out.

Upon our arrival, I reached for the handle of a gas pump and saw a small picture of a young Bobby taped just below it. I pointed it out and said, "I think they're expecting us," to which he laughed.

We walked in and I saw my dad beaming like only a proud father can. Then, the 15 people there started to applaud as Bobby strolled across the floor. He did his usual wave and I just smiled at the affection they showed him.

A few folks came up for pictures and two women had something they wanted him to sign. We sat at a table and some folks wanted to know if we had any books they could buy. That's always my cue to run out to the car and get a box.

While I was at the car, five more people wearing NASCAR items walked in the door. As I got to the door, four more held the door for me to enter. As they came in behind me, I heard one man say, "Holy crap, Bobby Allison IS in here." This wasn't a publicized stop and the only person who knew we were coming here was … Dad.

We sold an entire box of 20 books in the next 30 minutes. During this time, Bobby signed autographs, posed for pictures and was his usual people-loving self. I noticed how crowded and busy the place had become in the last half hour.

The original 15 people grew to 40 in minutes, and by the time we ordered lunch there were 60 people filling the Filling Station. My dad was still smiling and talking to his friends, and some folks I hadn't seen for years came in as well. Some sat at the bar and just stared at Bobby being in "their" place while talking amongst themselves.

I heard words like "amazing, cool, unbelievable, wow" while cell phone calls were being dialed and answered by the small crowd that formed in minutes. After we finished lunch, Bobby was holding court with about 30 people at the table while my dad sat behind me on a bar stool.

Upon glancing at Dad, I think—for that one moment—he forgot about the broken windows, the nights coming home late and the load of dumb crap I'd done growing up. Because right now, in "his" place in his hometown, his son had NASCAR legend Bobby Allison hanging out with his friends.

Bobby answered questions and even went behind the bar to pour some draft beers from the gas pumps for pictures. Stop in; they're still hanging on the wall. When it was time to leave, I announced to the crowd, which now numbered about 75, that we had to go to another signing.

As he strolled across the wooden floor, everyone stood and applauded Bobby Allison. They saluted this NASCAR legend who had come to their hometown for an impromptu 90-minute visit on a Saturday afternoon.

We drove up Main Street and I felt like the luckiest person in the world and still in awe of what just took place. I turned to Bobby and said, "Well, I think they loved you." To which he replied with a smug grin, "They did," and we both laughed.

At that point, I simply said, "They should; you're a superstar," and from that day on, I have always addressed Bobby Allison as … Superstar. I can't think of anyone more deserving of that name.

~Tim Packman

How Mark Martin Turned Me into a NASCAR Fan

The final restart of the 2005 NASCAR Sprint Cup Series season occurred with 11 laps to go in the Ford 400 at Homestead-Miami Speedway. During the final run, Greg Biffle, Dave Blaney, and Mark Martin battled for the lead. At one point during the run, they were three-wide going into Turn 2. Biffle eventually shot between Blaney and Martin, grabbing the lead. Blaney was on old tires so he began to fade while Martin charged hard after Biffle. Martin and Biffle were side by side as the white flag flew, signaling one lap to go.

They were still side by side coming out of Turn 2 and they raced down the back straightaway. Neither driver could shake the other and they entered Turn 3 door to door, just inches apart. Martin dipped to the bottom of the track while Biffle went up high, taking a slight lead. Martin charged back in Turn 4 and they raced to the finish line. Biffle crossed the line 0.17 seconds ahead of Martin to win the race.

I don't think I've ever seen such an exciting finish to a sporting event. The funny thing was, I didn't know who many of the drivers were and I didn't understand racing strategy or what it meant to race a competitor clean.

NASCAR was new to me. A few months prior, a publisher came

to me with an idea for a sports book. The editor told me which sports he wanted me to write about and one of them was NASCAR. I told him I had never followed the sport so writing about it wasn't going to be easy. But I had some time, so I began to research it.

Once I had an understanding of the points system and a basic grasp of the lingo used in the sport, I decided to watch the last three races of the 2005 season, not having any idea what was about to happen. I didn't have a favorite driver in mind as I watched the first two races and I didn't have one in mind as I watched the Ford 400. But my heart was racing after the exciting finish in Miami.

Then Martin got out of his car for his post-race interview.

"Man, it was close," Martin said. "I thought we were going to pull it off. We were just inches short. I guess maybe we needed another lap—or maybe I'd have crashed trying. I raced Greg hard and I raced him clean and vice versa. And he was in front when it was over."

I was fascinated by a sport that provided such high drama while also honoring a code of racing each other cleanly. Of course, I learned later that not every driver adheres to the code quite so strictly, but I had an instant respect for Martin. At that moment I became a NASCAR and a Mark Martin fan and I've been following both ever since.

The more I read about Martin, the more I learned that what happened that night in Miami is the norm for him. He has finished second in the overall standings five times in his NASCAR Sprint Cup career that dates back to 1981. He also finished third three times—all of which often prompts analysts to refer to him as the best driver to never win a championship.

If you asked his competitors to sum up how they feel about him, the vast majority would simply say "respect." Although now that he's driving for Hendrick Motorsports, he might just end up with both respect and a championship. But I imagine that having the respect of his fellow competitors means more to him.

That's why I'm proud to consider myself one of his fans.

~Lee Warren

Lasting Legacies

In a four-month period in 1993 NASCAR lost two of its brightest stars in aircraft accidents, leaving the racing community heartbroken and grieving.

Only four months after having been crowned the 1992 NASCAR Sprint Cup Series champion, Alan Kulwicki, along with three Hooters employees, died in a plane crash while en route to Bristol, Tennessee, for a race. The 38-year-old Kulwicki had been in Knoxville earlier that evening for an appearance. He and the three Hooters of America employees boarded the corporate Merlin Fairchild jet and headed for Bristol on that chilly, misty night. The plane was on its approach to the Tri-City Regional Airport when it suddenly plummeted into a mountainside. Both engines had lost power simultaneously due to probable ice ingestion.

Kulwicki and Davey Allison, along with Bill Elliott, had been locked in an intense battle for the 1992 championship, and as Allison left Kulwicki's wake he remarked that he now understood why it wasn't meant for him to win the title. Sadly, Allison never got the opportunity to compete for another championship. The former Daytona 500 winner lost his life a little more than four months later.

On July 12, Allison and veteran race car driver and family friend Red Farmer had flown to Talladega Superspeedway in Allison's helicopter to watch Neil Bonnett's son test his race car. Allison had acquired the Hughes 369-HS helicopter only weeks before the accident. He was attempting to land the aircraft when, within 6 to 12 inches of touchdown, it began oscillating from side to side. The helicopter then rose suddenly about 25 feet into the air, began spinning counter-clockwise, banked to the left and crashed, striking the media parking lot fence and a gate allowing access to the garage. The 32-year-old Allison died July 13 from severe head injuries.

Heartbroken, the motorsports community trudged on through the 1993 season, but it was an extremely difficult time for competitors and fans. At the time, I was the editor of the weekly publication *NASCAR Scene* and the letters the newspaper received, as well as the baskets of letters, cards and poems that arrived at the race shops following their deaths, provided insight into the tremendous impact the two men had on people's lives.

After Kulwicki's death, something was received at his race shop from every state, as well as the country formerly known as Czechoslovakia, Germany and Canada. Former NASCAR Sprint Cup Series team owner Martin Birrane also sent a letter from London. Many of the letters sent to Kulwicki's shop came from children.

Scene received hundreds of letters and poems after each man's death, and they showed that Kulwicki and Allison affected their fans differently, even though the thousands who loved and admired them called them "hero." Those who wrote about Kulwicki told how the Greenfield, Wisconsin native's work ethic, independence and intense determination had inspired them.

One man said the inspiration he received from Kulwicki turned him from a high school dropout into a student seeking a mechanical/electrical engineering degree. Another said Kulwicki motivated him to do what he believed in his heart could be done and not to let others tell him what could and couldn't be done. Kulwicki was described as a quiet hero who gave of himself; an inspiration to the small business owner who showed everyone how to compete against big companies and emerge victorious.

The effect Allison had on his fans was much different, but generated emotions just as strong. They talked about how they would miss his smile, his interaction with his family, and the twinkle in his eye. Perhaps one fan summed it up best when he wrote, "I feel like I just lost my best friend." Allison also was cited for his hard work, honesty, competitiveness, sincerity, determination, and loyalty to his fans.

One fan noted the young Allison had taught her a new meaning to life, proper perspective and priorities. Another called him a "fine example" for today's young people.

Today, the two men live on through the things that epitomized them—family and education. Allison's smile and personality are clearly evident in son Robert Grey and daughter Krista Marie. Engineering students at UNC Charlotte and Kulwicki's alma mater, the University of Wisconsin-Milwaukee, will benefit for years to come thanks to scholarships and new facilities created by trust funds established by his stepmother, Thelma H. Kulwicki.

We will never know what achievements the two men could have added to their already stellar resumes, but more than a decade later it has become evident the inspiration they provided remains.

~Deb Williams

JPM: Just Talking

Juan Pablo Montoya was already talking when he walked through the door of Alsace 1, AKA the teleprompter room, at the Wynn Hotel in Las Vegas on Wednesday morning of the 2009 NASCAR Sprint Cup Series Champion's Week.

"I don't want to read this stuff," he said as he strode briskly to the front of the room. "Can't I just talk?"

The teleprompter room is the place where all those smooth, carefully worded speeches TV viewers and the live audience hear on Friday night at the NASCAR Sprint Cup Series awards ceremony come together.

Long gone — and lamented, by some — are the days when celebrities would pull handwritten speeches out of their pockets at awards show when their names were announced, stumbling over the words and invariably forgetting to thank someone really important, who probably never let them live it down.

Nowadays, most drivers work hard at Champion's Week on their speeches. It's like assembling the ingredients to cook a perfect meal: Take equal parts of congratulating the champion, thanking the owner, the team, the sponsors, the family, and the fans, mix well and serve.

Visible to the speaker but not the listeners, the words scroll across the teleprompter, which looks to me like an ordinary TV set. The driver reads them, the audience applauds and that's it. Bring on the dessert.

But like all of the world's great chefs, Montoya prefers not to adhere too closely to the recipe.

"I just want to say it, not read it," he said again. "It doesn't sound natural when I read it."

Of course, Montoya was given the green light to "just talk." As if he needed anyone's permission.

He took his place behind the podium and let it fly. It had a stream of consciousness vibe, how one might imagine an actual conversation with him might go.

He acknowledged the 2009 series champion Jimmie Johnson, noting that "I've been in NASCAR three years and he's kicked my ass all three years. I admire him, but I don't like getting beaten."

He thanked what sounded like a trio of pop bands from the 1960s—"Target and Partners, Brian and the Team, and Connie and the Kids."

He thanked his team owners, Teresa Earnhardt, Felix Sabates, and particularly Chip Ganassi—"I've known Chip for 10 years. I won my CART Series championship with him in 1999. The guy is crazy."

A speech that is systematically written and then read aloud in front of a large group all too often sounds, for lack of a better word, stiff. It isn't anyone's fault. That's just the way things are. Professional athletes aren't movie actors, paid to make words on paper sound like normal dialogue. Nor are they motivational speakers whose purpose is to make crowds jump up from their seats and get excited; NASCAR drivers use stock cars for that particular job.

One of the best things about JPM is his knack for keeping things real. It's refreshing and makes him fun to be around. He uses all the correct ingredients in the proper amounts; he just likes to spice things up a little bit. He keeps you on the edge of your seat, because whatever pops into his head is likely to spill right back out of his mouth, whether it's suitable for family audiences or a little more R-rated.

In Montoya's case, the term "speech rehearsal" was a misnomer. When he stood in front of that mostly empty room and talked about NASCAR and all the people associated with it and what it has meant to him to be a part of this sport, you believed his words came from the heart. He wasn't reading something to you, or parroting phrases he had memorized and then practiced for hours to perfectly recite.

He was just talking. That's a rare thing these days, and definitely something worth listening to.

~Cathy Elliott

The Secrets
to Success

NASCAR's Strong Family Foundation

I n a race near the end of the 2009 NASCAR Sprint Cup season, the championship points leader, Jimmie Johnson, was caught up in an accident and had to take his car to the garage on Lap 3. Crew members from other Hendrick Motorsports teams rallied around their teammate and worked together to get the car back on the track as quickly as possible. The next day, everybody was talking—and a lot of them were criticizing—their efforts.

It's funny. I was listening to some of these people complaining about crew members from other Hendrick Motorsports teams coming over and helping to fix that car. And I thought to myself, "What is wrong with these people? Have they lost their minds?"

Teamwork is the very essence of our sport. That is why we are successful. And that is why when people look at the selfishness it takes to be successful in other sports, sometimes they miss the fact that in NASCAR, things just don't work that way.

Through the years, there is not a one of us who has been around for any length of time who has not needed help from somebody else. I've had to borrow engines from other competitors to put in my car to go out and race. I've borrowed crew members because I've needed somebody to change a tire. I've borrowed trailers, and I've borrowed trucks, just so I could get to the race.

That's what makes NASCAR different from all the other sports.

When we say we're a family sport, people think that means all those people in the grandstands are actual families who come with their wives and their kids—and they are, and they do.

But what I'm talking about here is the garage area, the camaraderie and the respect that we all have for each other. We all know how hard you have to work to just show up at a race track, particularly back in the day. And so when someone's there and they need something and you've got it, you never give it a second thought. Even if you loan an engine to somebody and then they go out and beat you with it, you take pride in the fact that your engine was in their car, and boy, look how it ran. Or that's your tire changer, and boy, he did a great job for you guys, didn't he?

That's something that so many new fans do not understand about our sport and how we all feel about each other. This is a fraternity in every sense of the word. These people live together, probably 325 days a year. We're all in the garage together. We police each other; we're accountable to each other. It's a different atmosphere in NASCAR than it is in some locker room somewhere, or out on some field. It's just not the same.

Things never stand still. They always progress; they always evolve. The atmosphere I grew up in was different, because we truly did depend on one another a lot more. Nowadays, some of the guys are more independent. There's a lot more money, and there's a lot more opportunity out there for guys to sort of isolate themselves. For the amount of exposure this sport gets, the kind of coverage it gets, and the kind of microscope that everyone involved with it is under, you have to admit that it's a quality product, with quality people. Every driver is a role model. They all have a lot of morals, a lot of values and a lot of ethics, and that is what makes our sport great.

In every part of society and every part of life, there is a season of change, and I think we're going through some of that right now. You don't want some things to change, and sometimes you don't understand why they have to, but that's just a product of the times.

But I still look at the core people in the sport today—the Hendricks, the Yates, the Pettys, and the France family—and those are the people that built the foundation of NASCAR, and they built it strong. As long as we don't shake that foundation too bad, I think we'll be OK.

~Darrell Waltrip

Nice Guys Finish First

I was lucky. I grew up in North Carolina, where college basketball is amazingly huge and accessible, and NASCAR is the same way. One example of that accessibility has made a big impact on my life and the way I deal with people.

My dad was a huge race fan, and when I was a kid, my dad and my uncles were big hot rod guys. They worked on hot rods and drag racers and all that kind of thing, so I was always around cars. We had the old apple tree with the chain over it pulling the motors out of the cars, and all that kind of thing. So I grew up tinkering with cars and tractors and stuff like that.

You know, as a kid of 6 or 7 years of age, there are particular things you remember from your childhood. Every weekend my dad would sit down and watch racing.

It was really interesting. Race broadcasts have come a million miles since then. I remember very vividly sitting there with my dad watching the Holly Farms 400 from North Wilkesboro or something like that, and it would be on ABC's *Wide World of Sports*. It would be weird because you'd watch Lap 1 to Lap 40, and they'd say, "Now we're skipping ahead," and then they would show something like diving for a while, and then the race would come back on and they'd be at Lap 265. My dad would get so excited, and we'd sit and watch those races together.

Then we started venturing out to the local race tracks. We'd go to places like Asheville Speedway and North Wilkesboro, places within driving distance of our farm in Black Mountain, North Carolina. My dad was a big man physically, and we were the only African-Americans there. It was a different time in our culture and our society, but my dad and my uncle would do these kinds of things. We were right in the middle of everything. But nobody ever bothered us.

The first time I ran across Richard Petty, I was with my uncle. We were in Daytona. He was walking through the garage area and we were on the access road. He was walking across there and I was just a kid, maybe 8 or 9 years old, and I said, "Look, there's Richard Petty." So I hollered out, "Hey, Mr. Petty!"

I didn't think he'd heard me. But he wandered over and started talking to me. He asked me questions about myself, like my name and where I was from. He said he knew where Black Mountain was, and that he raced in Asheville a lot. It seemed like he took forever to talk to me.

That made an indelible impression on me.

Just a few months later, I was at North Wilkesboro, and the same thing happened. He was coming around a corner, and again I said, "Hey, My Petty!" And here he comes again. He came over and he stood there and talked to me. It seemed like he stood there for five days, but it was probably more like 15 seconds.

I remember telling myself that if I ever became famous, I would always speak to people, especially if they spoke to me. And as time went on, and I got older, I always remembered that.

Time went on and I went to Chapel Hill and started having a little bit of success playing college basketball. Then I got to the NBA, and the guys were always kidding me about my Southern twang. I had a great backup, though, because in my third year in Cleveland, Larry Nance came to the team. Larry's a big gear head; he still drag races.

In our spare time we would work on his race car all the time, and when we'd come to practice we'd have cuts and burns all over us, and the coach would say, "What are you guys doing? We're paying you all this money and you're coming to work with oil under your fingernails?"

They thought we were the biggest bunch of rednecks they had ever seen.

In the NBA, it's like you're always in this little cocoon. You're always concentrating on what you're doing. I guess one major thing NASCAR has taught me is that it's a good thing to be accessible to people. They couldn't get guys in the NBA to do anything. They wouldn't even make eye contact. They act like people don't exist.

You get catered to and you start getting a little full of yourself, but those encounters when I was a kid would always ring true in my head. If someone asked me a question or wanted an autograph, sometimes I would think, "Man, I don't want to go over there and sign that hat." But the day that Richard Petty took the time to stop and talk to me would always pop back into my head.

And so many times when I did walk over to sign that autograph, I would end up talking to that person for 10 minutes because they were just so interesting.

It happens to me today all the time, especially at the race track, because you're always in a hurry to get somewhere. But every time you stop, you meet someone incredible.

This is the most remarkable professional sport as far as accessibility that I have ever seen. These guys are getting ready to go and put their lives on the line, and it blows me away. You can walk right up to these drivers while they're getting in their race cars and talk to them. You can walk up to Jeff Gordon and ask for an autograph and he'll sign it.

I have had the great honor of getting to know Richard Petty over the years. We have shared a lot of conversations about a lot of things, but probably none of them will ever have as much of an effect on me, and on the way I deal with people, as the day "The King" took the time just to stop and say hello.

~Brad Daugherty

Barney Hall:
A Legend, a Friend

I have been with MRN Radio since the early 1980s, but in comparison with my co-anchor Barney Hall, I am still a relative newcomer. Barney has been around since the inception of MRN in 1970. He was announcing stock car races well before the idea of MRN was ever conceived: we like to joke that he called Ben Hur's first win in a chariot race.

I was an avid listener and fan of Barney's well before I went to work for MRN. I worked as a turn announcer for 20 years and eventually moved to the position of co-anchor.

I can't even begin to describe the honor it was to be moved into the "booth" and named Barney's co-anchor in 2001. We have worked together for more than a decade, and it has been one of the most rewarding experiences of my life. I am proud to call Barney a friend as well as a co-worker, and I have learned an extraordinary amount from this legendary broadcaster.

Barney never fails to be the heart of any broadcast in which he is involved. Sometimes an MRN broadcast can get rather hectic when several things are happening at the same time during a race. It isn't unusual to have a pass for the lead about to take place while one of the frontrunners is coming into the pits with a problem, our producer is telling us we need to take a commercial break, and a guest has just stepped into the booth for an interview.

Barney somehow remains the calm in the storm, and has the uncanny ability to crack one of his famous jokes in order to relax everyone on the crew.

His sense of humor is unmatched. During the 2009 season, Talladega President Rick Humphrey came into the broadcast booth to promote the upcoming Amp Energy 500, which fell for the first time on Halloween weekend. Rick explained the event would be named "Hallow-dega," and many of the staff members would be in costumes in honor of the holiday.

There is always a certain amount of levity that occurs when Rick comes in to be interviewed, so I looked over at Barney and asked him what he would be for Halloween. Without missing a beat, Barney responded, "The Booger Man." This unexpected response threw all of us into a fit of gasping laughter, from which we didn't completely recover until several laps later.

A few weeks after that, we were at Richmond International Raceway. We called on our three pit reporters for an update on stops about midway through the NASCAR Sprint Cup Series race. Winston Kelley did his report, and Alex Hayden reported on the teams in his section of pit road.

Barney then asked for a report from Steve Post. Apparently, Steve was talking to a crew chief and didn't hear us. After a few seconds of dead air, Barney said, "I wonder if he got run over," sending us all into fits of laughter once again.

Known not only for his quick wit and comedic timing, Barney is truly one of the most respected and admired individuals in the NASCAR Sprint Cup garage. He has helped launch the careers of most of the broadcasters on television and radio today. I don't think there is a single person, from Richard Petty to the newest crop of interns at MRN's Sprint Vision, who has not been touched in some way by him.

Though small in stature, Barney is truly one of the giants of NASCAR racing.

Despite all of this, Barney has remained unbelievably humble.

He hates having attention called to him in any way, which posed a special challenge for the MRN crew in December 2007.

Barney and I were scheduled to anchor the broadcast of the season-ending NASCAR Sprint Cup Awards Ceremony at the Waldorf Astoria in New York City. David Hyatt, president of MRN, had informed me the day before that Barney had been chosen as that year's recipient of the Bill France Award of Excellence, probably the most prestigious award in NASCAR.

David really wanted to surprise Barney with the announcement, which was proving to be tricky as Barney and I were always on the air when the award winner was announced. We had to think of some way to get him down to the stage in the middle of the broadcast, and Barney wasn't likely to simply get up and walk away with a show in progress.

We decided that a few minutes before the scheduled announcement, David would simply say he needed to "see" Barney for a minute. We knew Barney would be suspicious, but we couldn't think of any other way to do it. We only hoped he wouldn't realize that the Bill France Award was up next, since our broadcast always follows the ceremony as it unfolds and there is rarely any rigid format.

Fortunately, everything went according to plan. David interrupted us pretty much mid-sentence and said he needed to see Barney for a minute. Barney looked at me with what appeared to be a combination of panic and utter bewilderment, but I just shrugged and motioned for him to go. I was terrified I would give something away if I acted like I knew what was going on because we both knew the usual protocol—if David needed to tell us something, he would at least wait for a commercial break.

Barney was very reluctant to leave, and for a moment I thought he was going to refuse outright. David, though, was quite insistent, and in the end almost had to drag the poor guy down the stairs.

Moments later, Mike Helton stepped up to the stage and announced that the recipient of the Bill France Award of Excellence for 2007 was Barney Hall. The audience roared, especially the table in the balcony containing the MRN bunch. Barney sheepishly stepped onto the stage to receive the honor, but he never lost his composure and had the audience in laughter shortly into his acceptance comments.

He came back to the broadcast booth and everyone on the crew congratulated him during the next commercial break. Humble as ever, he slid right back into the role of professional broadcaster.

I'm sure Barney's award was not mentioned in many newspapers or television broadcasts the following day; in fact, I doubt he got any mention at all aside from the inclusion of his name in the column with all the other award winners from the weekend's ceremonies.

However, for the MRN crew, the pride we feel in claiming Barney Hall as our own is hard to describe. He may not be remembered as a "mover and shaker" in NASCAR, but in his own quiet way he has made an impact that will last as long as there are cars racing under the NASCAR banner.

In one of the suites after the awards ceremony that evening, NASCAR President Mike Helton stated that if he had not listened to Barney on a little radio station in Bristol many moons ago, he himself might not be involved in the sport today.

If that is not evidence of Barney Hall's accomplishments, I'm not sure what is.

~Joe Moore

The Business Card

When we built Pocono Raceway, we made some mistakes with the construction, and we got into some pretty serious financial trouble. Back in the early 1970s, things were rough. I got fed up with it, and decided to put the race track up for sale.

The next day I got a call from Bill France, Sr. down in Daytona Beach—"Big Bill," they called him—and he wanted to come up to New York and have me go and meet him over there. So my son and I went over to New York, to one of the old hotels, and we met Big Bill at the bar. We were talking, and he was trying to convince us not to get out of the business. Apparently he didn't think the conversation was going very well, because after a few minutes he finally got disgusted with me. He pulled out one of his business cards and wrote something on the back of it.

Then he handed the business card to me.

Now, Big Bill France was an intimidating man. He was about 6 feet 4 inches tall, and when he handed me that card, I looked up at him, and then looked back down at the card. And this is what I read there: "On the plains of hesitation lie the bleached bones of millions, who when within the grasp of victory sat and waited, and waiting, died."

I said, "OK, Bill, you win. We'll stick it out and see what we can do." Then we all sat back down at the bar and had dinner together that night, and that was it.

Not too long after that, a couple of years or so, Bill and his son, Bill, Jr., gave Pocono Raceway a second NASCAR race. He helped us over the years, right up until he died. He gave us a lot of good advice, and he brought his wife, Annie B., to our races for the next two years after our meeting in New York to show their support.

I've told this story before, and over the years I've gotten calls from different people asking where this saying came from. I never really found out, and no one has been able to track it down that I know of. Was it original? I really don't know.

But I do know this. Bill France, Sr. cared enough to make the effort to come to New York to try and talk me out of what he thought was a bad decision. As it turned out, he was right.

Had it not been for him, Pocono Raceway would not be here today.

~Dr. Joseph Mattioli

Editor's note: The quote, "Upon the plains of hesitation bleach the bones of countless millions, who on the dawn of victory paused to rest, and there resting died," is attributed to John Dretschmer.

Jack Roush's Random Act of Friendship

Never at a loss for words, Jack Roush has always had a reputation for being one of NASCAR's most colorful—and, at times, controversial—personalities. A competitive fire burns in Jack Roush, a fire that some say makes him great.

He's probably a genius. He can make a race car do things that most NASCAR crew chiefs only dream about, possessing a vernacular that only engineers and rocket scientists understand.

I've been told you either love him or hate him.

I landed my dream job in NASCAR in 2000 when my husband, an active duty lieutenant colonel in the U.S. Army, got orders for Kansas. I snagged a good job when I accepted the position of public relations manager at Kansas Speedway in Kansas City, Kansas, the NASCAR Sprint Cup Series' newest speedway that opened in 2001.

I thought it would be temporary. The Army makes advance planning difficult. But I loved my job at the speedway so much that we did what we could to stay near Kansas, commuting where possible and maintaining two households, his and mine.

It was strange for me to call Richard Petty, Dale Earnhardt, Jeff Gordon, and yes, Jack Roush "colleagues." I used to be a race fan. I remember sitting in the cheap seats of a NASCAR race track, focusing my binoculars on all the NASCAR types scurrying around and wondering, "How do I get a job like *that*?"

Now I had one. It was exciting … and fun. I was really lucky and I loved it!

One day, life threw me a curve ball.

In 2003, my husband was deployed to Iraq and I was left alone in Kansas. My parents were in Texas; his in Massachusetts. His military unit was in Fort Riley, Kansas, about 125 miles west of where I lived. My support system was basically my work colleagues who, despite their best efforts, would never truly comprehend a husband being sent to war.

So Cathy Elliott, my counterpart from Darlington Raceway, invited me to help her out at the Southern 500. She probably needed help, but I suspect she wanted to get my mind off my husband's deployment and be my friend.

I had traveled to Darlington before, but this year was especially memorable. My NASCAR colleagues did their best to take my mind off Iraq—and Cathy spared no expense, even suggesting dinner at my favorite restaurant, Chik-Fil-A.

In my excitement over chicken sandwiches, I raced to Cathy's car, only to fall down her doorsteps. A tumble, a roll, and man, did my knee hurt! Probably a sprain, I thought; nothing ice, Motrin and an apple martini wouldn't cure. But the next morning, it was worse. So I visited the track's infield care center for some relief.

The doctor suspected I had torn a ligament in my knee and fitted me with a temporary cast to stabilize my leg. The weekend was pretty much a bust and I was useless as a helper. I limped back to Kansas and saw my doctor.

X-rays and tests proved nothing significant. So my doctor ordered an MRI to get to the root of the problem—a tumor in my right femur.

A tumor? Was it cancer? Would my leg be amputated? What was in store for me? My husband was in Iraq and I had a tumor; what more could happen to me?

Doctors recommended immediate surgery, with a simultaneous biopsy to see if it was cancerous. But because the tumor was inside the bone, surgery would be difficult and recovery would be long.

I talked the doctors into postponing surgery for two weeks, until after the race. They agreed, with conditions: I had to stay in a zero-mobility leg brace and off my feet. Doctors felt if I stood on my leg, I could break a bone and split the tumor, releasing it into my bloodstream. Not knowing if the tumor was cancerous, they didn't want to take any chances.

Anyone who has ever been on crutches knows how much they suck. And anyone who's been to a NASCAR event knows mobility is essential; I might as well have walked on my hands. It was brutal.

That weekend was unusually hectic, and Saturday was especially dramatic. Then, with the day almost over, a staffer knocked on my office door and said, "Jack Roush is here to see you."

I wondered what a NASCAR team owner could possibly want from me, as he came into my office. I wanted to stand, but couldn't. Sensing my angst, he sat down, grabbed my hand and said: "Sammie, I heard you aren't feeling well and thought I'd see if I could help."

Jack Roush helping *me*? Wow. He doesn't even know me. What could we possibly have in common?

He reminded me of his near-fatal plane crash the previous year, and described the team of doctors who repaired, among other injuries, the multiple fractures in his left leg and a compound fracture of his femur. He knew what the fragile uncertainty of learning to walk again felt like, and wanted to reassure me.

Then he did something incredible: produced two cards—his personal business card and that of the doctor who saved his life in Alabama. He told me to call him if I ever needed anything and suggested getting a second opinion from his doctor. He even offered his plane to pick me up.

He left me with a fatherly hug as I tried unsuccessfully to hold back tears. It was a simple, warm and genuine gesture that meant a lot—he gave support to a stranger who needed some strength.

When the race weekend ended, I geared up for a five-hour

surgery. Doctors removed a benign, giant cell tumor from inside my femur, stitched me up and sent me home for a long, six-month recovery of learning to walk again.

The night I got home from the hospital, my phone rang: It was Jack Roush. He wanted to see how the surgery went and how I was doing. I explained my road ahead and how much I appreciated his call. That kind of follow-through and attention to detail is what makes Jack Roush so successful in business.

Years later, I'm at Michigan International Speedway—Jack's home track!—and doing great. My husband has retired safely from the Army and my knee is like new. I even ran the Detroit Marathon in 2009.

I have never spoken to Jack about those 30 minutes at Kansas Speedway. I'm not even sure he remembers me, what he did, or the impact his visit made on me all those years ago.

I've come to realize that the measure of someone's greatness isn't in the number of championships they win, or how competitive or smart they are. It doesn't matter if someone's aloof or outspoken, controversial or competitive.

Sometimes, a single act of kindness—no matter how big or small—can make all the difference in someone else's life. Giving up those moments freely, without any notion of payback or credit, is what matters most and what makes people great.

Love him or hate him, in my book Jack Roush is great.

~Sammie Lukaskiewicz

Racing in the Hinterlands

So there I was, a long-haired rock and roll singer growing tired of beer joints and high school dances when a phone call came ringing into my life like a church bell in the distance, beckoning me to a destination that would change me forever.

Ten years prior, I was a young boy sitting in the grandstands with my family, enjoying our typical Sunday afternoon—the stock car races at Portland (Oregon) Speedway. The 1974 season was wrapping up, and the "Armstrong's Radio Electronics" Chevrolet with Ernie Trujillo at the wheel was on the track. That was all that mattered to this 13-year-old boy. We were part of the sport, and that gave me a sense of belonging.

My father's death months later would change all of that. For 10 years, racing would disappear from my life.

That phone call in the summer of 1985 was a rather innocent request from my brother Craig to join him up at Pacific Raceway in Seattle, Washington for a NASCAR Grand National Division West race where he was to work PA duties pit-side. The main announcer didn't show, so Craig went to the booth, and this rock and roll kid picked up his first pit microphone and went to work. A guest driver—the late Dale Earnhardt, Sr.—won the event that day, my first Victory Lane interview.

I'll never forget that smile, and his graciousness to a rank rookie asking totally dumb questions. I think I actually commented on his "Southern" accent. Yikes.

The bug bit again and before I knew it, Craig and I were diving headlong into NASCAR, hell-bent on bringing our "entertainment" flair to the hinterlands of an exploding sport.

First stop, Portland Speedway. A local cable TV show was the vehicle for our invasion. Donning blue blazers, we fumbled through the play-by-play and stand-ups, hoping to impress the management. The following season, the effort paid off, as Craig and I stood side-by-side, announcing the action at the track that provided so much joy to us for so many years.

That next year was a literal whirlwind of activity. Before we knew it, we were running up and down the coast, from Sears Point in California, to Washington's Evergreen Speedway, hawking our talents for whatever dollars we could muster.

There was some trepidation on my part that we might meet with resistance from the NASCAR establishment. Quite the opposite; we were welcomed into the family like long-lost kin by the likes of venerable West Coast NASCAR announcer Gary Cressey, NASCAR PR guru extraordinaire Owen Kearns, and Evergreen Speedway promoters Bob and Mickey Beadle.

I often wonder why they took to us so quickly. Perhaps it was our willingness to work—wherever and whenever—without hesitation. Regardless, they all took me under their collective wings and counseled me through many mistakes, misstatements, and misadventures.

My announcing career would have short-circuited, I believe, had I not had the pleasure to work with Shasta, California's Gary Cressey, truly one of the most talented announcers in NASCAR and a West Coast staple. Relaxed and confident, he is quick with the wit and genuinely passionate about the sport.

Gary literally wrote the book for me, inspiring what would become my "Announcer's Creed." Double-check the proper pronunciation of a driver's name and sponsor. Never speculate. Always promote. Never fan the flames of fan disdain. Sell food for the promoter. Most importantly, make the fans feel as if this is THE place to be right now.

Gary's words of wisdom and patience with my clunky mistakes guided me through those early years when I might well have stepped in the "poo" often enough to warrant an early exit from the sport. I'm still here.

You didn't announce for the Grand National Division West without support former NASCAR Camping World Truck Series PR Manager Owen Kearns, Jr., whom I regard as one of the hardest-working men in all of motorsports.

My fondest memory of working alongside Owen was the inaugural 1986 Tacoma Grand Prix NASCAR Grand National Division West event. The race would be a first for the series—running around the Tacoma Dome between concrete barriers and fence, spilling out onto city streets, and back to the dome. Craig and I had scored the turnkey PA gig up there, converging a group of hinterland announcers on rooftops and connecting them by miles of wire back to our PA loft atop a dome outcropping.

I have a photo that I cherish, of Gary Cressey and me with our headsets on, and Owen in the background—nose to the grindstone as always—feeding us storyline after storyline. He and his lovely wife Kathy always offered words of encouragement to this scruffy, still unpolished announcer. Following a race at Willow Springs where I was shagging stories on pit road, Kathy came up to me and said, "Wow. You were running all day. I'm gonna call you 'Flying Fred' from now on." It was that kind of endearing dialogue that gave me a feeling of acceptance. Of family.

Evergreen Speedway in Monroe, Washington was our second home track. Craig, Dad and I used to drive up there for the Grand National Division West shows. So, when promoters Mickey and the late Bob Beadle invited Craig and me to come up and work pit road, we jumped at the chance.

The 1986 Peterbilt Winston Washington 500—starring guest driver Bill Elliott—was the 5/8-mile oval's first 500-lap NGND event.

The place was packed; everyone wanted to see "Million Dollar Bill." He finished second to Washington native Chad Little that day, but it didn't matter. Awesome Bill was right here. In the hinterlands. The "wow factor" was high that day.

With Gary Cressey at the helm of the PA show, Craig and I went to work, using a two-way walkie-talkie as our pit mic. We had no communication with the booth, so I'd just key up the radio and say, "Fred! Fred! Fred!" Gary would then take his microphone, stick it into our custom "radio coupler"—a cardboard box with a radio inside and a mic hole—and cue us by waving his red hat out of the PA booth window.

Innovation was critical in the hinterlands. We used our wits and whatever tools we had at the time to do the job. Garage-band style. I have always loved that challenge.

Motorsports is my livelihood. For me, it's a merger of my two greatest loves—automotive competition, and show business. I work with some of the brightest people in all of sports, and with some of the most advanced audio and video tools available.

But I cherish those times out west. The racing was good, the people were dedicated, and there was a sense of family. One didn't have to dig too doggone deep to find another's motive for being there. We just loved it.

Just as it was to a 13-year-old boy watching his family-sponsored late model beat and bang on a Sunday afternoon, being there was all that mattered. It still is. And that's the way it should be.

~Fred Armstrong

Lynda Petty:
A Woman to Emulate

When Richard Petty decided 1992 would be his last season as a driver, the announcement was made in the fall of 1991 at the Petty Enterprises compound in Level Cross, N.C.

Lunch was served following the announcement and that's when Al Pearce of the *Newport News*, Thomas Pope of the *Fayetteville Observer* and I engaged in a conversation about the Petty family and how well it had treated the fans and the media throughout the then 54-year-old driver's illustrious career. During this discussion, I told my fellow journalists that if I ever married and I could be half the wife that Lynda Petty had been, I felt I would have been a good wife. Thomas looked at me and said, "Well, you might try being the woman she is." I told him he had a very valid point and I had never thought of it that way.

At the time, I was an associate editor with *Winston Cup Scene*, a weekly trade publication that 13 years later would become known as *NASCAR Scene*. My assignment for the 1992 season was to shadow the Petty family, specifically Richard. Little did I know that it would be a year that would provide me with the opportunity to learn many lessons from Lynda.

I had done an in-depth interview with Lynda in 1988, but it was during the 1992 season that I truly came to understand the woman who epitomizes what I consider a true Southern lady. She is gracious, but very strong. She is staunch in her beliefs, a firm believer in ethical behavior, and a fierce defender of her family. The woman who has been Richard Petty's wife since his racing career began in 1958 possesses a silent strength that has enabled her to endure the heartache stock car racing has sent her way and yet still greet people with a smile and a warm embrace.

The sport that has brought her family so much success, fame and joy has also left her with many lonely nights, little privacy, numerous frustrations, anger, tears and a pain in her heart. It took her only brother, Randy Owens, in a pit road accident at Talladega Superspeedway when a compressed air tank exploded in 1975. And on Mother's Day weekend in May 2000 she lost her first-born grandchild, Adam Petty, in a NASCAR Nationwide Series practice session crash just two months shy of his 20th birthday.

Lynda has watched her husband barrel roll down the frontstretch at Darlington Raceway and become airborne and flip on the Daytona frontstretch, a track where at age 23 his car sailed over a turn and landed outside the 2.5-mile track.

Motel swimming pools and race track infields were the playgrounds for the couple's children, and in some instances, the birthplace of an entrepreneurial spirit. At one track Lynda was making peanut butter and crackers for her children. Suddenly, it occurred to her she was making a large amount of the snack food. She decided to follow her small children after giving the crackers to them and discovered they were selling them to the fans.

When Richard's popularity exploded in 1967 with his 27 victories, she had to deal with finding fans in her family's yard, photographing their home each morning when she opened the curtains on the modest brick house's picture window. At the time, the family's home sat beside her in-laws and only a few yards from the race shop.

Yet, despite the flood of fans, Lynda never forgot how to make strangers feel welcome. One evening during a dinner at the Charlotte track, there was a young couple no one knew seated at the Pettys' table. Lynda, however, was very much aware as the conversation progressed that this young couple was being ignored. It was obvious they felt uncomfortable. Lynda turned her attention to them and began asking questions, drawing them into the conversation. It was discovered they had won a contest and the prize was to have dinner with Richard and Lynda Petty.

In addition to raising four children, hosting fan club cookouts at her home, preparing surprise birthday parties and often traveling with her husband, the civic-minded woman worked tirelessly in the racing wives auxiliary and served on the Randolph County Board of Education.

However, it was Lynda's thoughtfulness of other people that always provided me with security and comfort while covering the sport, spending nearly 30 weekends a year on the road. True, my parents were only a phone call away, but I could always walk into the motor home lot at a race track and have a conversation with someone who truly cared during a tough weekend. It was a relationship that began more than two decades earlier when I delivered a batch of sugar cookies to Richard and Lynda Petty in the infield at Asheville-Weaverville Speedway. And upon high school graduation I received a philosophical book she had given to her friends at the local high school when they graduated.

Yes, Thomas Pope was right that sunny October day in 1991. Lynda Petty is a very special woman.

~Deb Williams

Dreams with Deadlines

S etting goals is human nature.

As a University of Notre Dame graduate, Coach Lou Holtz's self-proclaimed list of things to do before dying served as impetus for me to create my own list while in my mid-30s.

It included items like a happy marriage and being a good parent along with a healthy dose of adventure items like sky diving, flying a plane and traveling to distant lands.

A whirlwind of events kicked off the year 2001. Triumph, when Aimee accepted my proposal of marriage on New Year's Eve, and tragedy — Dale Earnhardt's fatal accident on the last lap of the Daytona 500 — punctuated my tenure as Vice President of Daytona International Speedway.

Then came transition. In March, after 10 years in various positions with Daytona and International Speedway Corporation, I was tapped to succeed Jim Hunter as president of the track "Too Tough To Tame" — Darlington Raceway.

Hunter was a tough act to follow. Thanks to the physical improvements he had overseen during his time at Darlington, the track's physical plant now matched its reputation as one of the pillars of NASCAR. At a point during that growth, however, the increased seating capacity coupled with growth at other Southeastern tracks crossed the fine line between demand and supply, and Darlington's string of sellouts suffered.

Between accepting the position and moving my family to South Carolina, I slated a golf outing with my friend and mentor D.C. Williams. We navigated early morning dew, tight fairways and protected greens, talking about family, life's priorities, racing and the usual questions and answers to the world's problems.

Inevitably the conversation turned to my impending marriage, move and professional challenge at Darlington Raceway. In the middle of the 18th fairway, D.C. asked—"What do you want to accomplish there?"

I knew the answer, and verbalized it for the first time—"I want to sell the place out"—the result of which would be the largest crowd ever to witness a race at Darlington.

I was embraced by the staff and welcomed to the communities of Darlington and nearby Florence, right on up to the state capital in Columbia. We settled in as a family, and I got to work.

My list was getting shorter as many of my dreams had already come true. Now it was time to focus on the next one.

In March 2003, the track hosted the first of Darlington's two annual race weekends. An unfavorable weather forecast cropped up late in the week, and rain forced the postponement of the NASCAR Nationwide Series race to Monday.

Sunday of the Sprint Cup weekend dawned with gray skies and an iffy outlook on running the race. But what unfolded was one of the most epic duels in NASCAR history.

Wrestling 3,400-lb. stock cars around the notoriously difficult egg-shaped oval, Kurt Busch and Ricky Craven were at the front of the pack after 393 miles of the advertised 400. With five laps remaining, they swapped the lead several times, bouncing off each other and the retaining walls along the way.

Around the final turn, with the checkered flag in sight, Craven got the nose of his Pontiac underneath Busch's Ford, they steered into each other, and crossed the line locked together door handle to door handle. The top position on the infield scoreboard read "32," and NASCAR confirmed that Craven had edged Busch by .002 / second—that's TWO ONE-THOUSANDTHS of a second—in the closest finish in NASCAR history.

To top it off, in the postponed NASCAR Nationwide Series race, the last lap saw Todd Bodine and Jamie McMurray side-by-side coming out of Turn 4. They touched, Bodine kept his Chevy straight to win and McMurray crossed the line for second place in his Dodge ... BACKWARDS.

Talk about a selling point for the Labor Day race.

But larger issues would come into play with the announcement of another step in a process called "Realignment," which basically meant the schedule was rearranged. NASCAR announced that a Sprint Cup Series race would move from Rockingham to Auto Club Speedway in California. California gained a second event as part of this realignment, and to everyone's surprise, it was announced that the newly acquired event would be held on Labor Day weekend, Darlington's traditional place on the NASCAR calendar.

Darlington's race weekends in 2004 were to be its regular March date and November, in the penultimate race of the season.

Everyone was shocked that Darlington's Labor Day tradition was coming to an end. But I reminded them we still had a race to run—the final Labor Day running of the Southern 500.

Everyone rolled up their sleeves and got to work to send Labor Day out in style. Working with NASCAR, we were able to secure the renowned pop/rock band Smash Mouth to do a pre-race concert. Thanks to an opportunity presented by U.S. Senator Lindsey Graham, Admiral Vern Clark, Chief of Naval Operations for the U.S. Navy and a key figure in the post-September 11 team tapped by President Bush to respond to the terrorist attacks, accepted our invitation to serve as Grand Marshal.

Anyone involved in the sport will attest that even under the best of conditions, a certain element of luck is necessary for a race weekend to come off as planned. As race weekend approached, Darlington enjoyed plenty of publicity given the seismic changes to the race calendar. All advertising, every speaking engagement, even the drivers themselves, reminded the ticket-buying public what had transpired in March at that tough old track.

But in the conversations amongst the staff as we tracked each day's ticket sales, there was still that uncertainty that we wouldn't make it. Just one week before the race, a sellout was not a certainty.

A lot happened during my time at Darlington. After the realignment of its two race weekends for 2004, we announced that in 2005 one of Darlington's dates would move to Phoenix, leaving our track with just one annual race weekend. Lights were added, helping to move Darlington into the next chapter of her long history, running on the Friday and Saturday nights of Mother's Day weekend.

All of these were challenging, nerve-wracking, life-changing and gray-hair-causing occurrences. But something was missing. I still had not achieved that one specific goal.

Race week began. The weather forecast was good, the last push of advertising hit, and those in the know tabbed the race as "one you don't want to miss." The pre-race festivities played out, the politicians and celebrities greeted the crowd, the band played. And on race morning, ticket director Norma Nesbitt summoned me her office for what she called "something I was going to want to see."

Upon arriving, Norma informed me I was there to witness the last pair of tickets being sold to a customer from North Carolina. The race was sold out.

It is said that goals are dreams with deadlines. Selling out the final Labor Day running of the Southern 500 was not the closest finish in NASCAR history—we had achieved that one six months earlier—but to me personally, it was the victory of a lifetime.

~Andrew Gurtis

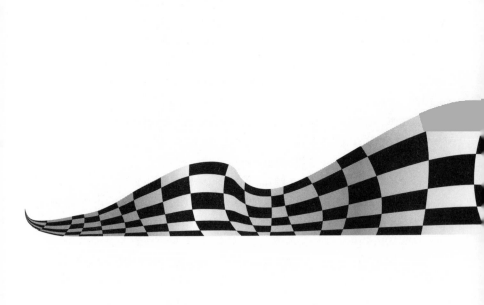

Heroes,
Everyday and
Otherwise

A Championship Friend

I wonder where to start.

In 2002, Ricky Hendrick and I became friends, and we had raced together a little bit, but we hadn't spent a whole lot of time together.

Then, at the last race of the year in Homestead, Florida, Ricky invited me over for a party he was having on his dad, Rick Hendrick's boat. They were looking for someone to replace Ricky in the No. 5 NASCAR Nationwide Series car, which he had decided not to drive the following year.

Ricky wanted it to be me. He called me up and said, "Hey, do you want this job?"

I said, "Absolutely."

It was a tough decision for me. I was racing for my family team at the time. We were pretty much done; we were out of sponsorship and were going to shut down anyway, but it was tough to make that choice. But this was the opportunity of a lifetime!

Rick had asked Ricky to run the team, but at the same time he wanted to be in control. He had a hard time letting go. He had someone else in mind to drive the car, but Ricky stood his ground. He basically said, "If you want me to run this team, this is who the driver is going to be. If you want to run it, that's fine. I'll do something else."

I didn't really know Rick at that time. Actually I had never met him, and I wanted to introduce myself and talk to him. So at the end of the race weekend, I went by his boat. I never told him how I knew where it was, though, until later on—I knew where it was because the party was on it!

Rick and I sat and talked for more than an hour. Then I went down to the Keys and spent some vacation time with my family. A little while later, Ricky called and said, "If you want the job, it's yours." So I went to Hendrick Motorsports, worked out the details, and started driving for Ricky.

I remember we signed the contract at Rick's office. Rick had a garage out back and he had this awesome car, a Porsche Carrera. Ricky was showing me around, and Rick made some comment, jokingly—"If you win the championship, I'll give you that car," or something like that. He's always throwing carrots out there. He's a great leader. He definitely knows how to motivate people, but obviously he didn't think we were going to win the championship our first year.

That was a great year. We were fortunate and ran very well. We won our first race together, Ricky and I, at the Indianapolis Raceway Park (IRP), which was a very special moment. It was a hard-fought win, but everybody did their job and we had a fast car.

At the time, Ricky and I and a few other guys lived together in Charlotte. We had a lot of good times. We became really close and had a lot of fun and made a lot of great memories. So we went back after the race and threw a big party to celebrate the win, and it was great.

Later on in the year we won some more races, and then we ended up winning the championship. Being able to win my first championship and win it with Ricky, the youngest owner ever to win a championship, is one of my most memorable moments in racing. I've never seen Rick more proud than when his son won the championship as an owner.

It was definitely a very, very special year.

The following season we raced in the NASCAR Sprint Cup Series.

There were some ups and downs; your first year in Cup is usually a struggle.

Then in October, in Martinsville, Virginia, there was a plane crash. It killed Ricky and a lot of other good people. It was a very sad day. It was my 21st birthday; we had a big party planned that night.

It was a very hard time in my life. Ricky was like a brother to me.

But he accomplished a lot in the short time that he had. He impacted my life in so many positive ways, and gave me an opportunity I can never repay him for. He taught me by example to accomplish as much as you can every day, because you might not get another chance.

For the longest time I couldn't even talk about Ricky's passing, or think about it. I still think about him every day, every time I get into a race car. He was a great man and I think he was going to do a lot of great things.

I miss him.

~Brian Vickers

The Jack of Hearts

In May 2009, an old friend of mine phoned with a story he knew I'd appreciate. At the time my son was a spry, gregarious 3-year-old who lived in constant motion. He was oblivious to the backwards world in which he lived. He was all hope and happiness, ever-infectious to those in his midst.

As my friend began telling me the scenario that left young Preston Loyd critically injured and turned Jeff Kerr into a hero, I looked over at my own little boy and wept.

Kerr is the jack of hearts.

Like almost every NASCAR Sprint Cup Series crew member, he strolled into Time Warner Cable Arena in Charlotte, N.C. on May 14, 2009 focused on earning the $10,000 prize for individual skill supremacy in NASCAR's pit crew challenge. He was motivated like never before.

Ten grand was a pretty penny, not to mention the bragging rights an individual skills winner carried up and down pit road. Kerr knew all about that. He'd won the jack man contest before.

But Kerr wasn't interested in gloating about his prowess or spending the cash.

He wanted to give it away.

In April, Kerr heard the story of Preston Loyd, a 4-year-old boy whose family attended the same church that Kerr and his family attended.

Young Preston had been watching television one afternoon and ran outside, unbeknownst to his grandfather, who was mowing the lawn on a riding mower.

Grandfather never saw Preston—who had uncharacteristically exited the house through the back door—and accidentally backed over him. Below his chest down to his waist, from his spinal column over, the entire left side of his torso was sheared off.

He lost all the ribs on his left side, his entire stomach, spleen and left kidney. His liver was lacerated. His arm was cut badly. Preston was airlifted to Charlotte Medical Center, and upon arrival the trauma surgeon gave him less than a 50 percent chance of survival.

Kevin Clark, a 23-year veteran volunteer fireman at Lake Norman Volunteer Fire Dept., now deputy chief, was en route to pick up his own 4-year-old when the call came from dispatch. He knew immediately it was bad. He was the first responder to the scene.

"It was a terrible injury," Clark said. "In all my years of experience, a young child doesn't have that much blood. My opinion was he didn't have anything left in him."

Clark took Preston from the grandfather and rolled him over. That's when he noticed the gaping wound. Preston's lung was severed, so Clark used his hand to try and seal the wound. Two other volunteers arrived to assist his breathing. He was losing air quickly.

"I thought it was over," Clark said. "He was in rough shape."

And that wasn't the only emergency situation on site.

"I thought we'd actually have to figure out who to work on first—I thought the grandfather was going to have a massive coronary, right there," Clark said.

• • •

"One of the paramedics said that it was the most intense seven minutes he'd ever been involved in at a scene," said Ashton Loyd, Preston's father. "One of the nurses told me everything had to happen perfectly for Preston to be alive."

Ashton is a former athlete, having played and coached football at

Davidson College before choosing a career as an agent for Nationwide Insurance.

"I can't really put into words what this has been like," Ashton said. "One of my biggest struggles, as an athlete, a coach, a guy in general, is we're used to being fixers. We didn't run that play right. We didn't have the camber adjusted right. We can fix that. That's not the case in something like this."

Kerr was heartbroken upon hearing the story. He has a little boy around Preston's age. He couldn't fathom the pain. So Kerr sent Ashton a text message the Sunday before the pit crew competition to deliver a message: If I manage to win, the money is yours.

"He was very broken down about it," said Kerr, bashfully. "It was just one of those things I felt led to do. They're a good family in a bad situation."

Thing is, it's not like they were best friends.

"I would call us casual friends," Ashton said. "Misty (Kerr's wife) found me and said, 'Jeff told me to remind you if he wins anything in the pit crew challenge, he's giving it to you.'"

Ashton watched the competition intently, and when Kerr posted the quickest time among NASCAR Sprint Cup jack men it took a moment to grasp the magnitude of the gift.

"I kept tabs on it, yeah," Ashton laughed. "It was like, 'Wow.' I hadn't processed it at the time—OK, he's going to donate. Then you see him standing there with the big check and I'm thinking, 'He can't give me $10,000.'

"Then I thought, 'Well, if he does donate that money, the government will send him a 1099. I have to give him the tax dollars back!'"

Ashton said the experience made him a better man, more patient. He wouldn't wish that hell on anybody. But his faith, already quite strong, became stronger. He and his wife, Cinamon, were humbled by the outpouring of generosity.

Gorgeous sympathy cards arrived in the mail with stories from folks they didn't know who had experienced similar tragedy. Oddly, they comforted the Loyds. Checks showed up from anonymous donors.

Doctors were hesitant to predict a timeline on Preston's recovery, but using "country boy logic," Ashton estimated they would have their little boy home by the end of the summer.

Three days after the accident, that seemed infeasible. Preston experienced a hypoxic brain injury during the accident. He never stopped breathing, but his brain was deprived of oxygen during the trauma. The prognosis for future cognition was concerning.

There were challenges in the beginning with bleeding. Ashton was uncertain his son would ever have a stomach again. For the next year or so, Preston would rely on a spit fistula (his esophagus terminates outside the body).

The future held much rehab, including plastic surgery and skin grafts. But after 32 days in a coma, Preston was awake and jovial. And as Preston improved, so did his grandfather.

• • •

"Is it absolutely Preston all the time? No," Ashton said. "But the neurologist came in yesterday and Preston was talking to the nurse. The neurologist said, 'I think that's about all I need to see.' The progress we have made has been crazy. We're already out of ICU, which I didn't think would ever happen this quickly."

Back at the race track, Kerr's teammate Mark Kennerly handed him $200. A random fan offered another $200.

"It's the most amazing thing," Ashton said. "The human spirit's not so bad, after all."

Indeed. Jeff Kerr should be an example to us all.

"If I was in that position I'd hope somebody would do that for me," Kerr said. "I think about the grandfather—that would be the worst punishment of all. They need that money more than I do."

I see Kerr weekly at race tracks all over the country. He's not much for words, so when we see one another we grin, nod. I sought him out in Richmond, Virginia, for some information. I'd planned to nominate him for a national humanitarian award, and as we spoke he told me I could make a felon sound like Mother Teresa. We shared a laugh, and nearly a tear.

He'd provided this amazing story of the human spirit, and for whatever reason God chose me to tell it.

The world could use a few more Jeff Kerrs.

~Marty Smith

Ode to a Mentor: NASCAR Style

I have worked at NASCAR for nine years. Prior to that, I was a sportswriter for 21 years; much of that time was spent writing about NASCAR.

Thirty years ago, if someone had told me I would one day be writing the previous two sentences, I would have called them crazy.

Breaking news: I did not always particularly care for NASCAR. But I came by my disinterest honestly; I'm from Indianapolis. One of my earliest memories is of the noise of roaring engines outside my front door, coming from the speedway a mile-and-half-away, when the month of May arrived and practice began for the Indy 500. And then, my first job at my old newspaper, *The Tampa Tribune*, was in the sleepy Central Florida town of Sebring, which awakens each March to host one of the world's legendary sports car races, the 12 Hours of Sebring.

And so, 30 years ago, an inherent open-wheel sensibility was being tempered by up-front exposure to exotic sports cars. NASCAR seemed, at best, interesting but no more so than when I had tuned into ABC's *Wide World of Sports* as a kid to watch taped-delay broadcasts of the Daytona 500 or Firecracker 400.

Tom Ford, though, said I needed to get interested. And by God, he was going to make sure that happened.

Tom, a witty and opinionated guy from Hollywood, Florida, was only the second auto racing writer the *Tribune* had ever had, following a courtly Southern gentleman named Bob "Wheels" Smith. Ford was doing more than following. He was making his own mark, turning auto racing—and NASCAR primarily—into one of the paper's showcase beats.

Tom liked all forms of auto racing and wasn't shy about proclaiming it the "greatest sport in the world." And while that was collective praise, NASCAR was always the catalyst. Tom was enamored with everything about NASCAR, starting with the men who drove the cars and their ability to do so.

He especially relished the annual IROC (International Race of Champions) event at Daytona International Speedway each February, held a few days before the Daytona 500. He took considerable joy in pointing out the dominance of NASCAR's entrants into the IROC Series, which matched drivers from different racing disciplines in identically-prepared stock cars. Oh, he would acknowledge the skill of an Al Unser, Jr. or Derek Bell but at the same time also established some parameters: "They're not as good as *these* (NASCAR) guys."

It didn't take long before Tom's wisdom's sunk in. Of course, watching stock car dramas unfold at places like Daytona, Talladega and Darlington helped that process along. And in the late 1980s, when Tom stepped away from the racing scene to concentrate on pro football coverage, I had evolved into a full-blown disciple. I was the *Tribune's* third auto racing writer ever and like the first two, favored NASCAR.

Fast-forward to 2001. Much had changed by then. I had also gone on to cover other sports, while Tom had evolved into one of the *Tribune's* best editors.

But the two people who had followed me on the racing beat had taken jobs at other papers. And so, at Daytona 2001, Tom and I were back on the scene again, in a "patchwork" role, covering the 500 because there basically was no one else around.

You know what happened that year.

Let me tell you that it shook Tom to the core, when Dale Earnhardt didn't climb out of that damn car after smacking into the Turn 4 wall.

Tom had written a piece earlier that week suggesting Earnhardt was perhaps past his prime and too interested in his "brand" to continue challenging for championships. Suffice it to say Tom regretted that piece. He vowed to never cover another NASCAR race. He was done with the sport, he said.

By late summer, I was immersed in it, having accepted an offer to join NASCAR's expanding public relations department. Tom cheered me on throughout the application/interview process. And when I got the job, no one was happier than he was; after all, he had convinced me, way back when, that NASCAR was cool.

He almost joined me at NASCAR. He interviewed for a position in our department in the fall of 2001, after abruptly quitting the *Tribune* to join his wife in her work-at-home, medical transcriptionist business.

Tom didn't get the job.

Two months later he got cancer.

He spent Christmas Eve 2001 in the hospital. Extensive surgery had removed the tumor. Given a clean bill of health, he returned to journalism, welcomed back by the *Tribune*. Over in Daytona Beach, I looked forward to working with him from the PR side in coming years, certain he'd be back covering races again, at least occasionally. We would have a great time, I told him. We'd raise a little hell like the old days, he said. What serendipity this would be!

It didn't happen.

The cancer returned. Tom died in November 2003, leaving behind a wife, two young sons and friends throughout two industries — newspapers and motorsports.

I was devastated.

Years back, when he was young and I was younger, we didn't really get along that well. As the years passed I came to love him like a brother. He felt the same, which he said the last time we talked, over the phone on Halloween 2003, just four days before his death.

In 2004, I authored a book titled *The NASCAR Family Album*. When it came time to write the acknowledgments, remembering Tom was a given. After all, he will forever get the credit for getting me interested in the remarkable world of big-time stock car racing.

To honor Tom's ever-lasting influence, I came up with this:

> *"And finally, a well-deserved acknowledgment of an old mentor from another life, who's now gone behind the sun, as they say.*
>
> *"Former fellow journalist Tom Ford preached the NASCAR gospel long before it was fashionable among media, and predicted the sport's popularity boom long before it seemed feasible. Tom always touted the stories NASCAR offered. Even more so, he touted the people involved in NASCAR. I guess what I'm getting around to saying, is that I hope he would've thought this book was OK."*

And now, all these years later, I guess what I'm getting around to saying is that I hope Tom Ford would've thought this story was OK.

~H.A. Branham

Repaying the Debt

hen I covered my first NASCAR race as a fledgling sports writer the assignment was thrust upon me. I wasn't given a choice.

It was 1971 and I had just been hired by the *Martinsville Bulletin*, which had taken a chance on a kid just out of college whose only credentials were that he had served, for a year, as the sports editor of his college newspaper.

For me the job was going to be temporary. I needed to make money for six months before reporting to Marine Corps boot camp at Parris Island, South Carolina, to begin the fulfillment of my reserve enlistment.

After that I was headed to law school.

As a quick aside, I never went to law school.

I became enraptured with sports writing. It was stimulating and gave me a sense of purpose. More than just reporting about games, news and meeting the challenges therein, I was afforded the opportunity to get to know a vast array of people. I told their stories, and what intriguing stories many of them told.

In Martinsville, Virginia in 1971 only one professional sport existed—NASCAR racing at Martinsville Speedway. It is the same today.

One day my sports editor told me I would have to cover a NASCAR Sprint Cup Series race at the track.

I was petrified. I had no knowledge whatsoever of stock car racing other than I had heard of Richard Petty.

My sports editor gave me one piece of advice. He told me to contact the speedway's public relations director, Dick Thompson. He would give me all the help I needed.

I didn't know it at the time but Thompson had been a veteran sports writer at the Roanoke Times. Just a few years before I arrived at Martinsville, he was hired by the speedway's owner and president, H. Clay Earles, to be one of the very, very few speedway public relations officials tracks then employed.

When I called Thompson I spoke to someone who sincerely wanted to know all about me. I admitted I didn't know anything about racing but he told me he would take care of me.

I took him at his word.

And he kept it.

Much later it occurred to me that Thompson was being the consummate professional. He wanted his speedway's hometown newspaper to have a writer that, however raw at first, could be cultivated into a knowledgeable ally.

When I arrived at the track Thompson left his office and took me into the pits where he introduced me to the competitors—Petty, David Pearson, Bobby Isaac, Bobby Allison and lesser known drivers such as Buddy Arrington and Earl Brooks.

I told Thompson that I wanted to do something enterprising; something out of the ordinary. Perhaps, I suggested, it would be interesting if I could explain, as a raw rookie writer trying to express his naiveté to the readers, what it was like to discover NASCAR and its drivers.

He pointed to Brooks and said, "This is Earl Brooks. He'll tell you all you need to know."

Brooks, indeed, told me everything. He answered every dumb question with a bemused smile on his face.

Somehow, the story delighted many readers, which offered me a great measure of relief.

Thompson wasn't surprised.

He told me that I had gone beyond the boundaries of race coverage; beyond the facts and figures.

"Give your readers something new," he said. "They always know who won the race. You can — and have to — tell them how. Earn the drivers' trust. When you do, get inside them and let them reveal things about themselves. Let them tell their stories. That's when you will give your readers things they don't know.

"And they will read what you write — always."

He made it clear that every competitor — in fact, everybody in NASCAR — had a personality, a life of his or her own and certainly a tale to tell.

Thompson was the best at his job. In the days before instant communication via the Internet and e-mail, writers had to rely on the telephone and the post office.

Thompson's releases came regularly. Some were about Martinsville Speedway in terms of facts and figures but many were compact features about drivers or other notables.

He provided them because his goal was to stimulate a writer; prod him to tell a story that would interest his readers and, perhaps, steer attention to his speedway.

When the media arrived at each Martinsville race, the information they needed would be waiting for them. No one had to ask for anything. Entry lists, schedules, track information, driver records, manufacturer records, previously sent releases and much more were available for the first reporter who entered the press box.

Thompson always made sure of that.

But he had another quality. He loved to laugh. He never took everything seriously. He was always proud of the gag photos that were a part of each race program — unique to Martinsville.

His philosophy was that if his job, and racing itself, couldn't be fun, then why bother?

After 1971 I was fortunate enough to advance to the *Roanoke Times*. For years afterward I traveled to races, often in the company of Earles and Thompson.

Through their anecdotes, opinions and recollections, which I duly reported, I soon knew as much as the seasoned media veterans.

As I advanced my career beyond Roanoke, from executive editor to publisher and vice president, Thompson remained a fixture at Martinsville.

He was there after others came on board to meet the increasing demands of marketing and promotion.

He was there after sinus cancer cost him an eye.

I am ashamed to say that, in time, I didn't stay in touch with Thompson as much as I should have. Sure, I talked to him by phone and we always conversed when I showed up for Martinsville's races.

But while I might have been far busier as my career advanced, I had the nagging feeling that I had ignored the man who gave me my start.

That dissolved somewhat in 1999, when, as president, I was able to present Thompson with the National Motorsports Press Association's Joe Littlejohn Award for outstanding lifetime service to the organization.

I had never seen him so humbled.

In 2004, I willingly took on the task of editing his delightful book, *A Funny Thing Happened On The Way To The Checkered Flag*, a hilarious collection of stories and anecdotes that provided a unique insight into NASCAR and its people. It came complete with his beloved gag photos.

But it wasn't enough.

I have never fully repaid my debt. I doubt I ever will.

I hope that in your life you have found someone who, while serving his or her own goals, has found it more rewarding to serve yours.

That person has realized a quality in you and wants to cultivate it for your benefit.

In his role as Martinsville Speedway's public relations director Thompson did his job.

But, at least with me, he did more than that. He encouraged me to go beyond boundaries. He wanted me to be more than a reporter.

He wanted me not only to inform but also to entertain. He wanted me to tell stories about people.

He wanted me to be a chronicler of lives and all that they entailed. If that benefited Martinsville, so be it.

But if it made NASCAR a sport so much more intimate to its fans—and lured those who didn't know much about it—that was even better.

He became the most influential force of my career.

A mentor? Yes. For those of us who have had one, have not we been forever grateful?

Please repay the debt—somehow, some way.

I'm still trying.

~Steve Waid

Editor's note: Dick Thompson died on Oct. 28, 2009 at age 74.

Fast Cars
and Freedom

When the 2009 NASCAR season kicked off in February, one thought filled my mind: Hallelujah! After months of watching NASCAR clips on YouTube, I needed the real thing. Plus, the season opener brought me one step closer to my favorite race.

Despite my private pep talks, the Memorial Day weekend race seemed like a small dot on the distant horizon. We were smack-dab in the middle of a cold New Jersey winter and I was still adjusting to a major household change that occurred weeks before on January 3.

But Father Time proved me wrong. As I adapted to my new role of "happily married single mom," the days rushed by in a blur—every day except May 24. No matter how I filled my time, the hours preceding the Coca-Cola 600 dragged by slower than a pace car with four flat tires.

Finally, after what seemed like an eternity, I was only minutes away from viewing a patriotic ceremony unlike any other. I placed my peanuts, M&M's and Diet Pepsi on the end table, found a comfortable spot on the couch and settled in to watch the opening events.

I promised myself I wouldn't cry when the Celtic Force Pipers played "Amazing Grace" on the bagpipes, followed by the 21-gun salute. But it was a promise I struggled to keep. When the 82nd

Airborne bugler played "Taps," memories of my beloved grandfather's funeral flooded my mind.

And then my thoughts turned to the living. "Please keep him safe," I silently prayed. Not wanting my 8-year-old son, Dakota, to see me in tears, I took a deep breath and concentrated on the remainder of the beautiful ceremony.

And then I waited. And waited some more, while rain soaked Lowe's Motor Speedway. After much deliberation, NASCAR officials postponed the race to Monday. Memorial Day.

I downed my soda, returned the snacks to the pantry and pondered how I'd fill the extra hours of unexpected free time. Despite my disappointment, I was delighted at the thought of a Memorial Day race.

At noon the next day, Dakota and I headed to the family room. With munchies in hand, I returned to the couch, while my son sprawled on the floor amongst a sea of Legos and Hot Wheels cars.

"Carl Edwards is gonna win," he said, lining up his collection of droids and cars.

"No way. We both know Tony Stewart's going to Victory Lane," I teased back as we eagerly waited for Darrell Waltrip to shout, "Boogity, boogity, boogity. Let's go racing, boys." And when he did, Dakota yelled, "Wahoo," but I wasn't sure if he was referring to the race or the NASCAR versus space invaders battle being waged on the carpeted floor.

The race had been underway for almost three hours. Shortly before 3 p.m. on Lap 167, with Brian Vickers in the lead, the caution flag waved. Not another rain delay, I thought to myself, frustrated with Mother Nature. It was still early in the race and already they'd halted the event three times for sprinkles and light showers.

"Who crashed?" Dakota asked as he concentrated on the fantasy skirmish playing out before him.

"I'm not sure. The caution might be for rain or debris. I don't think it's anything major."

Seconds later, Mike Joy's voice came across the airwaves and informed viewers there wasn't an accident. Nor was there debris or rain on the track. In an unprecedented move, NASCAR officials were stopping the race to observe Memorial Day's National Moment of Silence.

Dakota's attention snapped to the wide-screen TV. "Mommy, did you hear that?" he asked, scrambling to his feet.

"Yeah, I did." Reaching over, I retrieved an unframed snapshot from the end table and rose from the couch. Careful not to step on any renegade Legos, I joined Dakota in the middle of the family room where we quietly observed Memorial Day.

Beneath dark rain clouds, Old Glory, now lowered to half mast, whipped in the wind. Thousands of NASCAR fans stood as the cars slowly came to a stop along the front stretch. Crew members formed a solemn line along pit road. I blinked back tears and smiled when Tony Stewart waved a small American flag out his window. Goosebumps peppered my arms when silence overtook Lowe's Motor Speedway.

"Do you think Daddy's watching?" Dakota asked in a hope-filled voice.

Probably not. "I don't know," I answered.

Despite my best attempts, my eyes misted as I clutched a three-week-old photograph of my husband, dressed in full battle gear, standing next to an MRAP. Unlike the Dover race on September 23, 2001, my husband wasn't in the grandstands. Nor was he sitting next to me as he did during last year's Memorial Day weekend race. No, this year he was thousands of miles away in Baghdad.

I glanced down at my son and felt my throat tighten. His small right palm rested over his heart and he stood tall and proud, like a miniature soldier. I imagined that in his mind he saw the little picture, like the 4x6 I held in my hand, whereas I saw the big picture — the paying homage to and honoring of all service members, past and present.

I counted my blessings and sent up a silent prayer, thanking God that my husband was in Baghdad and not part of the deeper meaning of Memorial Day.

Seconds later, the somber tribute came to a close and the track roared to life when the drivers restarted their engines. I gave Dakota's shoulder a gentle squeeze and he looked up at me with his big brown eyes and smiled. "Mommy, NASCAR loves the troops."

I knelt and wrapped my arms around him. "Yes they do, honey. And that's why I love NASCAR."

~Kim Wilson

T. Wayne Robertson: A Friend Indeed

"You want me to drive home?"

It had been a long day at Bristol Dragway. Rain and an unusually high number of oil downs had pushed the finals of the race until the early hours of a Monday morning. The photos and trophy presentations seemed endless, and we still had the three-hour drive home ahead.

"You can navigate," he said. We'll get home quicker if I drive."

Three hours later, we reached my house in Winston-Salem, N.C. After unloading my very tired family, I asked him what he was going to do with a rare day off.

"You headed home to get some rest?" I said.

"No. I'm headed to work. I promised Ralph I'd get some reports done by noon and he won't care what time we got back."

That's when I knew that one day, Wayne Robertson would be my boss.

All Wayne Robertson had ever wanted to be was a fireman; he really couldn't think of anything he'd rather do. In the early 1970s, he honed his firefighting skills by working shifts at the Mt. Tabor VFD in Winston-Salem while pursuing a Fire Science degree at Rowan Technical Institute.

But then fate intervened, in the form of the aforementioned Ralph

Seagraves, who befriended Wayne at a NASCAR race in Darlington, S.C.

Seagraves was one of several R.J. Reynolds executives charged with the responsibility of giving the Winston brand a presence in NASCAR. It started with race sponsorships but Seagraves had a larger vision — Winston would sponsor the entire NASCAR Grand National Series and use its considerable promotional expertise to show the folks in Daytona Beach the way to grow the sport on a national stage.

But Seagraves needed help. His newfound buddy Junior Johnson, one of NASCAR's all-time greats, had convinced him the public needed educating when it came to NASCAR, and part of that education was seeing a real race car up close.

Seagraves was a world-class salesman, but it took very little of that talent to convince Wayne to become the first Winston show car driver, in 1971.

He hit the road, taking the red-and-white Junior Johnson Chevrolet to shopping centers, supermarkets and malls, making friends for the sport of stock car racing.

Everybody liked Wayne. He combined a ready smile with considerable street smarts and a passion for what he was doing. He couldn't believe he was actually getting paid for being part of the sport he so dearly loved.

Wayne's impact on the NASCAR garage was immediate. He could talk the talk with the mechanics and officials, but also impressed his managers with his natural leadership style. He would do anything, anywhere, anytime for any friend of NASCAR or R.J. Reynolds. He became a known quantity in the sport at an early age.

The show car job didn't last long and Wayne got a series of promotions. He literally flew past more experienced, better-educated people, but none of them, including me, minded. Wayne outworked us all and was fiercely loyal to his managers. That philosophy served him well.

In 1984, Seagraves decided to retire after establishing the Winston sponsorship of NASCAR as one of the most effective sports marketing programs in America. There was no question as to who his successor would be. My prediction of a decade earlier came true—Wayne was everybody's boss now, and his influence began to grow.

By that time the R.J. Reynolds portfolio of event sponsorships had expanded dramatically, taking on drag racing and rodeo along with sports car and motorcycle racing and the Senior PGA Tour.

All the while Wayne was making friends. He became a trusted confidant of the top executives at R.J. Reynolds and was their "go to" guy when trouble struck, professionally or personally.

Wayne not only impressed the people he worked for but he also spent countless hours improving the quality of life for the 100 people who reported to him. Every one of those employees would go to war for "T. Wayne," as he had come to be known in the outside world.

Wayne's people were friends first and employees second. He took care of them, lending them money when times were tough. He talked them through family crises and showed up at every wedding, funeral or graduation. No one doubted his primary concern in the world was his people. He was just built that way.

However, trouble was on the horizon and the perfect world Wayne had built turned upside down when Kohlberg, Kravis Roberts & Co. (KKR) completed what at the time was the largest leveraged buyout in American business history, acquiring RJR Nabisco. The deal was later immortalized in the book *Barbarians at the Gate: The Fall of RJR Nabisco*. Wayne's biggest supporters were gone and his keen business instinct gave him an inkling of what was to come.

In an effort to strip R.J. Reynolds down, making it a more attractive acquisition target, a hoard of experts descended on Winston-Salem with the goal of extricating the company from every sports marketing alliance it had forged since 1971. The battle was on.

Contracts were scrutinized and costs to end the relationships assessed. All the while, Wayne was preaching the gospel of his programs' effectiveness and his people's expertise. He was evangelical in his belief that his programs had done more and could do more in the future than any other form of advertising a tobacco company could buy.

After six months of study, the experts made a full report. Not only were R.J. Reynolds' sponsorship programs effective, it was their view that the involvement should be expanded. Wayne had made some unlikely new friends.

His legend continued to grow and in 1991, *The Sporting News* named him one of the 50 most powerful people in sports—select company for someone who started out just wanting to be a fireman.

One aspect of Wayne's legacy was assisting NASCAR car owners and drivers to secure sponsorships by citing the success that R.J. Reynolds had experienced in the sport. That took him to Louisiana in January of 1998 as he attempted, with others, to convince a new sponsor to stay the course with NASCAR.

A duck-hunting trip was scheduled and when the boat assignments were distributed, Wayne decided his boss would have a better time hunting with the folks originally scheduled to be with Wayne. In typical fashion, he took care of his friends and convinced his boss he would be better off in the other boat.

The next day, the greatest newspaper in the world, in my opinion—*The N.Y. Times*—had this to say.

"T. Wayne Robertson, who became one of the most influential leaders in American motorsports, died … during a hunting trip in Louisiana. He was 47.

"Mr. Robertson was one of six duck hunters killed in a boating collision with an oil rig crew boat near the Intracoastal Waterway in Vermillion Parish …

"Just as important as his company's financial largess was Mr. Robertson's role in leading lobbying efforts to spare motorsports from recent Federal efforts to ban tobacco sponsorships of sports events."

In the end, as always, Wayne was just taking care of his friends.

~Jeff Byrd

Son, Brother, Husband, NASCAR Fan

For those who live in Southern California and love sports, Louis Brewster is an institution. As sports editor of the *San Bernardino Sun* and *Inland Valley Daily Bulletin*, Brewster keeps fans informed about all sports, but his heart and his sports section save a special place for NASCAR.

He can be gruff and grumbly—at times a real curmudgeon—but that occasionally rough exterior hides a heart of gold. He's not a homer. But while we may not always agree, he is always fair and balanced in his reporting and really makes an effort to know his beat, which often means spending a lot of time at the track. That is why it wasn't really a surprise to me that when I met his son, it happened at Auto Club Speedway.

We were outside the media center and "Louie" grabbed me. "Come meet my son," he said excitedly. He did not need to say that. There was no mistaking that Bryan was his son; they had the same twinkle in their eye that said, "I have a secret, which I'll let you in on when I'm good and ready."

He was wearing a credential around his neck in one of those plastic holders, emblazoned with U.S. Army logos, and I pulled on it playfully. "Are you a fan of Joe Nemecheck?" I asked. Louie quickly jumped in, saying," Bryan's a soldier." There was so much pride in his voice it brought a lump to my throat.

"I'll bet you're a good one. Thank you." Then I pressed on to wherever I was headed, but I am so grateful now for that moment, however brief.

Louie said Bryan was born a soldier and from the time he was 4 or 5, he would go to school wearing camouflage. He was Jr. ROTC, then ROTC, and enlisted at 18. When I met him, he had already completed his second tour of duty. In a very short time, he had risen to the rank of Sergeant and was leading 30 men, well on his way to accomplishing his goal of becoming a helicopter pilot. No wonder his father was so proud.

His father was dedicated too, in supporting Bryan's passion for service to America. At each race, Louie would gather up leftover media gifts, along with press kit folders and notebooks, basically anything with a NASCAR team logo, to send overseas to Bryan and his "guys." Louie would be the last one out of the media center on Sunday and would come back on Monday to "help clean up," in order to send a bigger haul over to Bryan and his buddies. Bryan's fellow soldiers always told him what a cool job his dad had, and would ask questions about the drivers and teams as he handed out goodies from his father's latest care package.

One day in May 2006, I got a cell phone call from Dennis Bickmeier, the speedway's director of communications at the time. "I have some terrible news," he said. I could tell from his voice that what followed was going to be devastating. "Have you heard about that helicopter that went down in Afghanistan?"

I had. A CH-47 Chinook helicopter crashed during combat operations while searching for al-Qaida and Taliban fighters east of Abad in the Kunar province. Ten American soldiers were killed. Then Dennis said, "Louie Brewster's son was on the helicopter." Bryan was 24 years old.

In times like that, we are helpless. Nothing can make it better. But I was reminded during the next several days and weeks why NASCAR refers to those who love it as being part of a family, because that is how everyone behaved. People came out of the woodwork to pitch in, helping with arrangements, donations or a shoulder to lean on. The service was beautiful and Bryan was remembered as he lived, with humor and honor. Louie told many stories about Bryan's childhood, including how he learned to count—by playing with his father's NASCAR die-casts.

It was a terrible time, but the coming months were busy at the speedway and helped us regroup. We were in the midst of a major capital project, building the new FanZone for the track, including a concert stage, Apex by Wolfgang Puck (a full-service restaurant), and a retail store; and adding landscaping, shade and a dedicated tram route. Although we were busy, my thoughts would often go out to Louie, who I knew was suffering and working to keep Bryan's memory vibrant.

In late July, I was out checking on the construction progress when I noticed they had completed the loop for the tram turn-around. They were installing flagpoles in a giant circle of dirt. I tracked down our construction team and said the four words everyone on our staff has come to fear … "I have an idea."

Over the next several weeks, a dedicated team worked to make it a reality.

The Opportunity, California FanZone had a pretty spectacular announcement event. Wolfgang Puck and Jeff Gordon were there, and Wolfgang handed out No. 24 frosted, race car-shaped cookies.

The Asian-themed Grand Opening of the FanZone was even more spectacular, with hundreds of VIPs from San Bernardino County and NASCAR eating Chinese Chicken Salad and drinking Opportunitinis, the signature drink of the Opportunity, California FanZone. Carl Edwards built a giant chocolate race car with the help of Wolfgang Puck's award-winning pastry chef Sheri Yard, and fans were out in force to watch him make it and help him eat it. That's when I learned the fittest driver in NASCAR occasionally sneaks some chocolate.

Despite all the hoopla, the FanZone opening event that will remain forever the most meaningful to me was a private tour, given hours before the public ones.

The media was invited to see the facility first and the usual characters were circling the wagons, waiting to get in, sample the food and tell the world about it. I told Louie Brewster I wanted to show him the place myself, so we jumped in a truck and off we went as I described all the ways this new FanZone would create everlasting, meaningful memories for fans.

I parked the truck outside the same circle I had seen several weeks earlier while checking out the construction. The bare dirt was gone. The turn-around was now a circle of pristine green grass and thousands of pansies in an enormous flower bed bursting with color. The flagpoles were gleaming, standing tall, and the American flag was flying proudly.

I got out of the truck and Louie followed. He took a step toward the flowers as he pointed to a mounted plaque beneath the flag. "What's that?" he said. I shrugged, and he took another few steps forward before stopping and falling to his knees.

The plaque beneath the American flag reads, "In loving memory of Sgt. Bryan Brewster. Son, brother, husband, NASCAR fan."

Every time I pass that turn-around, I remember Bryan Brewster, the twinkle in his eye and the sacrifice he and his family have made to protect us from harm. And I am reminded of my promise to his father to create everlasting, wonderful memories for race fans.

~Gillian Zucker

And the Winner Is ...

Our family had been big NASCAR fans for as long I could remember. I'd purchased two tickets in anticipation of the upcoming race in our town. My college student son Mark and I couldn't wait to cheer our favorite driver on to victory.

When I arrived at work early Monday morning, my supervisor greeted me.

"MJ, you're a big NASCAR fan, aren't you? Would you happen to know how I could get my hands on a couple of tickets for Saturday's race? It's for a foster child."

As a social worker, I was always looking for resourceful ways to put a smile on a child's face. Was God giving me another opportunity to fulfill a little one's dream?

My supervisor went on to tell me about a foster dad who had raced stock cars when he was younger. When he and his wife had taken in a little boy, they'd decorated the child's room using a NASCAR theme, complete with race car bed and all. The little boy grew to love NASCAR, but had never had the opportunity to attend an actual race. The dad hadn't been to a race in years, either.

I couldn't help feeling the excitement welling up inside me like a volcano about to erupt. "It so happens I have two tickets for Saturday's race!" I said. "I need to make a quick phone call before I hand the tickets over, though."

I made my way outside, dialing Mark's number at college. Soon I'd filled him in on all the details.

"Mom," Mark replied, "remember when I was 7 years old? Attending an actual race meant more to me than a hundred birthday parties put together! Give the father and son our tickets with my blessing."

I hung up the phone beaming with pride at having such a terrific kid. Giving up those tickets hadn't been that big of a deal after all.

Race weekend finally arrived. There wasn't a cloud in the sky. "It will be a perfect evening for NASCAR," I chuckled, cracking four eggs into a frying pan. I couldn't help whispering a prayer of gratitude as I fixed breakfast for my husband, Vince, and my mother, Thora.

All evening long I wondered how the father and son were making out at the race. Were they creating happy memories together like Mark and I had done so many times over the years?

Several days later I reached into the mailbox. My fingers pulled out an envelope addressed in unfamiliar handwriting. I opened it and began to read.

Dear Mrs. Hart,

There are no words to describe how grateful my son and I were to be able to attend the NASCAR race last Saturday. We had the most wonderful time! I wish you could have been there to see Danny's eyes light up like a Christmas tree as he watched the cars racing around the track. We'll remember that evening together for the rest of our lives. And to think you made it all possible! Danny and I want you to know something — YOU were the real winner of this year's NASCAR race. God bless you!

I clutched my first fan letter tightly against my chest. God couldn't have blessed me with a better trophy.

~MJ Hart as told to Mary Z. Smith

NASCAR to a "T"

When racing lost one of its pioneers October 7, 2008 with the passing of T. Taylor Warren, one of the few remaining original members of the world of NASCAR was gone. Taylor lost his battle with ALS (Lou Gehrig's Disease), silencing the shutter of his Nikon camera for the last time.

"T," as his many friends in all echelons of the racing world called him, gained renown for his now infamous shot of the finish of the 1959 inaugural running of the Daytona 500 on the shiny new 2.5 mile tri-oval track that is, to this day, NASCAR's equivalent of the Super Bowl. The race found its new home at the monster track after being moved from its original sandy beach course.

Johnny Beauchamp and Lee Petty finished the day in a dead heat, and Beauchamp was declared the winner. It took officials three days of developing and combing through the black-and-white still photos that Warren had shot to reverse the decision and proclaim that Petty was the winner of the race. To this day, there hasn't been another decision to change the position of the winning car at Daytona.

Taylor Warren started his racing career in 1947 at the Milwaukee Fairgrounds photographing Sprint and Midget races. He was given his first part-time NASCAR deal by Bill France, Sr., who hired him to photograph the Daytona Beach races in 1952.

In his 60-plus years chronicling auto races, he became known as the father of photography on the NASCAR circuit, photographing all 50 races held at the Daytona International Speedway. His last was in

February 2008. He also captured photos of all the Darlington races, from September 1950 through May 2008, the final Darlington event preceding his death in October.

T was the only photographer to receive the International Motorsports Hall of Fame's prestigious Henry T. McLemore award. He was presented this coveted award in 2006. He was one of the most respected photographers in the history of the sport. He was best known for his smile and easygoing demeanor both on and off the track.

I sat at the table with T for the 2008 National Motorsports Press Association's inductee banquet, in January. He was in high spirits and I teased him about being dressed in a coat and tie instead of his trademark yellow suspender britches with the matching yellow Goody's fishing hat. You never saw him at a race track when he wasn't wearing these two specific items.

Our paths didn't cross again until Mother's Day weekend in May. He didn't look well at Darlington, but was as always a trouper, lugging his camera equipment all over the track's expansive grounds, trying to get that perfect frame.

He told me on Saturday evening after the Southern 500 race had taken the green flag that he wasn't feeling well. He had seemed not to be himself all weekend, tiring easily, something that wasn't in his demeanor. He was typically one of the first people at the track and one of the last to leave, long after the race had ended. He enjoyed staying around and reminiscing about events that had occurred during the weekend's festivities.

But this time it took only one look for me to tell him that he should just go home and rest, and I'd get him any photos that he might need. He said, "I think that's what I'll do." He left the track about halfway through the race, telling me he'd see me at the race in Charlotte at the end of the month.

He did make it to the Coca-Cola 600 weekend, but told me that he hadn't bounced back like he thought he would. We shot Victory Lane together and talked briefly after the race in the media center. I left, telling him I'd be off the circuit until the October race in Charlotte, and I'd see him then. As always, I told him to give me a call if he needed anything, and I'd do the same.

I never saw or spoke to T. Taylor Warren again.

Numerous racing colleagues attended his funeral in Darlington. Photographers, writers, public relations directors, track officials, racing personalities from television and radio, NASCAR officials that included Mike Helton, President of NASCAR and Jim Hunter, the Vice President of Corporate Communications for NASCAR and former president of Darlington Raceway.

T's final memorial was a Nikon camera and that yellow Goody's hat arranged alongside a large picture of a smiling Taylor, a very fitting memorial for someone who devoted his entire life to the task of snapping photos of the sport of auto racing.

I was indeed fortunate and blessed to have known T. He made me a better person just by being in his presence. He took me under his wing and helped me succeed in a tough business.

T never forgot a name or face in all the years I knew him. I was and always will be honored to have called him my friend. He was an inspiration to me as well as to legions of other photographers over the years. He made me aspire to be the best that I can be when photographing and providing print coverage of the various types of racing, from the NASCAR Sprint Cup Series to the Saturday night dirt tracks.

To this day I'm continuously trying to live up to that standard, and hope that every now and then, I'll get that perfect shot that brings it all together through the camera's lens. Taylor captured the core essence of auto racing in his tens of thousands of photos. The racing community is a better place for having him in it. There are few that will ever be able to live up to the high standards he set during his illustrious career.

Always let your photograph tell a story and the printed words will follow. If you succeed in accomplishing this task, then you've done your job well, and that would have made T. Taylor Warren proud.

~Tommy Dampier

When You Can't Say No

During my four years in the communications department at Dale Earnhardt, Inc., I couldn't count the number of times people wrote, called or e-mailed requests to have Dale, Jr. call them, Martin Truex, Jr. come to a birthday party, or just wanting a job.

One day in early 2006, I received a letter forwarded by Claire B. Lang of Sirius/XM Radio from one Zachary Campbell in Weaver, Alabama. While reading his story, I was taken with the emotion and care that went into writing this letter. All he wanted was the opportunity to meet and talk with his favorite driver, Martin Truex, Jr., reigning champion in the NASCAR Nationwide Series.

Normally, I'd let someone like Zach know where Martin was going to be making an appearance and guide him in that direction. But, the thing about Zach Campbell is you can't just brush off someone filled with and driven by such determination.

I was amazed by his back story. Struck and moved are good ways to describe the emotions one gets from looking at his life.

A good-looking kid with an infectious smile greets you on the home page. The tale begins by talking about a kid who loves to race. At age 14, a motocross accident left him paralyzed from the waist down. While others would have abandoned their dream to drive, all this did was spur Zach onward to bigger things.

Doctors told him he would never stand again, much less walk. Six months later, Zach went to that same doctor's office. With the help of leg braces and forearm crutches, he stood in the doorway to let the doctor know he was wrong. Zach doesn't take the word "no" too kindly.

A year after his accident, he achieved another goal through grit and determination, as he stood at the doorway of his ninth grade classroom ready to attend classes.

So, if this determined young man was going to defy medical advice and prognoses, who the hell was I to tell him "no" about coming to Talladega. I called and asked if he was interested in being an honorary crew member for the No. 1 Bass Pro Shops Chevrolet team. If I had a dollar for every "thank you" I heard, I'd almost be retired by now.

DEI put him on the No. 1 Bass Pro Shop credential list, Talladega provided a media parking pass for him to park near the garage, and Bass Pro Shops gave him a hat and crew shirt for the weekend. When I asked if he needed a credential for his dad to drive him to the track, he simply said, "No, man, I'll drive myself there." ... OK.

I met him at his Jeep, which was equipped with hand controls, and handed him his crew shirt and hat. The wonder in his eyes as he held them and put them on was incredible. He swung his legs out, straightened his crutches, smoothed his shirt, tightened his hat and said, "Let's go."

Off to the garage we went with Zach pivoting on his walking sticks, swinging his legs forward each step of the way in his official crew attire. While there, he met Bobby Allison and Dick Berggren who posed for photos with him. If I had a dollar for every, "Oh man, that was cool," out of Zach I WOULD be retired by now.

He met every member of the Bass Pro team, hung out by the garage, talked with the crew and finally got to meet and talk with Martin before qualifying. On race day, he returned to the track and I took him to the pit box. I had some pre-race duties and left Zach with the crew on pit road. I figured he'd sit in a captain's chair behind the pit box and watch the action from there.

But a person like Zach is always looking forward ... and upward.

While walking back to the pit box for the race, I nearly cried at what I saw. There was Zach, all stretched out, being lifted up the pit box ladder by the pit crew so he could sit on top of the box. While some might have been embarrassed by this, he just smiled and gave me a thumbs-up. This kid who had gone through so much pain, therapy and determination to get to this point was being given the royal treatment—and rightfully so.

As the race played out, I kept looking at the smile on Zach's face and he actually looked like he belonged up there. Toward the end, it looked like we were going to win the race. Sure enough, Martin took the checkered flag and we all jumped up ready to take off for Victory Lane.

Before darting from the pit box, the same crew members who helped Zach up made sure he got down to come to Victory Lane. As we piled in, waiting for Martin and the car, here came Zach, laying down a qualifying lap of his own because he was moving so fast.

He stood tall and proud with "his" crew, got sprayed with beer and champagne while taking part in Victory Lane, and literally soaked in the moment. For him, the path to this Victory Lane was a victory all by itself. Johnny Morris, owner of Bass Pro Shops, made sure Zach was front and center for photos with Martin and the trophy. If it had been nighttime, Zach's smile could have lit up the entire track at that moment.

Zach's determination to meet Martin was for more than a photo op. Zach wanted to tell Martin how he still had the desire to race, to get behind the wheel and compete. Martin listened and gave him words of encouragement.

Since that spring weekend in 2006, Zach's dream has taken off with impressive results. He started out in a specially-built Legends car with hand controls, then to a Truck and then to Late Models. While writing this story, word came from Zach that he had secured a ride in the Pro/Super Late Model local and CRA South Series races for the 2009 season. They fielded the No. 81 F&S Body Shop/United States

Marines Chevrolet Monte Carlo for Coffman Motorsports across the Southeast.

Zach isn't getting these opportunities because folks feel sorry for him. It's because his passion and determination drive him to succeed and others to believe in his efforts.

And if everything he's gone through to get to this point works in his favor like it has before, look for Zach Campbell to return to Victory Lane again real soon. But this time, he'll be the one driving in to claim the trophy and accolades.

His talent, grit and determination already make him a winner and an inspiration to all for one simple reason—he won't take "no" for an answer.

~Tim Packman

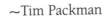

The Great Guy Who Made Me an "OK Guy"

Sometimes chance meetings have a life-changing impact, but, getting to know Lou LaRosa, whose engines propelled Dale Earnhardt to three NASCAR championships, was no coincidence.

I had been photographing, then writing, about races since the 1970s, but was unable to make inroads into the then very regional NASCAR garage. I was born in Brooklyn and have lived in New York City virtually my entire life.

Covering the Daytona 500 was a must, but, NASCAR wasn't my main beat at the time. Infrequent trips to cover races, back then, made me a stranger in a strange land inside the garage gates. Oddly enough I connected with Benny Parsons because I had many assignments to photograph him and we shared a love of mystery novels.

Still, walking around the garage there wasn't a friendly face for me to have a chat with. Every time I opened my mouth, my native New York accent was a giveaway. As a Yankee, that didn't win me any friends—then.

When the late, great Earnhardt won one of his NASCAR Sprint Cup Series titles in 1986 or 1987 (darn it, can't recall which year exactly) I read that Richard Childress Racing's motor shop boss,

LaRosa, was from Brooklyn. Chevrolet was giving its own awards party on the Saturday night following NASCAR's annual banquet in New York and I thought I should meet the only other person I could talk with—without a translator.

The Chevrolet public relations folks were kind enough to make an introduction and Lou and I quickly got into a discussion about Brooklyn trivia.

About six weeks later I was in Charlotte for the annual media tour of the race shops. It's a wonderful opportunity to see where all of the race craft starts and get interviews to preview that year's Daytona 500.

Even though reporters come there from the four corners of the globe, the sheer numbers of credentialed media, now running close to 200, make it almost impossible to have an actual one-on-one conversation with any of the principal players.

As the bus pulled into the RCR facilities in Welcome, N.C., I wondered if my fellow Brooklynite, LaRosa, would remember me. I saw him lurking in the background, got a big smile and he waved me over.

The other 199 or so credentialed media went over to interview Dale or Childress and LaRosa said in a quiet voice, "Come with me."

He took me into his part of the engine shop, which was not part of the media tour. I was elated he remembered me. Then he started to show me around the place where he made the power for Dale.

Now, I'm not a technical guy. Especially then, while I could identify a piston from a connecting rod, he could have been showing me engine blocks from tractors for all I knew. Still, I knew that I was in some special place.

Before this private tour was over he told me—then off the record—he was buying some of his piston heads from Cosworth Engineering, which was based in England. I didn't think anyone in NASCAR was doing anything like this at the time.

Then he said to come see him in the garage in Daytona.

I never printed a word of that, until now, when you are reading this anecdote.

When I arrived in Daytona I found LaRosa. He greeted me with a big smile and said to look him up anytime he didn't look busy.

While I wasn't covering the entire Cup season in those days I made it my business to find Lou as often as I could. Sometimes he would introduce me to other RCR crew members and rival crew guys. Getting an introduction from a championship engine builder was like passing a test.

It's true that I don't spend enough time in the garage (because I think the crew teams are so busy), but there are quite a few crew chiefs who will stop and say hello, and ask how I am.

Without that not-so chance meeting with LaRosa, and his "OK guy" stamp of approval, I don't think I would have continued to write about NASCAR as much.

It wouldn't have been so much fun, and I wouldn't have gotten to meet some dedicated and hard-working people. I'm very grateful.

~Lewis Franck

The Book

Blaise Alexander was a promising young race car driver, from Montoursville, Pennsylvania. As a reporter, I used to tease him. He was charismatic—and popular. The girls loved him for his charm and he made everyone, young or old, feel as if they were special.

He'd always shout from across the garage, "You're looking good today!" I'd holler back that he was to stop hitting on me immediately as I was old enough to be his mother. Then, we'd laugh so loud it would rival the roar of the engines dashing in and out from the garage stalls. The girls loved Blaise and he was a magnetic young gun at the beginning of his career.

Blaise began racing in go-karts and he won the World Karting Association East Regional Championship in 1992. He moved to North Carolina to enter the ARCA Series and earned that series' Rookie of the Year title in 1995, tasting the sweetness of success. He began running in what was then the NASCAR Busch Series and had signed to run for Team Sabco in 2000, finishing 25th in points. He lost sponsorship and had to drop back to the ARCA series after that season.

I felt for Blaise at the time and didn't want him to lose his confidence, so I got him a book that I thought would be great for him at that moment.

The book, a New York Times best seller, was called, *Failing Forward*, by John C. Maxwell. The book's premise is that while our parents teach us how to succeed they don't teach us how to fail and that learning how to fail is the most important tool to achieve success for anyone who has attained it.

On October 4, 2001 I was at home in Charlotte preparing to head to the speedway to cover events there, when I heard some horrible news. Alexander was battling Kerry Earnhardt for the lead during the EasyCare 100 when their cars touched and Alexander crashed into the outside retaining wall nearly head on. He was pronounced dead at the hospital 25 minutes later.

How could Blaise be gone, his youth, his smile, his personality snuffed out so quickly and brutally? I vowed to mention his name on the air every year since, so that no one would ever forget Blaise Alexander.

Recently, nearly seven years after his death, I was approached by a tire changer in the garage. The story that he told me stopped me cold. After Blaise's death his parents let his friends remain living in his house. One by one, the friends got married and moved on. Finally, the house was empty and needed to be cleared out for sale.

Blaise's parents kept his room exactly as it had been left at the time of his death. This tire changer/friend and his wife had volunteered to clear out Blaise's room to spare his parents the emotional grief of doing it so many years after his death.

The young tire changer was moved emotionally as he told me they found a book that had been lying on Blaise's desk in his room all those years, with an inscription in it from me. They wanted to know if I'd like the book back.

I froze for a moment as I was moved again by the loss of Blaise, so tragically. "Yes, for sure," I responded, my voice cracking.

Several weeks later, they brought the book to the race track and gave it to me. Here was the book I had given to Blaise Alexander now back in my hands, years after his death. I held it in my hands, not moving, and said a quick prayer for his parents and his soul.

I opened the book and read the inscription. *"Blaise, You are going straight to the top!"* it read.

I treasure that book now, and know that Blaise did go to the top.

He's watching from above, still smiling and, as we race, he's enjoying the heck out of having the best seat in the house.

~Claire B. Lang

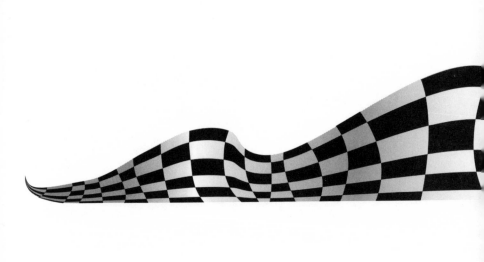

The Business
of Speed

Behind the Scenes of the Earnhardt Investigation

In late March of 2001, I was in my office at the PR agency of Powell-Tate in Washington, D.C. I had been at Powell-Tate almost four years and had transferred a political background into a concentration on strategic and crisis communications.

I took a call from former colleague Tom Griscom, who told me that he had recommended me to NASCAR as someone who could help them manage the communications issues on safety that the sport was facing as a result of the death of Dale Earnhardt. I was flattered by this recommendation. Tom, a veteran communications expert with R.J. Reynolds and then the Reagan administration, is someone for whom I have enormous respect, even though I was a former Democratic Party consultant.

There are many more bipartisan relationships in D.C. than most people might think. Even the firm I worked for, Powell-Tate, represented the best of bipartisanship. The company, formed by former Carter administration Press Secretary Jody Powell and former Nancy Reagan Press Secretary Sheila Tate, managed high level clients from both sides of the aisle.

I got off the phone with Tom and immediately called Jody to let him know we had the opportunity to work with NASCAR. Jody was truly one of the great figures in modern American politics. He was at the forefront of one of the most difficult times in U.S. history—in his role as Press Secretary, he faced the national media 1,245 times—and always did so with honor, accuracy and occasionally, wit.

The death of Dale Earnhardt transcended sports. You didn't need to be part of NASCAR Nation to understand the importance of Earnhardt. At the time, I was a casual NASCAR fan who typically watched the Daytona 500 and the Coca-Cola 600 each year. I had two rooting interests. One, as an avid fan of the Washington Redskins I wanted to see Joe Gibbs succeed, and two, Ward Burton and I attended the same high school in Chatham, Va. so, I liked to keep up with how he was doing.

However, neither Jody nor I were versed in the crisis that was swirling around NASCAR and the media over the recent deaths of Earnhardt, Kenny Irwin, Adam Petty and Tony Roper. We prepared for the meeting by researching the media reports since the loss of Dale and then digging deeper to better understand the circumstances around the deaths in 2000. While no one in our position could fully understand what NASCAR officials had experienced, we became acutely aware that they had lost not only a national icon, but a friend, as well.

About a week later we hosted a meeting at our offices with NASCAR President Mike Helton, Senior Vice President George Pyne, NASCAR confidant and then-president of Darlington Raceway Jim Hunter and NASCAR consultant Cliff Pennell. The group had visited a few other agencies before the visit to us. I later confirmed that most everyone else they met that day were among the "bow-tie and suspenders" crowd, as I'd expected. Clearly, none were a fit for the NASCAR team.

Jody and I thought our group, however, might be.

We held the meeting in Jody's office, which was, to say the least, "rustic." In one corner of the office was a carved wooden wild turkey covered in spent 12-gauge shotgun shells; on the walls were portraits of hunting dogs and Georgian landscapes.

It was clear this group had been through a lot—not just on the day Dale was lost, but over the previous six weeks. They were all business, but Jim Hunter was remarkably engaging. He wore a maroon tie with palmetto trees on it. I made a complimentary remark about South Carolina and he lit up and began telling stories of Darlington and his alma mater, the University of South Carolina. We had a good conversation about the situation and how we might help.

We told the group they needed a message. Up to that point NASCAR had been overwhelmed by negative press. The sanctioning body was being defined by their critics and the circumstances. They needed to start turning the tide; they needed to say something positive.

We were hired a couple days later and invited the team back to D.C. for a strategy session. That meeting included everyone who had made the initial visit, plus NASCAR's Chairman, Bill France Jr. Soon after the meeting got started we were treated to the first of many colorful sayings by Bill. He described what the sport had gone through by saying, "The world is on fire and there's not a fire engine in sight."

I made the point that at the time NASCAR was losing by a score of 100-0 on most of the news stories because it wasn't truly communicating to the media; NASCAR didn't have a message. I said it was important to come up with a limited but positive message and to convey it consistently.

This didn't make Bill, Jr. happy at all. After the negative press NASCAR had received over the past weeks, further engaging the media wasn't high on his list. He let me know that, as only he could.

The room fell silent for what seemed like an eternity. Jody leaned back in his chair, took a long drag off his cigarette and said in his Georgian accent, "Look, I have learned over time that bitching about the media might feel good in the short term ... but in the long term, being pissed off is not a plan."

Once again the room fell silent. Bill, Jr. stared at Jody, then started to laugh, which in turn caused Hunter to crack up. There was a chain reaction of laughter around the table; one by one everyone started to laugh. It may have been the first time in weeks the group had actually laughed about anything.

Jody and I became official participants in NASCAR's Earnhardt accident investigation, working closely with the team and especially Jim. The next six months included intense marathon meetings with the NASCAR team and their outside consultants, biomechanics expert Dr. Jim Radon and Dr. Dean Sicking, Director of the Midwest Roadside Safety Facility at the University of Nebraska.

We would present the facts of the accident to the media August 21, 2001 at the Hyatt Regency in Atlanta. While we all agreed that presenting the facts would be important, we also agreed that it would be even more important to discuss what NASCAR would do going forward to avoid another fatality.

We spoke to Hunter on a daily basis. He educated us about the sport, the media, the drivers. More than anything he taught us about NASCAR's history, culture and personality. He knew all the media, the team owners, the drivers—everyone.

We also learned about biomechanical kinetics, g-forces, delta-v, energy dissipation and the rate of deceleration. Jody, a former Air Force Academy student, had a good grasp of the physics and explained them to me, sometimes on the back of a cocktail napkin—with the help of a cocktail.

Finally, the day came to present the facts. We printed a 300-page, two-volume book set that included every bit of information we had. It included photos from the No. 3 car, plus photos, the medical report, and background info on NASCAR's outside experts. This book was so secretive that we made the printing company actually shut down while we had the book printed.

The books were flown down on a chartered freight plane. I was assigned to accompany them. I arrived at a special FBO at BWI airport to be greeted by the plane's captain, a grouchy character who reminded me of Captain Wild Bill Kelso, the fictional pilot portrayed by John Belushi in the movie 1941. The plane seemed like it was built in 1941—a twin-prop freight plane that took five hours to get to Atlanta from Baltimore!

Some 350 media members showed up to hear what we had to say. Most predicted a "whitewash" of the facts. What they got was a detailed and scientific review of what happened and why. There were specific diagrams, crash videos, and photographs. Everything was laid on the table, every question answered.

Raddin analyzed the biomechanics of what happened inside the car, while Sicking explained the impact of the crash outside the car. By most media accounts the presentation was thorough and convincing.

NASCAR went even further that day, announcing new enhancements designed to improve safety. Mike Helton took the podium and announced that NASCAR would be implementing or researching the following:

1) The creation of a full-time medical liaison to travel to each race who would have knowledge of the medical history of each driver.

2) The institution of in-car data recorders.

3) The development of a safety team that would head and intensify efforts to improve safety in the sport.

4) More research in the area of belt and restraint systems to help understand and prevent belt separations, such as what happened in Earnhardt's car, known as "dumping."

5) More research on how the design of the cars could be improved.

6) More research on the development of a soft-wall system.

7) Continue ongoing studies on seat designs.

I'm proud to say that every one of these items was implemented, making the sport safer today than ever. The full-time medical liaison initiative has evolved into a team of eight trained liaisons who are stationed at the infield medical centers in each of NASCAR's three national series.

All cars contain a crash data recorder and every impact is analyzed and used to identify opportunities to make further improvements. The safety team makes up the bulk of experts employed at the NASCAR R&D Center. NASCAR announced new safety belt guidelines later in 2001. The car was redesigned in 2007—the new car is safer, tougher, more competitive and more cost-efficient. The research in the "soft wall" technology has become the SAFER Barrier system implemented at all tracks. And driver seat technology has been significantly upgraded.

That year, NASCAR moved Jim Hunter from Darlington back to Daytona to serve as the Vice President of Communications. Hunter began hiring key people to fill positions on an updated NASCAR PR team. I continued to work with Hunter as each of the safety enhancements were announced. Eventually, he asked me to come to Daytona to work full-time for NASCAR. I accepted and that's how my career with NASCAR began!

I have been blessed to have mentors like Jody Powell and Jim Hunter. Both are legends in their professions, both are great teachers and both have a great sense of humor.

I'm forever indebted.

~Ramsey Poston

Editor's note: Jody Powell passed away on September 14, 2009.

One Phone Call to Success

Ialmost missed my chance at true NASCAR success — because *of one simple phone call.*

In 1975, I had a small well-drilling business in Susanville, California. I worked extremely hard to support my wife. Then suddenly, my life changed.

"Look out, you fool!" I shouted at the oncoming car. It was too late. I was run off the road, my 1971 Plymouth Road Runner damaged.

"Totaled," the insurance company said. A friend suggested I buy it back from the company; build it into a race car. For some reason, I took that advice.

In my first race at Susanville's Lassen County Fairgrounds, I was leading to the white flag when the car's right front ball joint broke coming out of Turn 2. It rolled end over end, landing on its roof. But I was hooked on racing. Drilling wells by day, racing cars by night, I won three dirt track championships in the late 1970s.

But I wanted more. I wanted to race in the big time, the Daytona 500. At my wife's urging, we moved to Level Cross, North Carolina in 1983. It was not an easy time. Work was hard to come by. Racing opportunities were even more scarce.

However, there was promise. A former Susanville resident, Terry Elledge, worked at Petty Enterprises, building engines; he signed me in 1983. When both Richard and Kyle Petty left to drive for other teams the following year, I hired on as a crew member for rookie driver Rusty Wallace. Cliff Stewart owned the team.

The work was hard and laborious, but I did it all. I worked in the shop, packed wheel bearings, did body work, and at the track I was the rear tire changer on Rusty's car. It was pretty grueling, but I knew I would eventually get my chance behind the wheel.

Basically, I did everything from cleaning toilets to driving the crew to the track. We didn't fly teams in those days, except to the West.

To break in, I raced a few NASCAR Sprint Cup Series and NASCAR Nationwide Series races as a car owner, and for others. I opened my own body shop to make ends meet while I raced Late Models in North Carolina.

In 1994, I got my best chance. Gene Petty, Richard's first cousin, tapped me to drive his Late Model mount. Success began to show; we won the local track championship.

Gene Petty and I also began competing in the NASCAR Nationwide Series, campaigning the No. 88 Kentucky Fried Chicken Chevrolet. I scored one pole, but didn't win a race that season.

But I stuck it out, working and racing as much as I could, pursuing that dream.

In late '94, while thrashing on Late Model and Nationwide cars in Petty's shop, I got a phone call. It was Richard Childress, owner of Richard Childress Racing. I remember the conversation well.

"Hi, Mike, I'm calling to see if you're interested in driving my truck."

I paused. My heart sank. I was already driving a hauler to and from the tracks. Driving another hauler for Childress Racing was definitely not the way to further my racing career, even if Childress was doing the hiring. My response was quick, concise.

"No, Richard, I'm not interested in driving your truck, but if Dale Earnhardt, Sr. calls in sick, give me a call. I'll drive that No. 3 car for you."

On the other end, Childress laughed; I hung up. I went back to thrashing on the cars; thought no more about it. Several weeks later, while competing at a NASCAR Nationwide Series race at Indianapolis Raceway Park, I heard some strange new talk. Four men from California, together with NASCAR, were starting a NASCAR *truck racing series*, called the NASCAR SuperTruck Series by Craftsman.

At first, I didn't believe what I was hearing. Later that week, I found out the rumor was true; the upcoming new truck series was legit. I was devastated. Apparently, Childress had called to hire me to *compete* in a truck!

I got a huge knot in my stomach. Thoughts raced through my mind, like how Richard had probably already hired his driver, and how I had really screwed up my career.

So I gave Childress a call.

Too embarrassed to tell him that I hadn't figured it out when he first called, I asked Richard, "Hey, do you have a truck driver yet? Do you think I could come and talk to you?' Fortune smiled on me; the job was still open.

When we met at RCR, Childress gave me the "entire 50-cent tour" of his phenomenal truck facility. At that time, I was making $300 per week driving for Gene Petty, and paying taxes out of that.

After the tour, we sat down in the RCR office together. I held my breath; my heart was pounding inside my chest. Finally, Childress spoke.

"Well, I can't guarantee you anything," he said, "but I think we can start you out with about $120,000, plus 40 percent of the purse."

Now my heart was almost pounding *through* my chest. I kept a poker face, but at that moment, what I really wanted was to reach across and give Richard a big hug.

"You don't have to give me an answer now," Childress continued. "You can let me know in the next week or so, if you're interested."

He walked me out to my passenger truck. Getting in, I rolled down the window.

"Richard, you have yourself a deal."

"What? You don't have to tell me right now."

"No, I'm in."

"You don't have to tell me now."

"Darn it, Richard, I'm in! Sign me up, I want to do this!"

A big smile creased Childress' face. Reaching forward, we shook hands.

I now had my first really big break. I was the hired driver for RCR's No. 3 GM Goodwrench Chevrolet Silverado!

In 1995, I competed in the non-points Winter Heat races, and captured a pole at Tucson. Then I competed in the inaugural NASCAR SuperTruck Series by Craftsman race—the Skoal Bandit Copper World Classic at Phoenix International Raceway.

In qualifying, things did not go well. My engine broke. I ended up 16th on the grid. But I was determined to win. This could make or break my future racing career.

Threading my way through the pack to the front, I caught Terry Labonte on the last lap of the race, charged past him sideways off Turn 4, and took the checkered flag. I went on to win six more races in the series that year. Then, in the final contest of the season, tasting full victory, I raced hard, passed Ernie Irvin, and beat *him* to the winning stripe.

With eight solid wins, I had just nailed down the first NASCAR Camping World Truck Series championship.

Many long years of hard work and sacrifice had finally paid off. At last, I was on my way up the NASCAR ladder to success.

~Mike Skinner as told to Kay Presto

Making—
and Taking—
the Right Call

O nce a year, like swallows seeking Capistrano, or stock-car bearing haulers headed for Daytona, I receive the inevitable phone call from Jim Hunter, who runs Public Relations at NASCAR. He doesn't even say hello. He just opens up with, "You stepped on your ying-yang, Androooo."

I hate those calls, which follow my latest gaffe—usually being too aggressive or snarky in my PR job with a NASCAR sponsor or running with an idea before getting the requisite sign-off. Yet Hunter (you can call him by his last name without disrespect) finds a way to make it clear that while I screwed up today, tomorrow I am expected to continue to swing for the fences. Get up. Dust yourself off. Take another cut. That's the perfect boss.

Hunter loathes political correctness. He says what's on his mind in that wonderful southern-fried South Carolina accent and has never been nailed for it. For example, a few years ago, we were interviewing a job candidate, and he opened up with: "Are you Presbyterian? Cause you look kinda stiff!"

What an ice breaker! I thought, man, I could work for this guy forever. The young woman being interviewed wasn't offended at all. She immediately warmed to the situation.

I'd come to NASCAR from McKinsey & Co., the global management consultancy. "The Firm," as it demanded to be called even before Cruise and Grisham, prided itself on collegial debate. In fact "Firm members" (we weren't employees) had "an obligation to dissent." You were supposed to speak your mind, always. A high-end London accent wasn't required but certainly helped.

First week on the job at NASCAR, I'm on a conference call with the Daytona-based PR team. I'm the lone guy on the horn; everyone else is in Florida. We were planning a press event, and I suggested we might do things differently.

Over the speakerphone came Mr. Hunter's booming voice: "That's B.S. thinking, Androoooooo."

He was right. It was.

At annual review time, I was used to McKinsey's voluminous reports. It felt like The Firm spent 11 months of the year preparing performance feedback. My first review with Hunter went like this: "Great job. But stop with all the damned e-mail."

Ironically, because I work in our New York office nearly 1,000 miles away, I know Hunter mostly through the computer screen and we've become true e-mail pals. I'll send him my daughter Gaby's latest cutting comments on life in these wacky times and her famous pie charts posted on a white board my wife hung on our refrigerator. Hunter gets a huge kick out of Gaby, whose biting sarcasm reminds him of his kids, Scott and Amy. We share a kinship as parents who encourage their kids to have a voice and exercise their independence.

"I don't mind getting old. I just don't want to hang around with old people," Hunter once told me.

He was a pretty wild guy, back in the day. There's one legendary story known to certain insiders of Hunter crashing a pace car. When the track was closed. Late at night. The car was messed up, as was Jim. Bill France, Jr., who ran NASCAR at the time, visited Jim in the hospital and laid down the law: the careening late-night revelry would have to stop. Or Hunter could simply get another job. He chose NASCAR and never did anything like that again.

Hunter was a fine athlete in his day, a running back for the University of South Carolina. He likes to joke that he wore a leather helmet on those teams. After graduation he became a sports reporter for the *Atlanta Journal-Constitution*. He enjoyed telling stories, and drivers like Joe Weatherly and the Flock brothers gave him ample copy as one of the first full-time reporters to cover NASCAR.

Hunter has great instincts, the kind you can't teach, as a writer, track operator at Darlington Raceway, and PR man for NASCAR. When you bring an issue or idea to Hunter, he'll give a quick, concise, common-sense answer. When I mentioned I was thinking about writing a book about remarkable NASCAR fans, he immediately exclaimed, "That's a book Bill Jr. would have loved!"

I don't think I would have embarked on a two-year project writing my book, *The Weekend Starts on Wednesday: True Stories of Remarkable NASCAR Fans* if it weren't for Hunter's support and encouragement. He taught me to always remember the fans who make every aspect of our sport possible. I worried I might not find strong enough stories, and he told me, "If anyone can turn chicken shit into chicken salad, it's you, Androoooo."

To all of us who've worked with him, Hunter has brought an invaluable connection to decades of NASCAR drivers and the sport's leaders, and its distinctive glory, swagger and deep-rooted traditions. He's not just a storyteller, although his stories are amazing. He's the embodiment of NASCAR, an old-school rebel who's made his way in a sterilized society without losing his sensibilities or sense of humor.

Everyone who has met Jim Hunter winds up influenced and touched by the man. For those of us in media, marketing and PR, he's as iconic as Richard Petty is to NASCAR drivers and fans. When I ponder how lucky I am to have stumbled into a job at NASCAR, the best part is to be exposed to the wit and wisdom of Jim Hunter.

And that's no B.S. thinking.

~Andrew Giangola

The Dirt on Bristol Motor Speedway

t Bristol Motor Speedway, the folks who run the place know how to think out of the box.

I covered the track for 15 years as a reporter and one of the best examples of their innovative thinking happened in the summer of 2000 when the "World's Fastest Half-Mile" was converted to a dirt track.

The plan was conceived by Wayne Estes, the track's Director of Communications.

Estes had the perfect background to pull off such a feat. He had earned a reputation as a guy who could get things done when he worked for the racing department of Ford Motors. Estes was well-liked in the industry and people always listened to his ideas.

Estes and his boss, BMS President Jeff Byrd, believed the track was under-utilized.

BMS sold out its two NASCAR races every year but Estes believed the area would support another major racing event. Estes had convinced the World of Outlaws, then the preeminent sprint car organization, to stage a race on the track's treacherously high banks.

There was a host of problems. First, you needed dirt—and not the kind that grows tomatoes. It needed to be red clay, soft enough to stick between your toes but hard enough to flatten like a day-old pancake. The dirt would have to be hauled in by the truckload.

Estes solved both problems by contacting Baker Construction. The company owned a farm a few miles from the track that was full of the "tacky" clay needed to make a racing surface.

Estes had a race, a date and the makings of a dirt track. Now he needed some luck.

I arrived early one morning to watch a parade of dump trucks cover parts of the concrete in dirt. There was only one problem. The dirt was too sticky. How would track workers clean it up once the race was over?

Bruton Smith, the owner of BMS, flew in some of his company's top engineers to solve the problem. A team of guys with degrees piled higher than the dirt filed out of a van. They came up with a bunch of solutions; black fabric, white fabric, plastic sheets, tar paper, but nothing worked.

Then a man with a deep baritone voice stepped from the back of a pickup truck and said, "You need some sawdust." George Wilson, a quiet, unassuming man, worked at BMS as a painter. But during his younger days, Wilson had hung around an old dirt track. "Just spread the sawdust on the concrete, and then roll it out like you're making biscuits ... and the dirt will stay in place," Wilson promised.

The college boys got a big kick out of old George's suggestion, but since nothing else had worked, they decided to give it a try.

The so-called experts couldn't believe their eyes. George was right. The School of Hard Knocks had trumped the Ivy League. The sawdust acted as the perfect buffer. The college boys packed their calculators and equations and flew back to Charlotte. Estes called several lumber mills for more sawdust and in a couple of days, the track was ready for its debut.

The World of Outlaws raced for a couple of years at Bristol, setting track speed records in the process.

Jeff Byrd was so impressed by George's solution that he gave him a bonus for coming up with the sawdust idea.

In fact, Byrd thought George might make a good spokesman for the track.

And so the legend of George the Painter was born. George has starred in a number of TV commercials for BMS and helped sell thousands of tickets.

In fact, George became so popular his bobble-head doll became one of the track's top sellers.

I just wish the bobble-head had been made of sawdust. Now, that would have been a fitting tribute.

~PJ Johnson

NASCAR's
Law of Attraction

I was born and raised in the Northwest region of the United States. It's about as far away from the World Center of Racing—Daytona Beach, Florida—as one can get. The irony (or total lack thereof) of a guy from the upper left-hand corner of the country coming to call the epicenter of NASCAR home still revs me up.

I've always maintained that the Universal Law of Attraction, which says like thoughts and experiences attract themselves, courses through all of us like a magnet to steel. So it's no wonder that on a cold, rainy Oregon Valentine's Day morning, 1988, *my* love for the sport was put into gear and the racing wheels of enticement were set into motion. The 30th annual Daytona 500 magnetized my energy to the raw steel chassis of 3,400 pound, 180 mile per hour rockets from over 3,000 miles away.

A young legacy of the sport chased his iconic father around the 2.5 miles of high-banked hallowed grounds that day. TV cameras following the dad and son duo through Turns 1 and 2 showed the horizon of the World's Most Famous Beach and everything in between. Somewhere in that shot was a place that would eventually bear my residential address.

The lad didn't catch his elder that day, but did congratulate him in Victory Lane by pouring a cold beer over his head in a loving thumb of the nose for finishing second in the sport's Super Bowl.

Of course I didn't realize it at the time, but the racing bait was cast that day and my soul had bitten, preparing to swallow it hook, line and sinker. I was about to be reeled in from the Pacific shore to the sands of the Atlantic.

As a kid I was fascinated by two things: sports and radio. I spent countless hours listening to the broadcasters of local sports teams on my parents' console stereo. Later when I turned my passion into a profession, it was me turning the action from the court, field and rink into a sports lover's theater of the mind. While starting out calling high school and college sports I was also introduced to something else — racing on the radio. On weekend mornings and afternoons one of my many duties at a couple of stations was to run Motor Racing Network (MRN) radio broadcasts of races from all over the country.

MRN had been airing NASCAR competition for 20 years or so but it was fairly new to us in the Northwest. The allure of 43 thunderous stock cars, roaring around the short tracks and superspeedways of the circuit, blaring out of radio speakers, captured my imagination.

It was also about that time in the not-so-coincidental world of Law of Attraction that I received an offer that would seal my fate for good. The owner of a local dirt track was looking for somebody to be his announcer and write up a story about the Saturday evening events for the area newspapers and racing trades. "You want me to do what? When? For how much? Sold!" Track announcer: a combination of race broadcaster and carnival barker, along with feature story writer and sports page stat compiler. Needless to say, a no-brainer decision.

Soon NASCAR would come to the Northwest in the form of what was then the NASCAR Camping World Truck Series. There, I met the owners (and part-time MRN announcers) of Portland Speedway. Not long afterward it was on to bigger, badder stock cars on a larger paved oval and my next link in the Law of Attraction chain.

One of the track operators eventually left the facility for the East

Coast and to take on responsibilities at MRN Radio full time. A year and change later, Yours Truly realized the track that started by watching a race take place from Daytona Beach some 12 years before had come full circle, as I would draft along the same radio route.

MRN's offices were just outside the walls of Daytona International Speedway. After interviewing for the job I was taken by car through the tunnel under Turns 3 and 4 and into the infield of DIS. There was nothing happening on the track, virtually nobody there but the history and ghosts of racing past. Even without an audience it seemed like a sold-out crowd to a kid from the Northwest. The towering, checkered flag-patterned grandstands in the distance and the familiar infield were sights I'd only seen on television and heard described on radio.

Taking a lap around the apron of the track, looking out the passenger's window and seeing nothing but pavement straight up the 31-degree banked corners, I was awestruck. At that moment it finally sunk in. The journey my soul set out on and was pulled toward via the Law of Attraction had hit the start-finish line. Not a checkered but a green flag to the next lap of life.

Seeing the track for the first time in person I couldn't help but remember that February day in 1988 watching the Allisons race each other over the same stretch of renowned real estate.

It is true that your soul knows which way to go if allowed to. Mine raced with the Law of Attraction to NASCAR's most famous address and into my own version of Victory Lane.

~Marty Hough

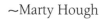

Batycki Never Takes Racing for Granted

I t's a Saturday night and I'm watching Lenny Batycki thrive in his element.

Wearing a Carhartt jacket, blue jeans, and an ESPN ball cap, he is at Highland Speedway, a dirt track near Gateway International Raceway in Illinois. He talks to anyone and everyone, be they fans or race car drivers or track staff. He preaches the power of racing with the fervor of a travelling minister, spreading the gospel of speed.

I met Lenny for the first time at a NASCAR Nationwide Series race at Nashville Superspeedway via an introduction by Mark Garrow of the Performance Racing Network. Batycki had badgered Garrow and PRN President Doug Rice incessantly in the late 1980s to work with them covering NASCAR races on the radio. Garrow has since said he finally gave him a chance, hoping Batycki would be terrible and they would be done with him. As it happened, Lenny was reasonably good and worked several races with what was then the Capital Racing Network.

I was helping Garrow that day at Nashville, as well as collecting audio for the motorsports radio show I hosted in St. Louis. With the introductions made, Lenny became my shadow, requesting with a polite ruthlessness that I interview his driver, Auggie Vidovich. And despite what Lenny may say now, I did, in fact, have the recorder on and did use the interview. That meeting would be crucial as it laid the foundation for his eventually hiring me as the public relations director at Gateway two years later.

Back at Highland, I watch him as he talks about race car drivers he knows, like Illinois native Justin Allgaier, and how he got his start on dirt tracks just like Highland's. He talks about the unity of racing, about how the sport is most successful when everyone is doing well, not just one facility. He talks about how racers and fans and track staff are his family.

And he means every word of it.

Going to area dirt tracks isn't something the former vice president at North Carolina Speedway in Rockingham, N.C., and Richard Childress Racing does a couple times a year; he does it a couple times a weekend. Every weekend. His resume gives him credibility with sponsors and media, but his education in the sport as an announcer at short tracks all over the South gives him credence in the eyes of the most important people in motorsports: the fans.

"Guys like Frank Wilson, Steve Earwood, Bob Harmon, Jim Turner, and Humpy Wheeler taught me a lot along the way. It's important to remember where we all came from," Batycki says. "We were all in the stands once, watching the cars go by and cheering for our driver. A lot of people in our sport forget that joy and take our fans for granted. We can't. Not now, not ever.

"We love the sport of racing. For us, it's not an act. It's who we are. We support the local tracks, just like the people who pay admission to go to NASCAR events, because at the end of the day, we're fans just like them."

The South Florida native has embraced every aspect of motorsports in the Midwest. A member of the St. Louis Auto Racing Fan Club, he won their outstanding media award in 2007 based on his local radio show. Batycki used that platform to not only promote the events at Gateway, but also the races at tracks throughout the region. I'm reasonably sure I won the award the following year thanks to his politicking of the Fan Club's board.

While he is masterful at working with the media, both local and national, in his efforts to promote, Batycki isn't above being a little devious in his efforts. A well-used phrase used to gain access to the public address mic or a TV camera is, "Hi, I'm Lenny Batycki. My PR guy said I was supposed to talk with you." More often than not, the ploy works, while the target of Lenny's deception looks at me as either a liar or an idiot. It's OK, though; I'm in the presence of a PR machine and would be taking notes if I weren't standing in amazement, admiring his chutzpah.

It worked in 2008 at the Chili Bowl, the wildly-popular midget race held every January in Tulsa, Oklahoma, where Batycki had the crowd of nearly 20,000 cheering his every word. The next year, he was invited to speak prior to the race and didn't have to rely on his "PR guy" to set up the interview.

So every weekend, we canvass the Midwest, Batycki and me, one of his oval-track apostles, spreading the word of racing. Of the pure joy of seeing cars whiz by at incredible speeds, of the smells of rubber and racing fuel, of fans getting that brief moment with their favorite driver. For Batycki, it's not his job, it's his passion.

He wouldn't have it any other way.

~Brandon W. Mudd

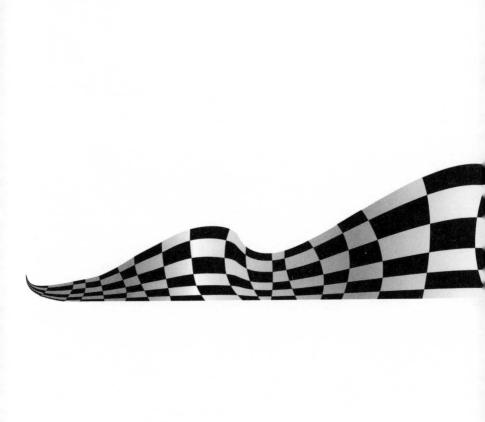

NASCAR
The Best Medicine

Short Stories, Long History

Racing has always been a part of my life, from day one. There are so many years of stories that it's hard to settle on just one. But a couple of things do stand out in my mind.

The first one is a story about my father, Buck Baker, and a couple of his employees.

Brad Hagler was the chief mechanic on my dad's race team, and Chick Morris, one of his very best friends, was the kind of guy who did just about everything. He was the tire guy. He would check the air pressure. He would run into town if we needed some parts picked up. He was just the go-to guy when you needed something done.

Back then, it wasn't like the race teams of today. We had a very small operation. And every time my father would win, this Brad Hagler character would get so excited and happy that he would just turn it on. He would party like crazy. He was a nervous wreck before a race, constantly checking back after himself to make sure he had done everything he needed to do. Then after the race, when all the tension was off, he would say, "OK, celebration!"

Chick was one of those people who could not stay awake. I mean at night, if he was driving, he would literally fall asleep and run off the road. It was one of those things everybody knew about Chick.

So my dad won a race in Columbia, S.C., and of course Brad did his normal thing—he started having a beer. My dad was pretty tired after the race, and he was offered a ride home with one of his best friends.

Chick said, "Buck, you don't have to worry about it. I'll tow the car back. Good grief, it's only a hundred miles. I'll have it back in a couple of hours."

Well, as it generally happened, Brad was loaded into the back of the car. This was when they carried their clothes, uniforms and everything in the back seat. Brad crawled up under some of the clothes back there, my dad rode back with his best friend, and Chick rode off with the car.

On the way, my dad and his friend came over the top of a hill, and he saw this black mark ... and all of a sudden he saw an embankment. He looked over and said, "Whoa, whoa, whoa, that's my race car upside down!" And the tow car was right there beside it.

So Chick came over and he said, "Buck, I'm so sorry. I know I'm fired. I know that.

"But I swear I've got to tell you something. When I ran off the road and got upside down and flipped back up, Brad was up under the clothes in the back seat, and he reared up and said, 'Can we get a beer here?'"

No matter what the situation, you can always find a way to laugh.

That's one of the funny stories, because there's been a lot of fun along the way. But there are other memories, too.

I watched my father win the Southern 500 at Darlington three times. I remember when he won his second race there. I was at the race track that day, and after the race, while my dad was in Victory Lane, I was sitting underneath the flag stand on the front straightaway. A little boy, just sitting there. I looked up and said, "Someday, I will win this race."

And as I was coming down that same front straightaway to win the Southern 500 in 1970, when I passed that same flag stand, I could almost see that little boy sitting there, saying, "Someday, that'll be me."

The greatest memory, though, came when after 18 long years of probably having the race won on eight or nine occasions, leading with less than 25 miles to go when something happened to prevent it, I finally won the Daytona 500 in 1980. It's a mark that still stands today as the fastest Daytona 500. I'm kind of proud of that one.

It's a short story that took forever to write, but it was worth the wait.

~Buddy Baker

Mok Security

*I*always encourage NASCAR fans to check out their nearby Saturday night short tracks.

There are two reasons that I tell people to go. One, the local race car drivers drive hard and put on some great racing, and two, the bullrings across America are filled with many, many interesting characters.

No local track had more character, with more interesting characters, than a little quarter-mile dirt track in northeastern Pennsylvania called Lake Moc-A-Tek Speedway. While "The Thrill Track" is no longer around, memories continue in stories about the races, the race car drivers and the cast of characters who made up a Saturday night at the track.

I spent a couple of years as track announcer at Moc-A-Tek and at times it was a two-sport gig: racing and fighting. Literally, when a fight broke out the announcer's role became play-by-play on that as well. Camping and partying were also part of the overall experience, and sometimes there was even racing to talk about.

I couldn't handle even one night of Moc-A-Tek at this point in my life, but I wouldn't trade my two years there for anything in the world.

One of the most colorful characters was a guy named Clarence, a grey-haired, 50-something, overweight guy who was track security. His credentials for getting that job were that he had a black security shirt, black pants and a pair of handcuffs, all probably purchased at a local flea market.

Clarence was there every week and NOTHING interfered with his security duties. Nothing, except a dirt modified (the featured division at the track) feature event. Truth is, he probably got in free, maybe got a little food from the concession stand, and his pay was being able to watch the races.

One night he was standing atop the back row of bleachers—basically planks on the side of a hill. A fan who was enjoying probably a bit too much of something stood next to him and fell into Clarence. The first time, no harm, no foul.

Then, the fan did it a second time and Clarence warned him that if he did it again, he would be asked to leave.

Of course he bounced off Clarence a third time and the chase was on—not the Chase for the NASCAR Sprint Cup, but an entertaining chase nonetheless.

Nothing at Moc-A-Tek ever just fizzled out. Every drama, fight or incident automatically became part of the oval racing experience. Part of that was because of another of the Saturday night characters at the track.

Ed Zigga, known as "Ziggy," was the flagger. He was always more interested in what was happening in the grandstands than on the track. If there was a pretty lady walking past, some crazy fan, or a fight, Ziggy had an eye on it.

In fact, Ziggy would automatically throw the yellow caution flag over the races when there was a fight in the stands, and at times was even known to leave the flag stand to join the fight.

But such was the nature of "The Thrill Track". At any other place, Clarence and the race fan would have run to the exit and the incident would have been over before it started. Not at Moc-A-Tek.

The errant fan and Clarence ran up and down rows through the stands, and Ziggy saw them and threw the caution. As the track announcer, it became my duty to call the chase. It was a combination of the *Keystone Kops* and a *Benny Hill* episode, minus the "Yakity Sax" music of Boots Randolph.

After a few minutes of fun, the fan made it to the exit and up the hill they ran, with Clarence in hot pursuit.

Racing continued and about 15 minutes later Clarence showed up in the announcer's booth, huffing and puffing, to let me know that he caught the guy.

We were in between races so I asked Clarence what he was going to do. He said he was going to call the state police. I asked how long before they would be here, to which Clarence replied, "I don't know."

"Have you called them yet?" I asked.

"Steve, are you kidding me?" he said in disbelief. "I left him handcuffed to a tree up by the road; he's not going anywhere. I'll call the state police later, but the modified feature is next and I can't miss that."

I've often wondered what was going through that guy's mind, handcuffed to that tree. But I suspect that in the manner of fans everywhere, he was probably just glad that the tree was close enough to the track for him to still be able to hear the race.

~Steve Post

The Politics of Mistaken Identity

Looking back, I'm not quite sure how I managed to grow up in South Carolina—I'm from Charleston—and become an adult without ever attending an event at Darlington Raceway, but somehow, that's what happened.

That all changed in 1996. I had been elected in the primary for the South Carolina House of Representatives, but I had never actually held office and again, I had never been to a race. My neighbor decided this had to change, so we headed to Darlington.

This was back during the time when Strom Thurmond was still coming to the races. That was Strom's last year to run for the Senate at the ripe old age of 94, and it was a neat, neat thing. I was 26 years old at the time.

I had never been a NASCAR fan. Actually being there changed my whole perspective about what I had heard about NASCAR, and I saw firsthand what the race meant to the state of South Carolina.

It was a completely different environment than anything I had ever seen in a sports venue before. The whole combination of things—the ambience of the race, how nice the heroes you had heard about actually were to people, the whole interaction—hooked me almost immediately. That's the best way to describe it.

That enthusiasm and appreciation hasn't cooled off, either. One year I actually went to 13 races. I've been to Charlotte, Bristol, and

Las Vegas; lots of places. Every track is special. One of the things on my bucket list is to visit every race track.

While I was at Darlington, one of the most memorable parts of the day was meeting a young driver who was really starting to make a name for himself. As a matter of fact, he won both races at Darlington that year. His name was Jeff Gordon.

I got to shadow Jeff that day, and spent some time with him and his wife. He was very hospitable and even as busy as he was, he let me go in his hauler with him and hang out. It was really a special time.

We may have gotten a few curious looks, but at the time I didn't think anything of it. I just assumed those race fans were all looking at Jeff Gordon. It wasn't until sometime later that several people remarked on the fact that the two of us look somewhat alike. The actual comment tended to be, "You guys could be brothers."

Since then, I have gone to some of his charity events where we've raced go-karts against each other and things like that, and Jeff and I have become friends.

And now, every race I go to, people ask me to sign something emblazoned with the number 24 on it for them. Regrettably, it is not because I am the Lieutenant Governor of the state of South Carolina. It is because they think I'm Jeff Gordon.

So here's what I like to believe, or maybe it's just what I'm hoping for.

I like to tell people that someday, somebody's going to walk up to Jeff Gordon and say, "Lieutenant Governor, can I get your autograph?"

~South Carolina Lieutenant Governor André Bauer

Kenny Wallace Gets No R-E-S-P-E-C-T

My very first public relations job was working for the Square D Company and their sponsorship of FILMAR Racing and driver Kenny Wallace. As is still the case with Wallace, there was never a dull moment when "Herman," as he's known, was around.

With the help of the track, we put together a media day in the city of Baltimore on the Thursday before race weekend at Dover International Speedway.

We got up early, flew from Charlotte to Baltimore and went to all the local television stations, met with local newspaper writers for lunch and hit some radio stations along the way, as well. This is a way for tracks to hype the races and sell the remaining seats before Sunday's big event.

Following the interviews, late in the afternoon we jumped in the car to head up around Chesapeake Bay and down to Dover for the race weekend.

When you traveled with Kenny Wallace, you ate a lot of fast food—generally in burger joints. But for some reason, on this day he wanted something a little different so we pulled up to a Subway restaurant that we found along the way.

Subway custom-makes sandwiches from a variety of options. Customers basically move down the row, tell the "sandwich artist" what is wanted on the sub, and they put it together.

Our sandwich artist on this day was a motherly African American woman who just beamed when she talked or smiled. Kenny started down the line cutting up with her while she was putting his sandwich together; I followed along as she was creating both of our meals.

We got to the end, the final pit stop, and she asked Kenny if he wanted oil and vinegar on his sandwich. To which he replied, "Why would I want oil and vinegar?"

"That's what Aretha Franklin started to do, and she lost all that weight," our artist said.

"Aretha Franklin?" said Wallace.

"Yes, Aretha Franklin, the singer," she replied.

"THE Aretha Franklin," said Herman.

"Yes, THE Aretha Franklin," said our new friend.

Kenny broke into song, in a not-so quiet, or melodic, voice.

"R-E-S-P-E-C-T, find out what it means to me. R-E-S-P-E-C-T!"

"That Aretha Franklin?" said Wallace.

She said, "Oh, Honey! You know who I'm talking about."

Kenny came back with, "If oil and vinegar is good enough for Aretha Franklin, then it's good enough for me. And, while you're at it put some on his, too," pointing to my sandwich.

Out the door we went. Our sandwich artist had no idea who Kenny Wallace was, but she—like us—probably laughed about that all night long, and for many nights afterward.

A driver doesn't always need a race car to make a lasting impression.

~Steve Post

Nuts, But Not Crazy

I've never been to a NASCAR race. I've never met a NASCAR driver. I've never even seen a NASCAR stock car up close. Still, I'm a certifiable NASCAR nut.

Here are some of the reasons why.

When I look up in the stands at football games, I still see mostly men. When I look up in the stands at baseball games, I still see mostly men. The same holds true for hockey, basketball, and pretty much any other professional sport you can think of.

But when the television cameras zoom in on the stands at NASCAR races, I see families. Blimp shots reveal infields filled with trailers and campgrounds crammed with BBQs, toys and family pets. Every race event is a family excursion.

There are serious, competitive business goings-on in the garage area for sure, but there is a real sense of camaraderie. Of family. Pre-race pit road crowds include the spouses and children of drivers standing beside their heroes. Truly, this is a family sport.

At football and basketball games the fans can't even get close to the players.

At NASCAR events fans get right up close and personal and rub shoulders with, and sometimes are lucky enough to get free autographs from, their favorite drivers.

At football and baseball games they play the national anthem before the event. Patriotic.

At NASCAR events they play the national anthem, but they rev things up a notch. They also have a military honor guard, a breath-taking military flyover, and a heartfelt prayer given by a local minister or pastor. Also patriotic. And respectful. And spiritual.

I have watched far too many sports interviews in my time with professional athletes who sicken me with their blatant arrogance and brazen cockiness. They are rich boys gone wild.

I have never watched a NASCAR driver being interviewed who was arrogant. Confident, yes. Sometimes, one is a little upset with another about an incident during the heat of battle on the track, but it is short-lived at best. Amends are made by the next race. But cocky? Never.

They are courteous, professional and true sportsmen. They love their real family, their NASCAR family, and their family of fans.

That's how it should be, no?

In my opinion, these things are reason enough to be a NASCAR nut, but here's a final one.

Baseball and hockey players go on strike.

Even if NASCAR had a drivers' union, I doubt the drivers would punish their fans with a season-long "drive-out." I'd certainly go crazy on any given Sunday if that were ever to happen. But I doubt it will.

I watch every Sunday afternoon or Saturday night race I can. You might ask why I'm glued to every race I can watch, yet have never attended one in person.

I guess I could say it's my geography, living up here in Canada, but that's just an excuse.

So, in the end, I don't have an adequate answer other than this: You're right. It's about time I went!

~Rick Beneteau

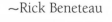

The Show (Car) Must Go On

Some of the good memories and stories come from experiences off the track.

This one has to do with a show car.

We used to make an effort to bring all kinds of show cars to Indianapolis in the week prior to our NASCAR Nationwide Series race at Indianapolis Raceway Park. That might sound easy now, but this is in the days before the Allstate 400 at the Brickyard, and Indianapolis wasn't always the preferred destination.

The summer the movie *Days of Thunder* was released, we managed to get four or five show cars and put them in front of theaters, suitably accompanied by posters for the race (Bob Daniels, our GM, never missed a chance).

I even took one of those stand-ups of Darrell Waltrip and pasted a poster over the Tide box he was holding.

Kroger, who was sponsoring the race, was great about putting cars in front of their stores when we could get them. Driver Tommy Houston said he didn't have a show car, but sent his superspeedway car a couple of times so we could use it. He even said we could use it in parade laps at prior races (with specific instructions that I wasn't allowed to drive it).

Anyway, there was one year when Darrell sent us his NASCAR Nationwide Series show car, and we met the driver for lunch at

Union Jack's, a very popular watering and feeding hole and gathering place for the race crowd, a mile or so from the Indianapolis Motor Speedway.

I explained that we wanted to show the car in front of the pub that day, then in front of the Speedway Motel the next day, then bring it to the track.

The driver asked if we could get a wrecker to move it, and naturally I wanted to know why.

Turned out that DW was using the souvenir trailer to transport the car, and once the guy had the trailer set up at the track he needed another way to move it.

I told him to sit tight and have lunch on us, then headed out on a mission.

First stop—Fately's Auto Repair, about halfway between the pub and the speedway. Two old friends from my ARCA days ran that place. I asked if we could leave the car there overnight, and they graciously agreed. I just asked that they put it back together after they finished checking it out.

Stop number two—the Speedway Police Department. Jeff Dine, the chief, was a race fan and a good friend. Just a couple of weeks before, he had stopped me and my 1965 Corvair on 16th Street. The speedometer cable was broken, and Jeff walked up and said, "Potts, do you know how fast you were going?"

"Uh, no, Jeff, I was hoping you knew."

After I explained how hard it was to find parts for one of those things, he let me go with a warning.

I walked into Jeff's office and told him I needed an escort to take a car from Union Jack's to Fately's, then to the Speedway the next day, and back to IRP.

"Why can't you just drive it?"

"Well, this car doesn't have a license plate, headlights, taillights, or mufflers, Jeff."

"Let me guess, does it have a great big number on the side and a sponsor on the quarter panel?"

"As a matter of fact, it does."

For the mere price of some comp tickets for Jeff and the officer who would perform the duty, we made the arrangements.

Made a pretty neat parade, really, a police car with lights on, the IRP pace car, and this race car headed down the road.

The only hitch came when we couldn't get it started the next morning, but the boys at Fately's took care of that with their battery charger.

As I walked back through the office door at IRP and headed for my office, I heard a familiar voice say, "John Potts, you'd better stop and talk to me."

I turned around, and there was DW at the front desk. As I've said before, we had been friends since I met him while he was in his teens and racing in the Owensboro area.

He wanted to know if I was on banker's hours, getting to work late.

I explained what I had been doing, and he was actually somewhat impressed by the whole deal.

"Didn't have any problems, did you?"

"No, just a little delay this morning. And we wouldn't have had that if you weren't using that cheap battery."

I resisted the urge to tell him that it was one of his sponsor's batteries.

~John Potts

Copycat That!

Communication between a driver and crew chief has always been a part of NASCAR racing. In the early days, it consisted largely of sign boards and hand signals. A driver's hand on top of the door window meant one thing, while a hand on the bottom of the door window meant something entirely different.

Today, thanks to technology like scanners, the Internet, and satellite radio, fans can listen in to the conversations all day long. Such was not always the case.

Radio communication changed on February 21, 1954 when Tim Flock—driving for Colonel Ernest Wood—entered his Oldsmobile in a race on the beach course in Daytona with a General Electric two-way radio.

From that day forward, radio communications evolved. And, so did "spying," where one team listened to another team's radio, trying to steal some strategy or find out how the other team was doing. These days, it's called a much tidier, more politically correct term, like "monitoring the competition."

Some driver/crew chief combinations use code words or speak in general terms like "what we talked about yesterday after practice," so as not to tip their hand to rival teams.

Back when it was still considered spying, in an accepted sort of way, I was the public relations guy for Texaco/Havoline and their sponsorship of Robert Yates Racing and driver Ricky Rudd.

Our crew chief was Michael "Fatback" McSwain, who was quite the character and a pretty shrewd "old school" crew chief. Not much got by Fatback, and he was always quick to find some humor in most situations—except of course when the car wasn't running well. He was passionate about his racing.

The pre-race parade lap ritual of the team was for McSwain to say something to the effect of, "All right, Ricky, can you hear me?" To which Rudd would reply that yes, he could.

Then Fatback would say, "How about you Cordell?" and Rick Cordell, our spotter, would give him a "Ten-four, loud and clear, Fatback."

Cordell would then communicate with Rudd, establishing that the three of them could hear each other. This was generally followed by some talk about the early-race strategy or any issues they had covered in the pre-race meeting. It's pretty standard conversation that happens even today within teams.

One particular night in Charlotte, Fatback just knew that Larry McReynolds , a popular current television NASCAR analyst who at the time was crew chief for driver Mike Skinner, was spying on our team.

So Fatback got on the radio and ran through his normal pre-race greetings with Rudd and Cordell.

Cordell and Rudd chatted for a few moments, so we knew everyone was hearing each other "loud and clear."

After the chit-chat ended, at the point when Fatback usually talked a bit about the car or strategy, he decided to change it up a little when, never missing a beat, he said, "All right, Larry Mac, how about you? Do you have a copy?"

We all jumped up and looked about six stalls up pit road where Skinner's team was pitting. There stood McReynolds atop his pit box, laughing because he knew he was busted. After a moment or two he waved in acknowledgement that in fact there was a "spy" listening in.

Lesson learned? In the immortal words of Lemony Snicket, "The key to good eavesdropping is not getting caught."

~Steve Post

The Soda Can

The sun was beating down as I stood behind the gate, peering into the garage of Infineon Raceway. My dad stood next to me carrying a bag full of pictures and a few die-cast cars. My best friend ran around snapping pictures left and right with her fancy camera, trying to get close-ups of our favorite drivers.

It had been a month since I had read about the testing session at the track. Carl Edwards and Boris Said were going to be there, along with my favorite driver of all time — Kasey Kahne. When I saw the article, I quickly called my dad and told him to take the day off, because we were going to spend the whole day there if that is what it took for me to meet Kasey.

There was no one better than Kasey Kahne in my eyes. It had only been the year prior that I had noticed him at the Infineon race. I had gone home and quickly looked him up, determining that he was going to be my driver.

Everyone in my family had their favorite driver. My dad was a huge Rusty Wallace fan at the time and my little brother cheered on Tony Stewart any chance he got. So here I was decked out in my Kasey Kahne gear looking for any sign of him. His car had passed by a few times heading out onto the track. Every time he passed, I waved and cheered hoping to get at least one little wave or nod. A few times I did, which made me ecstatic.

"Do you think they will come out and take pictures and sign things?" I asked my dad as I bounced around in excitement.

"I'm sure they will," he responded calmly.

"What do I say when I meet him?" I questioned, "Can I ask for a hug or is that wrong? What if I freeze up and miss my chance?" Different scenarios played through my head, quickly interrupted by my friend's laughter.

"Robyn, relax. He is just like any other person. Just say 'hi' and ask for a picture. You can also tell him you're his biggest fan like everyone else does. I'm sure if you asked he would give you a hug, too." She looked at me and snapped a picture of my confused face.

"But what if..." I started.

"No, don't think about it," she stressed, walking away. I turned to my dad for his answer, but all I got was a, "You'll be fine," as he took a sip of his Mountain Dew.

Around noon, a lady from the track had offered everyone waiting some refreshments. She had a box filled with different sodas and waters. My dad had pulled out a Mountain Dew, knowing that Kasey was sponsored by them at the time, and quickly came up with an idea.

"Wouldn't it be cool if I got Kasey to sign my Mountain Dew?" he asked. I told him it would, but I was more excited about meeting Kasey in person then getting anything signed.

Later that afternoon, when testing was finished, a car with tinted windows slowly drove up to the gate. "Do you think it's him?" I almost screamed as my friend again started snapping pictures.

"I think so. I see some people in the back," she answered.

The doors of the car opened and sure enough, Carl, Boris, and Kasey got out.

We made our way to Boris first. He signed a picture and took a photo with my friend and me. Carl was next. I had a picture from a recent win of his that he signed. Carl was also nice enough to pose for a picture with me, giving me a one-armed hug.

Finally, though, the moment had come. Kasey Kahne was literally 10 feet away from me, and I could not move. My worst nightmare was coming true.

"What are you waiting for?" my friend asked, pushing me up toward Kasey.

"Wait! I need something in my hand when I go up." I grabbed my dad's bag and pulled out my die-cast car, "OK, I'm ready now."

I slowly made my way up to him, going over what to say with every step. When I was finally there, he turned toward me with a smile. I couldn't believe it! This was the guy who I had cheered on every Sunday and dreamed of meeting in person. I had only seen him on television, but now here he was right in front of me. I had to admit, he looked even cuter in person.

I held out the die-cast car and said the first thing that came to my head, "Hi. Could you sign this, please?" Kasey gave me a quick smile and took the die-cast from my hand. I watched him sign his name and hand it back to me. With my hand shaking I took it back with a quick thank you and darted back to my friend and dad.

"That was it? Hi and thank you?" she asked looking at me, "What happened to the 'I'm your biggest fan' statement or asking for a hug?" I just smiled and tried to calm my nerves. I was too busy being on Cloud 9 to care.

That's when I realized I had forgotten to ask for a picture.

While I was trying to get the courage to go back up to him, my dad walked over to Kasey on his own mission. I heard him ask a question, and I slowly turned around to see a look of confusion on Kasey's face. My friend started to crack up along with a few other people in the area. There was no way now that I was going up to ask for a hug.

It wasn't until we were in the car on the way home that my dad brought up the incident.

"Why did he give me a funny look when I asked him to sign my Mountain Dew?" he asked. My friend just chuckled in the back as I turned beet red.

"He thought you wanted him to sign your bottom," I replied quickly.

"Oh, that would be awkward," he said, suddenly realizing this particular experience would go down in family history ... as the day my dad asked NASCAR superstar Kasey Kahne to sign his can.

~Robyn Schroder

Competitive Engineering

"Competitive engineering" is a really nice name for cheating.

I've gotten some e-mails asking if we ever did anything like that while I was with Harry Hyde and the K&K team in 1966.

I never said we didn't.

At Atlanta, there was something of a dust cloud on the backstretch during the pace lap when everyone who had chalk tablets in the front springs hit the brakes and busted the chalk tablets to drop the front end. A NASCAR official commented to Harry that he hoped we weren't involved.

Harry—the guy Robert Duval's character in the movie *Days of Thunder* was based on—didn't bother to point out that our K&K Dodge was equipped with torsion bars in the front rather than coil springs, and we hadn't figured out how to get a chalk tablet in there just yet.

By the way, Harry was the inventor of the taped-up front end.

He had his crew tape one up before qualifying one day after getting the inspiration, and NASCAR made him take the tape off.

Harry told the crew to get another radiator ready to put in after qualifying.

He then took his closed pocketknife and closed off all the vanes on the radiator in the car, bending them down flat and effectively cutting off the airflow.

Picked up almost half a second.

NASCAR later decided that taping up the front end was OK.

Still on the subject of competitive engineering, there have been many stories about Smokey Yunick's inventiveness.

Smokey was the guy who said that when the NASCAR rulebook declared "fuel additives" to be legal, he considered nitrous oxide to be a fuel additive.

One of the most frequently recalled and most classic Smokey stories concerned the time they tore down one of his engines and fuel systems completely. Left the car sitting there with no carburetor, no fuel lines, no tank, no nothing.

Smokey asked if they were through, and when they said they were, he got in, fired the car up, and drove it back to the garage.

I will relay the story about the time I was sitting on the pit wall at Daytona, timing practice (quite common in those days with no timing and scoring monitors), when Richard Petty was outrunning everybody by a pretty good margin.

I looked down at my stopwatches and noted aloud that Petty was really flying.

A noted car owner, sitting beside me, said, "Yeah, #&%*!"

I asked in a rather sarcastic matter how he could make such a statement about a fellow competitor.

"Because he's outrunning us by five miles an hour, and we're cheatin' a bunch!"

For the record, Richard won the Daytona 500 that year by a full lap, with it ending under caution two laps early because of rain. Cale Yarborough was second, right behind him but a lap down, driving Banjo Matthews' No. 27 Ford.

You very seldom remember second place finishers if the margin is that wide, but Cale and I had become friends that year because we were garaged side-by-side.

The previous September, Cale had tangled with Sam McQuagg

in a battle for the lead in the Southern 500. That crash showed up in the movie *Red Line 7000*.

Cale mentioned to me that he had led every race he was in the year before, and I said I didn't think he led a lap of that Southern 500 before he went out of the ballpark.

"Oh, yeah," he said. "Go look at that film. I never led a lap, but when I went over that wall, I was ahead of Sam by half a car length."

How did we (the K&K team) do in the 1966 Daytona 500? Blew an engine at 112 laps while running in the top 10. Gordon Johncock was our driver.

The car didn't sound right when it went through the tri-oval on the lap before, and I was hoping the problem wasn't terminal until Gordon pulled into the pit with what looked like milk running out of the exhaust pipes.

~John Potts

NASCAR Kryptonite

Every race track has its unique physical characteristics, you know. Pocono sports three distinct turns; Daytona has those dizzying high banks. Then there is stately Indianapolis, the only NASCAR Sprint Cup Series track born before World War I.

But on certain days, at certain times, this cluster of young and old speed arenas, which boast such a wide range of asphalt/concrete diversity, share the same level of joy … or misery.

Each of these unique individuals is at the mercy of the elements, such as wind, sun, dust, heat and cold, but all become positively dullards when assaulted by rain showers.

From the craggy hills of New Hampshire to the vast space of Texas, from the subtropical light of Homestead to the desert of Phoenix, each track on the NASCAR trail shares this personality trait.

Precipitation and race tracks—whether it's at a mighty super-speedway or a mouse-sized half-miler—just don't mix.

The guy in this seat has spent day after day inside race tracks where never a race car was seen or heard. When the rain starts falling, it grabs hold of all the excitement and emotion and promise of the day and takes it right down the drain.

NASCAR can write all the rules it wants, but even this sanctioning Zeus cannot contain the wrath of Mother Nature. Stock-car racing, one of professional sports' most proud beasts, goes running for cover when water descends from the heavens above.

Why does it happen? Why must NASCAR pull its head into the turtle shell when a few drops of harmless rain fall from the sky?

First, go out and take a look at the tires on the car in your driveway. See how they have grooved tread? When it rains outside a race track, we ordinary drivers can handle it because those grooves help keep our cars stable on the highway.

Now, take a close look at those Goodyear Eagle tires bolted on to any NASCAR national series car or truck. There are no grooves. They are smooth and slick, like the top of Todd Bodine's head. Those "slicks" have no traction in the rain, so if there is a shower, there's no racing.

Rain is to race tracks what Kryptonite is to Superman.

These rain events can last a few minutes or go on for days. The days of deluge are the worst. Hour after hour of rain can turn a normally active and upbeat garage area into a quiet barracks, where comrades play cards or catch up on their reading.

The brief shower scenario is OK, because it's like an unscheduled break. I have experienced some memorable bull sessions and heard tall tales of race days past during short rain delays. You end up in somebody's race hauler after running for cover and spend the next hour or so laughing so hard it's hard to grab a breath of air.

It's ironic, when you think about it, because the loudest storm imaginable can effect the one change at any NASCAR track that nothing else is capable of producing at these bastions of sound and motion.

Quiet.

~Godwin Kelly

The Dinner

A s a NASCAR Sprint Cup sponsor's public relations representative during the mid to late 1990s, I traveled to many of the races each season.

It was what I consider the heyday of NASCAR. Sponsorship money was plentiful, yet drivers and crewmen could still be themselves without corporate pressure and media scrutiny. It was a time when drivers would often go out to eat at local restaurants with their teams, friends or business associates.

This is a story about just one of those times.

A decade ago, the night race at Bristol Motor Speedway was just as popular as it is today. Its close proximity (just three hours) to Charlotte allowed drivers to bring family and friends to the festivities.

The sleepy, historically rich town of Abingdon, Virginia is just up the road from the speedway. Replete with bed and breakfasts, museums and quaint restaurants, Abingdon was, and still is, a popular destination for the NASCAR Sprint Cup dinner crowd. I'm not 100 percent sure which restaurant this little episode took place at, but it was in the historic district. It could have been Wither's or the Tavern or the Peppermill. We frequented each on the biannual stop at the world's fastest half mile.

On this night we had a fairly decent-sized party of 10 people including me, my father, and Paul, our friend who worked for Exide Batteries, the company that sponsored Geoffrey Bodine at the time.

Our over-sized party meant we were headed for the back room. The waitress seated us two tables away from Sterling Marlin, who was holding court with a group of about 15 people.

Now, Paul and Sterling worked closely together when Marlin drove the No. 94 Sunoco-sponsored machine several years earlier. The obligatory razzing went back and forth between the tables for the duration of dinner, much to the delight of the other two parties "lucky" enough to also be seated in this room.

Sterling and his party finished their meal before we did. As they left, Marlin stopped by our table for a few minutes to talk about the race, dinner and some other idle chatter. He left when our dessert showed up.

When our plates were clear and the last sip of coffee taken, Paul called for the check—and boy, did he get it. The waitress came over and politely said, "Mr. Marlin said it was your turn to pick up dinner." And she promptly handed Paul not only our check but Marlin's as well. Covering both would take well more than your typical share of Benjamins.

Paul did nothing but shake his head, mumbling, "I'll get him; I'll get him good." Half of our party was stunned; would Marlin really stick Paul with a check that big? The other half of us could clearly see the window in the door to the kitchen, which Paul's back faced. There in the window was Marlin, giggling like a schoolboy who just played the ultimate prank.

The waitress took both checks and Paul's credit card to the other room. Just before she reappeared, Marlin burst out of the kitchen—his entire party in tow - to the rousing applause of all.

Those kinds of pranks were not just an occasional occurrence in NASCAR in those days but more a weekly requirement. And Sterling was one of the kings.

By the way, the waitress never ran Paul's credit card (all part of the grand plan). Marlin took his bill back and paid it, much to the delight of Paul … and his wallet.

~Rob Fisher

On
(and Off)
Track

Moving Parts

*I*t takes lots of parts to put together a race win. Sometimes it seems like it's never going to happen. When it finally does, it's something you know you're going to remember for the rest of your life.

Especially when it happens at your home track. My dad has a business right down the street from Dover International Speedway, so I grew up with NASCAR right there in my backyard.

I came from a racing family. From as far back as I can remember, I was around race cars. I went with my dad and my uncle to watch them race. I remember when I was 4 or 5 years old and I had to stand in the seat of the race car to see over the steering wheel. I'd stand there and make race car sounds and pretend I was driving.

I played football and baseball when I was a kid, and I enjoyed them, but somehow I always knew that racing was what I wanted to do. After I started racing go-karts when I was 11, all that other stuff was just something to pass the time, something to do when I couldn't work on my go-kart, or race it.

I'm a do-it-yourself kind of person. I like to build things. I like to work with my hands and get dirty. I like to try to figure things out so I can beat the next guy, and that may be why I got into racing to begin with. I loved all the parts and pieces and trying to figure out how everything fits together and trying to learn about how it all works.

I pretty much always knew that I was going to do this. I didn't know whether I would ever get to the NASCAR Sprint Cup Series level. But I loved to go to the track on weekends, and I loved to work on my car during the week. And once I started driving, I did pretty well right from the start, and that was fun, but part of my passion was being in the shop and working on the cars during the week, and being a part of the whole process.

Some people think mechanics should build cars and drivers should just drive them, but I think it can be very helpful to know a lot about a race car if you go about it right. You can get in there and give your opinion without rubbing people the wrong way, because you know what you're talking about. I don't think there's any substitute for knowing the race car, and knowing what's in it and how it all works together.

Once I started racing in the NASCAR Grand National Division East, I finally got the chance to race at Dover, in front of the home crowd. It was the track where I started my first-ever NASCAR Nationwide Series race, too, in one of my cars that we built at my dad's shop. It's the place that kind of got my career going, in a lot of different ways.

2007 was my second year of racing full-time in the Sprint Cup Series. We were having just an OK season coming into the race at Dover. But that day, we were good. We led more than half the laps. We didn't only win the race; we dominated it. It was the first Cup win of my career.

To finally get that first win, and for it to happen there, was special. It really turned our whole season around. All my friends and family are there every time we go, and for me to be able to see them supporting me that day was really cool.

I think the biggest thing getting your first win does is change your mindset from trying to figure out how to win, and worrying all the time about what you need to do to win, to believing that you can win. You go from trying to do it, to trying to do it again. It's almost tougher in a way, because your expectations rise so much that you get disappointed when things aren't always that good.

But it gives you the confidence that you can do it. You've done it once, and there's nothing holding you back from doing it again.

I have Dover to thank for that.

~Martin Truex, Jr.

My First
Southern 500

It was 1961 and I wasn't too far removed from college. Ken Ray, Sports Editor of the *Columbia Record*, hired me as a sportswriter. Naturally, I was thrilled when he asked if I wanted to cover the Southern 500 NASCAR Sprint Cup Series race at Darlington on Labor Day.

My next-door-neighbor, Al Bailey, made the trip with me. We took my car, which was actually my first car, a blue 1955 DeSoto with the right front window missing. I replaced it with a form-fitting piece of thick cardboard because I couldn't afford glass. "Ole Blue" was an interesting car and was actually hit by a train with me in it, but that's another story. Let's just say me and Ole Blue lived to tell about it, and leave it at that.

Anyway, Al and I left on Sunday afternoon for Darlington. The race was scheduled for Monday morning at 11:00. The track's press agent, Russ Catlin, had arranged credentials and I was told we could pick them up on Sunday between noon and midnight. We took Highway 76 out of Columbia to Sumter and then took 401 to Darlington. We stopped at a country store outside Darlington and bought supplies since we were going to spend the night in the Darlington infield.

We didn't have much money, probably $10 or $15 between us, and no credit cards, but we had enough to buy gas (I think it was 28 cents a gallon), some baloney, Vienna sausages, saltine crackers, white bread, potato chips and Coca-Colas. What else could a man want?

I had never been to the track but had read everything I could about it, mostly stories in the newspapers when growing up in Charleston and then in the Columbia papers while attending the University of South Carolina. I was always busy on Labor Day with two-a-day football practices, first in high school and then in college. But I listened to the races on the radio. There was no television coverage. Best I remember, my TV set was black and white.

When we arrived at the track, we parked on the west end where a sign said, "Press Credentials." We walked into the screened-porch area of a house trailer and Catlin, the press officer, was sitting there in shorts, a loose-fitting shirt and sandals. He explained I would not be able to get a seat for my pal, Al, in the press box since he was not a working member of the media.

By the time we had driven inside and found a parking spot on the third or fourth row away from trackside, Al looked over at the press box and decided he would be better off watching the race from the infield, anyway.

The press box was a covered chicken coop structure of wooden bleachers and wire that sat just outside and above the guard rail lining the corners of the 1.366-mile track, NASCAR's original superspeedway and brain child of Darlington native Harold Brasington. The race had become South Carolina's biggest sporting event of the year.

Time trials were staged the week leading up to the race. There was no on-track activity on Sunday, but the infield and the surrounding parking lots were packed with partying people. Country bands were picking and playing. The smell of barbecue and hickory smoke filled the air. Horns blew. Flags flew. Al and I sat on the hood of Ole Blue and soaked it all in.

The noise didn't die down until well after midnight, but no one slept much anyway. Horns and loud cannons woke everyone up at daybreak. That's right; replicas of Civil War cannons were firing. Some folks just couldn't let go.

I went to the garage area when it opened at 8 a.m. and met quite a few drivers, who were mostly hanging around their cars, shooting the breeze. Several drivers were especially cordial as I explained this was the first time I had covered the race, drivers like Richard Petty, Jim Paschal, David Pearson, Ned Jarrett and Johnny Allen. They were regular guys and you never would have known they were going to run a 500-mile race a little later in the morning.

I attended the drivers' meeting, which was held beneath the pit road pagoda, Darlington's version of a Japanese tower, which served as a control tower for the race. This gave me an opportunity to see some of the sport's superstars up close, drivers like Fireball Roberts, Buck Baker, Junior Johnson and Joe Weatherly, men I would come to know in the ensuing years.

I went across the track about an hour before the race started and stopped to say hello to Catlin. He handed me a box lunch of fried chicken, a ham sandwich, an apple and a brownie, as well as a seat cushion and a pair of goggles. I didn't want to seem stupid since it was my first race so I didn't ask what the goggles were for; I waited until I got in the chicken coop. Bob Hoffman, editor of a racing newspaper, told me to wear the goggles. They would keep the dirt and stuff out of my eyes. The "stuff" turned out to be little specks of rubber off the race tires. When I took the goggles off after the race, I had a "tire dust" tan.

One of the biggest thrills I've ever had was the moment those 43 cars roared underneath the chicken coop to start the race. You could actually see the drivers wrestling the steering wheels (no power steering back then) as the big old stock cars sped into Darlington's slick, 24-degree banked first turn.

Nelson Stacy won the race in a bright yellow Ford with a big red No. 29, beating pre-race favorite and pole winner Roberts. Pearson was third and went on to become Darlington's all-time race winner with 10 victories.

Stacy was a rookie in NASCAR at the age of 40. He had won the ARCA Series championship three years in a row, 1958-1960. He was a strong, military-type tough guy, with a thick neck, big shoulders, and a crew cut.

Actually, it shouldn't have come as any surprise that Stacy would win the Southern 500 if you knew his military background. Darlington's tricky ribbon of asphalt was nothing compared to what he did in World War II. He drove a tank under the command of old "Blood and Guts" himself, General George S. Patton.

I think that's what I remember most about my first Southern 500.

Well, that and the goggle tan. Plus the fact that Ole Blue made it back to Columbia.

~Jim Hunter

My Memories
of Mud

*T*he year 2001 was eventful for NASCAR fans across the country. The sport lost Dale Earnhardt, but gained two tracks in the Midwest—Kansas Speedway and Chicagoland Speedway. But this story actually begins a few years earlier.

In 1997, International Speedway Corporation (ISC) was searching for a Midwest site for a race track and I was working with the Kansas City Area Development Council to help recruit ISC to Kansas City. As Lesa France Kennedy and Grant Lynch (vice president of ISC Strategic Projects) were searching for sites, Grant, who's an outdoorsman, and I started talking about pheasant hunting, one thing led to another and I started working at Kansas Speedway in 1998.

I let Grant and Lesa know that I didn't know the ins and outs of NASCAR and if they were looking for a NASCAR guy, I wasn't him. Over the past several years, I've become a fan of the sport as a whole because of how it brings people together and the impact it has on people's lives.

When this project started, there were a lot of skeptics saying we couldn't make this work and that NASCAR wouldn't be successful here. With Kansas Speedway celebrating its 10th birthday in 2010, I'd have to say we proved those skeptics wrong.

There's something exciting about seeing a project through from its beginning—the recruitment, land acquisition, construction, operations—to where it is today, a vibrant part of the Kansas City community, and it has had a huge part in helping the development of Kansas City, Kansas.

I was fortunate enough to be a part of the construction phase of the track and to actually see the rolling fields in western Wyandotte County transformed into a venue that becomes the fourth largest city in Kansas during a NASCAR Sprint Cup Series race.

It was difficult for people in the area to imagine the size of the race track when I first gave tours of the facility during the initial building phase. I had to compare the size of our facility to two other Kansas City sports arenas—Arrowhead Stadium (Kansas City Chiefs) and Kauffman Stadium (Kansas City Royals). You could see the amazement on their faces when I told them both stadiums would fit inside our infield.

There's also a misconception that Kansas is flat—trust me, it's not. We had to move 11 million cubic yards of dirt to start building.

Race cars were not the first equipment to race at Kansas Speedway. During the excavating process, some of the operating crews decided to race some of the scrapers around the tri-oval.

One of my favorite memories happened the day the late Bill France, Jr. visited in the early stages of building with one of his friends (John Cooper) and Grant. It had rained heavily the night before they arrived and I was concerned about driving them around the facility and getting stuck in the mud—we didn't have any jet dryers to help out with the drying process!

As we headed toward the infield, Bill told me to stop the "blank'n" truck, and took over driving duties from me. I expressed my concern to Bill that because of the mud he might get stuck. He told me not to worry, and proceeded to push the accelerator to the floor.

For the next 10 minutes, we basically four-wheeled throughout the infield and along the backstretch in my Tahoe. Mud was flying everywhere and Bill was like a little kid, enjoying every minute of it. When he finally handed me back the keys, he said, "That's how you drive in the mud."

It's memories like this that I'll never forget.

I've made a lot of memories as the president of Kansas Speedway and every time we host a race, I see all the families and friends that are here, and it's a great feeling to know that everything we've put into making Kansas Speedway the best guest experience in motorsports is helping these fans create their own lasting memories.

~Jeff Boerger

Not Too Tough
to Tame

The view from my desk gave me a front row seat to the comings and goings of the townsfolk, but it was the ticking of the motor that caught my attention.

I saw the old rustic-looking dump truck easing to the curb, and watched as an elderly gentleman with unkempt hair, dressed in a pair of ragged jeans and a buttoned-up plaid shirt, exited the vehicle and headed for the front steps. I had no clue who this man was but I did know one thing—he was about to enter the door of my workplace, and I was there all alone.

I became a little anxious as the man stepped inside. "Hello ma'am," he said in a gentle voice, "I am here to see Mr. Dargan. I do believe I have an appointment at 10 o'clock."

My boss—Mr. George Dargan—had phoned earlier to inform me he planned to come in the office later that morning, but had failed to mention the expected visitor. I called my boss to announce his client's arrival. "Put him on the phone and let me speak with him," Mr. Dargan said.

I handed the phone over to the gentleman.

Of course, I could not help but hear the conversation on my end because the man was using my phone and was standing right next to my desk. "Yes sir, I have been doing some work at the race track this morning," he said. "Oh yeah, things are going pretty good. OK, I will see you later, then." He handed the receiver to me and hastily made his way out the door.

I have never been a big fan of auto racing, and moving to a town known for its NASCAR mania really didn't change my opinion. If anything, it diminished whatever interest might have ever been there.

No matter where you lived in the small town of Darlington, South Carolina, you knew when race week began and when it ended. The roaring motors of those cars echoed for miles around. There was not a quiet moment for an entire week.

Hotel parking lots resembled ballparks on game day as guests packed rooms to capacity. Animated fans loitered in restaurants way past the usual business hours. A short trip to the grocery store seemed more like waiting in line at an amusement park. And even getting to church on Sunday was a race against the clock to make sure I didn't get caught in the incoming traffic.

Even back then, before the track was purchased by International Speedway Corporation, the residents of Darlington were well aware that the Southern 500 placed them on the map. The races may only take place on Friday and Saturday, but the locals and fans celebrate the town's livelihood with pizzazz. The enormous haulers that transport the race cars parade down Main Street and around the Public Square. Mini black and white checkered flags adorn the normally mundane-looking lampposts. Billboards lure you with big smiles from men in racing gear standing beside flashy cars. Long lines curve around like snakes in front of local businesses as anxious fans await their opportunity for that much-coveted autograph from their favorite driver.

Not being a big fan of racing, I didn't care much about such details. However, because my husband and children wanted to go, we visited the race track and its adjacent museum. So I had some small degree of knowledge of the sport and the track. However, I failed to let that information show itself at a most convenient time.

Shortly after lunch, the weary-looking man arrived back at the office, came in and took a seat. My boss had not yet arrived, so to buy some time I decided to strike up a conversation. In an effort to be more personal, I glanced at the file to verify the man's name.

"So you work at the race track, Mr. Brasington?" I inquired, pleased with my efficient attention to details.

"Well, ma'am," the disguised town icon replied, "I kind of own the race track."

At that moment I realized my lack of race knowledge had just revealed itself. Oh my, I did recall a set of grandstands at the track with the name Brasington on them. And yes, I had been informed they were named after the founder and owner of the race track. "How could I have been so dumb?" I thought.

I am sure Mr. Brasington thought the same thing, but he was too kind to express it. My body became very still. I felt as though I had just been run over by one of those swift contraptions of metal and rubber I heard whizzing around the track.

When I managed to regain my composure, I inquired about the race track and the race. It was the least I could do after making an idiot of myself. To my surprise, I actually found myself interested in what the man had to say. Maybe it had something to do with hearing the words from a pioneer of the sport and the builder of the town's livelihood, or perhaps it had something to do with smoothing over my previous faux pas. Either way, that day gave me a whole new perspective on the race.

I am no more of a race fan as a result of my experience. But I can say I am truly a fan of the race. The significance of a race like the Southern 500 to a small town like Darlington and its devoted race fans is nothing less than monumental.

We have since moved from that lovely town, but not without a souvenir—a big black and white checkered flag with "Darlington" stamped across it. It is a token that serves to remind me of the man who changed my opinion of the race—Mr. Harold Brasington, Sr., the man who built the track "Too Tough To Tame."

Thank goodness changing my perspective wasn't quite so tough.

~Rhonda Hensley

My Own
Victory Lane

I guess I'm just not cut out for a 9-to-5 job.

I've never really had one, except for a few months when I worked drawing blood in a laboratory. My first job was working on a serving line in a cafeteria when I was 12. As a teenager, I waited tables in a pancake house with mostly older, seasoned waitresses.

I started college unsure of what I wanted to pursue as a career. I began as a pre-med student, but quickly determined that my heart wasn't in it. A failing grade in freshman calculus hastened my decision.

What I really wanted to be was a paramedic. I'd wanted to ever since I was a pre-teen. But I also intended to go to college, and in those days it didn't take a college degree to become a paramedic.

So I switched my major from pre-med to education and eventually graduated with a teaching degree. In my junior year of college, however, I took an Emergency Medical Technician course as an elective, and that experience confirmed what I already knew: emergency care was what I wanted to do. By the time I graduated college, I was working as an EMT for a local ambulance company and training to be a paramedic.

I loved being a paramedic as much as I knew I would. It seemed like the perfect job, despite the long hours, hard physical labor, and very low pay. It was exciting and fast-paced and never the same thing twice.

I enjoyed the challenge and the responsibility, and the opportunity to make a difference in people's lives. I even drove the ambulance "code three" as we called it—full lights and sirens—sometimes (I can confess now) with one hand on the steering wheel and the other holding a cold can of soda.

I met my soon-to-be husband through the emergency field. He was a paramedic, too, but for the other ambulance company in town—our "competition." We ended up married for 23 years, together for 27.

When we got divorced a few years ago (not my choice), I found myself at a major crossroads—not just in my career, but also in my life. After five years as a paramedic, I had gone to nursing school and become an RN specializing in emergency nursing. The hours and pay were better than being a medic—especially with a young son at home - and it was still mostly challenging and rewarding. But I never felt passionate about being a nurse. It was a job and a necessity dictated by factors in my life at the time.

When my marriage ended, I was faced with the prospect of going back to nursing full-time. It was not an idea I relished. In fact, it made me queasy. Mentally and emotionally, I associated nursing with a particular phase of my life—my marriage—which had now come to a painful and unexpected end.

Financially, the sensible thing to do would have been to take the prudent path back to healthcare. But it wasn't where my heart was. I was convinced that returning to nursing would have been a huge psychological defeat. I panicked at the mere thought of it.

Meanwhile, in the back of my mind, I had been nursing a dream of a different sort: pursuing a career in NASCAR. Not as a driver, of course, but as a NASCAR journalist.

A few years before the divorce, I had begun submitting articles to a couple of Web sites devoted to stock car racing. I was already a diehard fan of the sport and felt I had a unique point of view that wasn't being expressed elsewhere on the Internet. There was no pay at first, but as soon as I started getting enthusiastic feedback from readers encouraging me to write more, I was hooked.

Writing in general was not totally new to me. I'd always been good at it in school and was frequently asked to help write and proofread term papers for my friends. In college, my answer to an essay question on an English test was included in a textbook that my professor wrote on how to succeed on college exams. After having children, I wrote some parenting articles that were accepted for publication.

It helped me break into the NASCAR field to be able to say with honesty that I was already a published writer. Still, I was quite uncertain whether I could turn my NASCAR passion into a well-paying job. But, at that point in my life, the gig was giving me something of even greater value: self-esteem.

Being rejected by someone you once loved is not an easy thing to shrug off. And as much as I adored being a mother to my two boys, I had to reluctantly admit that they'd grown past the stage where I could define my purpose in life as the room mom who made the best cupcakes for the class parties.

Gradually, my reputation in NASCAR grew, and I became comfortable seeing myself as a NASCAR writer in earnest. As even more doors opened, I gained confidence in the fact that I could have value in the workforce as something other than a nurse. Who'd have thought that the RN-turned-stay-at-home mom would be go-kart racing with Carl Edwards one day and taking hot laps with Kyle Busch around a race track the next? That I'd be rubbing shoulders (literally) in trackside interviews with Jeff Gordon, Tony Stewart, and Dale Earnhardt, Jr., or conducting a phone interview with a NASCAR legend like Darrell Waltrip?

I've done all of that and much more. I've been interviewed on radio and TV, attended NASCAR races as a credentialed media member, been published in numerous magazines and newspapers, and even parlayed my writing experience into a dream job doing motorsports marketing and public relations.

Looking back, the trait that helped me most to succeed as a

NASCAR writer was perseverance. British author Douglas Adams said, "Writing is easy. You only need to stare at a blank piece of paper until your forehead bleeds." And sometimes it felt that way. But when you're committed to a dream, you can't let anything stand in your way.

NASCAR was truly a blessing in my life at a time when I needed one desperately. I may have started from the rear of the field, but I think I finally found my Victory Lane.

~Becca Gladden

We'll Always Have Brooklyn

*T*his was a day my wife Kara and I had been looking forward to for months. We were about to see our first live NASCAR race, at Michigan International Speedway.

For years, we had talked about going to a race as a couple. As a surprise for my 35th birthday, Kara bought tickets for the two of us to go to a NASCAR Sprint Cup Series race in Brooklyn, Michigan.

During the 250-mile trip from our house in Chicago to the speedway, Kara and I were giddy with anticipation. The two of us had enjoyed many Sunday afternoons together watching races on TV. Now, we were on our way to our first NASCAR event.

Racing broadcasts look so awesome; we could hardly imagine what it would be like when we saw the cars traveling live at breathtaking speeds. Would the sounds of engines require us to wear earplugs? What does a pit stop look like in person? What is it like to attend a race with thousands of fellow NASCAR enthusiasts? We were on our way to having all our questions answered.

The entire trip we talked about whether Carl Edwards, Dale Earnhardt, Jr., Jeff Gordon, Kyle Busch, or Jimmie Johnson would emerge victorious at the race we were going to see.

As we got closer, there was a wrinkle in our plans—a steady downpour. Before we left, we had checked the weather forecast, which called for rain all weekend. However, Kara and I figured the weatherman was wrong. After all, there was no way there would be precipitation on our first trip to a NASCAR event. It couldn't possibly rain because we had been looking forward to this for so long.

Were we ever wrong. But as we pulled into the parking lot, there already was a sea of cars. Despite monsoon conditions, Kara and I decided to venture to our seats.

We hadn't thought to bring an umbrella with us so we had to buy ponchos to keep protected from the pellets falling from the sky. We scurried to our seats to see what our view would be like. From our vantage point, we were both amazed. The speedway's size was simply incredible. TV doesn't do justice to depicting the enormous capacity of a speedway that holds tens of thousands of fans.

My anger grew as the forecast became gloomier by the minute. This wasn't fair—we were supposed to see a race. I decided to look at our tickets to see, if the event did get rained out, how we could get our money back. I grew even more incensed as I learned there were no refunds for inclement weather. Now we'd lose the money we paid on top of everything else? My blood was beginning to boil.

I thought my wife would be feeling the same way. Wrong again. Instead of sulking, Kara suggested we make the most of our experience, as there was a lot to take in at this NASCAR environment.

It was like we had been transported to another world. Hand in hand, Kara and I, pardon the pun, soaked in the atmosphere. We were surprised to see how many haulers there were selling NASCAR merchandise. We enjoyed people watching as we saw countless men, women, and children walking in the rain wearing the apparel of their favorite driver. Entire families were dressed in the gear of their heroes. Even babies were clad in racing gear. I lost track of how many people I saw wearing Dale Jr. hats, shirts, T-shirts, or jackets.

I had never seen a scene like this before in my life. TV definitely doesn't capture sights like this on broadcasts.

To no one's surprise, the race was postponed later that afternoon. The forecast called for more rain the following day, but NASCAR would try to get the race in anyway.

We returned to MIS the next morning. There was a glimmer of

hope as the forecast called for a small window when the rain would subside. Kara and I returned to our seats and were enthralled watching the massive vehicles responsible for drying the pavement circle around the track. We were so happy that we took pictures of ourselves in our seats and turned our attention to the racing news now being shown on the Jumbotron.

My heart started beating faster as the pace car emerged and started zooming around the track to test the conditions of the pavement. We were amazed at how loud the pace car was. What would it be like when the real cars started circling the track? We gave each other high-fives and the thoughts of NASCAR drivers quickly filled our heads. We were only minutes away from seeing our first race — or so we thought.

After a few laps, the pace car pulled off the track because it started sprinkling. Not a big deal, I thought. However, those sprinkles soon turned into another downpour. Not again! In just a matter of minutes, an announcement was made that there would be no racing this day, either.

Rain two days in a row? Weather may postpone a race for one day. But two? What are the odds?

For whatever reason, we weren't destined to see any racing that weekend. Under the grandstand, Kara and I embraced and kissed each other gently on the cheek. Arm and arm, we started slowly walking back to our car.

I couldn't hide my disappointment any longer. We couldn't stick around for another day as we both had jobs to get back to.

"We drove four hours for this?" I complained sounding like a 3-year-old having a tantrum. "This isn't fair! I wanted to see some racing!"

"That's not true," Kara said optimistically. "We saw the drying trucks and the pace car go around the track. That counts for something."

With that, we both broke out laughing. Her comments really helped put things in perspective and I realized how silly I was acting.

That's why I love my wife so much; she helps keep me grounded and helps me to see things from a different perspective.

While the weekend was a washout and there was no NASCAR racing to be seen, Kara and I experienced it together. That's what marriage is all about—sharing your life with someone special through the ups and downs of life. With marriage, you can find enjoyment anywhere and anytime, even at a soggy race track.

I'll never forget that weekend with Kara. While the weekend didn't turn out as we planned, we left feeling even more connected.

There's a famous line from the romantic movie *Casablanca*, "We'll always have Paris." My wife and I will always have Brooklyn.

Brooklyn, Michigan, that is.

~R. Stephen Repsys

A "Normal" Night with the Earnhardts

"They're so normal."

That's how Greenville-Pickens Speedway owner Kevin Whitaker described his famous guests the night 10 members of the Earnhardt family caravanned to South Carolina for the dedication of the Ralph Earnhardt Memorial Grandstand.

Headlined by Ralph's widow, Martha, they gathered at the historic half-mile to honor a man who created his own legacy as "master of the power slide" long before his son Dale became one of the most iconic sports figures of all time.

Aside from undeniable driving skill, Dale and his dad—and NASCAR drivers in general—are "normal" people. Even the ones who achieve fame and fortune barely seem to notice, as they remain focused on the finish line. The secrets to their success are the ingredients of the American Dream, and their familiar approach makes the dream a little more attainable for the rest of us.

I grew up in Capps' Automotive Machine Shop, where my dad built his own hot rods. By the time I was a teenager, he had parlayed his talents into a dynamic engine-building business. Normal, for us, was working hard, paying your dues and never acting like you were any better than anyone else.

I remembered those values as I launched a writing career, but I never imagined the bulk of it would be related to something that was just a part of life for us. I assumed I would have to work my way up ladders and through ranks to get to the powerbrokers who would help me sell stories.

Nine years and a few disappointments later, I can tell you that the normal people of NASCAR have been my best sellers. I've never had a problem showing readers how warm, genuine and straightforward this everyday brand of the elite really is.

In July 2009, I was invited to GPS for the grandstand dedication. Thanks to Whitaker, I would not only be snapping photos with the other reporters, but sitting in a suite with the entire Earnhardt entourage during the race.

I had a familiar job to do, but that time, it was different. The Earnhardts were true heroes. Surely the family would be guarded when I tried to talk with them. I expected to give my readers nothing more personal than what fans in Japan can learn about the Earnhardts on the Internet.

That night, the Earnhardt clan proudly posed for pictures, but they had come for more than just a ceremony. Although they couldn't call any of the track's regulars by name, they settled on the porch of the Turn 1 suite and made an evening of it.

If you didn't know the Earnhardts were a racing family, you would have figured it out by the time three divisions of competitors battled their way to the checkered flag. Tiny gold charms bearing her son's famous number adorned Martha's necklace, bracelet and ring. Predictably, she tended to favor any car with a No. 3 on its side, while Dale Earnhardt's eldest son, Kerry, and his young cousins cheered for the drivers they had pegged for winners during practice.

Winning 20 to 30 features a year was the norm for Ralph, who eventually was able to leave his job at Cannon Mills to pursue racing full time. The 1956 Sportsman (now NASCAR Nationwide) Series champion, he took the GPS trophy in 1966 and 1967.

"Ralph built most everything right there in his shop in our backyard," Martha said.

Ralph died of a heart attack in that Kannapolis shop in 1973. He was 45 years old. They were married when Martha was 17, and at 42, she had to figure out how to make a living.

She rolled her eyes and grinned when she noted that Dale hadn't started making money from racing yet. Martha worked as a waitress before taking a job at a children's clothing shop, where she stayed well beyond her son's rise to the top.

"About seven months before (Ralph) died, the doctor told us he had already had one heart attack. He didn't know when it happened, but he told him he would have to stop racing. He cut back, but of course, he didn't quit," she said.

Martha couldn't talk about the good times at GPS or the accomplishments of any of her family members without smiling. The sacrifices that come with building a racing career are assuredly worth it for those who choose that path.

"There's been a lot of heartache, too," she said, perhaps alluding to her son's fatal accident during the 2001 Daytona 500.

The light returned to her face when she spotted a little girl of about 4 years old, clad in a full Dale Earnhardt, GM Goodwrench driver's suit. Martha has seen fans wearing her family name countless times, but she hopped off her stool, grabbed her cane and called out to the child who struggled to secure a tiny black helmet with one hand while giving us a wave with the other.

Martha was recovering from surgery on a broken femur, but she refused to cut the evening short. Between races, granddaughter Kristi, a recent nursing school graduate, made sure Martha was taking care of herself.

"You need to get up and walk around unless you want a blood clot," she said.

The response was a furrowed brow, the "not in front of company" face that is the hallmark of grandmothers across the world.

The only time the Earnhardts' eyes weren't glued to the track was when they happily mixed with fans. The main event actually started late because Kerry, Austin and Kristi had left the suite for the chance to ride around the track in the back of a pickup truck and battle over who got to shoot T-shirts into the crowd.

In addition to the memorial, the Earnhardts celebrated Martha's birthday that evening. Her daughter, Cathy Earnhardt Watkins, insisted I share in the festivities.

"What an odd day," I thought. "Dale Earnhardt's sister is serving me cake. They aren't acting like they're special. They're so ..."

Returning to the conversation, I asked Martha what it was like to have so many people fascinated by her family. Aside from the occasional book signing for the cookbook she penned with Carolyn Gordon, she said her daily routine wouldn't interest people.

Speaking for the people, I can say the Earnhardts most definitely interest us. But by the time the last flag waved, spending three hours with the most famous family in racing was everything I should have expected. The experience was what makes good writing, good racing and good families.

It was ... normal.

~Amanda L. Capps

Wild Blue Yonder

I t's hard to imagine the famous Air Force phrase "Off we go into the wild blue yonder … flying high … into the sky …" when talking about NASCAR racing.

Over the years, however, a few drivers have made some pretty spectacular exits from the high-speed ovals, particularly back in the days before the tracks had SAFER barriers and tall, cable-anchored catch fences.

Who could forget Cale Yarborough's famous swan dive between Turns 1 and 2 (now Turns 3 and 4) at Darlington Raceway after colliding with the late Sam McQuagg during the 1965 Labor Day Southern 500? Veteran motorsports journalist Joe Whitlock, amongst those in the wooden-framed, bleacher-like press box with chicken wire stretched across the front facing the track, almost beat Yarborough to the ground as Whitlock tore down the steps of the press box and was the first to arrive on the accident scene.

"Damndest thing I ever saw," Joe recalled. "The dust and dirt had barely settled and Cale was climbing out the window, grinning and shaking his head. He immediately walked back up the bank outside the turn and waved to the crowd to let them know he was OK. It was the most spectacular exit I ever saw in all my years of racing."

There were others in the early days of stock car racing. There were no SAFER barriers (energy-absorbing materials placed between track surface and concrete wall) but just standard highway guard rail. The biggest problem occurred when cars would hit in the space between the wooden posts supporting the guard rail. The impact would just rip the guard rail and posts right out of the ground, sending the cars off into never, never land.

In fact, the 1958 Southern 500 at Darlington was a doozy when it came to high-flying exits. Three drivers sailed out of the fabled old track that day.

Eddie Pagan (Hutcherson-Pagan) was the first, and carried a huge section of guard rail with him, not to mention the wooden posts. He suffered the lone injury of the day, a broken nose, a seemingly small price to pay when viewing photos of his accident.

Eddie Gray followed Pagan many laps later, actually (consider the odds on this) going through the hole left by Pagan's crash.

The great Jack Smith crashed through the Turn 1 guard rail in a different spot later in the race and young reporter Tom Higgins (21 at the time) of *The Charlotte Observer* could hardly believe his eyes. Smith continued to qualify and start races at Darlington but would quickly turn his machine over to a relief driver. He had lost his enthusiasm for the track "Too Tough To Tame."

Another out-of-control car had also gotten up on top of the guard rail in front of the press box, which Higgins said made him think about whether it was a good idea to be sitting there that first day. Or any day.

Higgins and several other writers were made even more uncomfortable several years later when Earl Balmer spun, jumped on top of the guard rail in front of the press box and splattered gas and debris everywhere. Several years later, the track built a new press box but the old chicken coop was indelibly nicknamed "Balmer's Box," for the time in between.

Perhaps one of the most spectacular exits was logged by Johnny Allen, one of the nicest guys in the sport. Allen's car hit the guard rail between Turns 3 and 4 at Darlington in the 1960 Rebel 300, a convertible race. His topless car sailed over the barrier and smashed into one end of the scoring stand, leaving that end dangling in the air like a broken crane hoist.

Fortunately, no one was injured in the accident. In fact, it's probably the only time in NASCAR history the scorers were the ones who had to be rescued by firemen.

~Jim Hunter

All in the
Family

To Dance
with My Brother

I was awakened by a thunderclap that Saturday morning at
the McLaurin Arms in Clio, S.C. As much as the farmers
needed a good rain, it saddened me to hear it.

On my way over on Friday afternoon, I had called my brother
before I got off I-95 to see if he needed anything, and he told me to
stop and pick up a can of red wigglers.

It sounds goofy to say it, but I was overjoyed. Outside of his
family and the late Dale Earnhardt, there was nothing Cheese—a
nickname; a story for another day—loved more than fishing.

Cheese had a tough time with the cancer that slowly drained
the life from him. The round of chemotherapy treatments before my
visit had him so weak that it must have taken great effort for him
just to get out of bed to peck at what at one time were his favorite
foods. But the last course of chemicals—and he said it was the last
one—seemed to have run their course. He was in good spirits and
had more appetite than I'd seen in months.

In a small way, it reminded me of a happier visit a few years
earlier. I was on my way from Columbia to Richmond for a race and
my car threw a timing belt—luckily enough—about a half a mile
from the Dillon exit, just a few miles from my hometown. Cheese was
the first one I called.

I wound up spending the weekend at the Arms and we watched

the race together that Saturday night. I don't remember the particulars, but I do recall that Jeff Gordon—a name spoken with great enmity at Cheese's house—got "taken out" late in the race.

Now you have to understand that the McLaurins are a mixed breed when it comes to racing. My brother Lauch was a Ford man to the core, and my brother Zeke didn't care what it was as long as it would crank.

But Cheese and all his immediate family believed the sun rose and set on Senior—he always swore that his grandson Brian's first word was "Dale"—and next to Earnhardt winning, he loved nothing better than to see Gordon lose. And the more spectacularly, the better.

That night when the "Wonder Boy" crashed, Cheese jumped up from the La-Z-Boy and, recollecting some offense real or imagined to his hero Earnhardt, began to dance around the room, singing, "Payback is hell! Payback is hell!"

I wrote about that night, and the punch line to the story was that my biggest regret was that I didn't get up and dance with him, because you don't get too many chances to dance with your brother. Little did I know.

The rain spoiled our fishing trip, but we still made a good day of it. The doctors wouldn't let him drive with the medication he was on, so I was his chauffeur.

We went to our cousin's house down on the Little Pee Dee River and he wasn't home, but we sat for a few minutes chatting with a fellow on the opposite bank who said they weren't biting. We rode by Moccasin Bluff, an old fishing hole that seemed hardly calf-deep in spots, just to see the river.

We stopped by Aunt Jewell's house and she called her boy Brownie over—hardly a boy, he's 50-something—and before we left Cheese had gotten directions to Brownie's latest hot fishing hole and an open invitation.

We stopped by his favorite bar, a place called the Racing Stables, on the way home. A horse had never been near it, but the walls were plastered with every sort of NASCAR memorabilia, and every TV in the place was locked in on the NASCAR race when one was going on.

I had a beer. Cheese sipped on a Mountain Dew, talked about how the young Earnhardt paled in comparison to his daddy, and soaked up the warmth of some of his old friends.

He had a good supper and went to bed not 30 feet from where I sat down to write that Saturday night. He was snoring softly as I recounted our day together. About an hour later while I was channel-surfing, I came across the fireball crash that ended drag racer Scott Kalitta's life in Englishtown, N.J.

Kalitta, the son of NHRA legend Connie Kalitta, probably never knew what hit him after his engine exploded and his car drove into the barrier at the run-off end of the track at 300 mph.

Somewhere during the inevitable and painful driver interviews that followed, one driver whose name I didn't catch rattled off the old axiom that he at least died doing what he loved.

The guy in the studio did a phone interview with a reporter who was at the track, and broached the same subject.

The reporter recounted a story he'd read about legendary driver Juan Manuel Fangio, the five-time Formula 1 champion.

He said Fangio was once asked about that, and Fangio asked the interviewer, "If you could choose, how would you like to die?"

I thought of Cheese. The drugs for his pain had a good effect, but they were at best a tradeoff, a devil's bargain between not getting any sleep and possibly never waking up again.

The interviewer pondered the question a minute, and then said he guessed if he had a choice, he'd rather die in his sleep.

"Then," Fangio said, "I don't know how you find the courage to turn off the light every night."

How, indeed?

~Jim McLaurin

Full Circle

Where I'm originally from, NASCAR wasn't that big of a deal. I grew up in Maryland, which is not far from NASCAR country (with Dover, Pocono, and Richmond easy half-day drives away), but not as entrenched in the culture, fever, and passion of NASCAR as the South.

But where you're *born* is not necessarily the same as where you're *from*.

I was *born* in Charlotte, N.C.

In fact, not long before I was born, my mom and dad lived within earshot of the stock cars on the super-fast speedway in Charlotte. My dad loved to watch the races on Sunday after church. We would leave church, and he'd joke with Mom and me that it was time to "put on the sunscreen and get out the binoculars," to sit on the couch and watch the race.

Nowadays, Dad just likes to "see the beginning of the race."

Dad loved Richard Petty, and loved to root against the likes of Dale Earnhardt, Darrell Waltrip, and Rusty Wallace.

My earliest NASCAR memory was watching Bobby and Davey Allison finish 1-2 in the 1988 Daytona 500. I also remember the next year, when Waltrip won the "Great American Race," and all Dad could do was shake his head.

We didn't go to our first race until the 2000 Coca-Cola 600. What a thrill! I couldn't believe the awesome power of those stock cars.

My brother and I wandered down to the exit of Turn 4. That was when you could still get right up next to the fence, and feel the wind and sound and power of forty-three cars going close to 180 miles per hour, just feet from your face. I will never forget that feeling, nor the first time I felt it.

My brother and I both managed to get a little closer than most to racing. Blake was a mechanical engineering major at Virginia Tech, and while at school, he interned with Morgan-McClure Motorsports out of Abingdon, Virginia. He worked closely with team engineers in the wind tunnels and engine dynamometers, and even got to accompany the team to preseason testing in Daytona Beach. He also attended races at Bristol, Charlotte, Darlington, Daytona, and Talladega.

I got my first job with a TV station in Florence, South Carolina, and the first race I covered was the final fall race at Rockingham, North Carolina in November 2003. As the field came roaring off the fourth turn, and I stood watching on top of the media center in the infield, I couldn't believe that a) I hadn't paid to be there, and b) I was *getting* paid to be there.

Since then, I've been able to cover three Daytona 500s, seven Darlington races, and I've attended four more races at Charlotte.

Blake and I spent time together while we both worked at the 2007 Daytona 500. I remember as we sat on the back of my television truck after the race, and watched the crowds pass, both of us lost in our thoughts. Blake, I am sure, marveled at the race teams as they scurried about with millions of dollars in equipment, all precision and engineering, math and science, and all for competition at the highest level.

At Daytona, or in the infield of any NASCAR track, it's hard to miss the rich and famous as they whiz by on golf carts driven, invariably, by some young woman with a walkie-talkie. I watched with wonder as golf cart after golf cart came by carrying network television personalities and NASCAR drivers and legends. I couldn't believe that while technically we were all there to do the same job, here I was working in the same place alongside those who really are at the top of their game — or at least look great trying to play it.

But maybe our NASCAR experience really came full circle when Blake got a pit pass for my dad and took him to see just his second race ever, the 2006 Mother's Day weekend event at Darlington. Blake was still working for the Morgan-McClure team then. He and Dad were able to watch the race (as best they could) from the infield, and even snuck some food from the team hauler.

But it was toward the end of the race that Dad came face to face with one of the true heroes of his life — The King himself, Richard Petty.

Dad mustered up his courage, approached the always very approachable Petty, and said humbly, "Mr. Petty, it's nice to meet you, and I've got to tell you, you're the only person here whose autograph I really want."

Anyone who knows a thing or two about Petty knows that Dad got that autograph. It's on a hat that sits proudly in his office to this day.

Even if I never make it to another race, it makes me happy to know that our family has come so close to experiencing NASCAR in ways that we never thought possible.

For as long as I work in television, I'll be sure to remember that, while we're supposed to be working, we have the power, in this one special case, to stop and listen to the awesome roar of the sport we love so much.

~Rusty Ray

A Big Heart for Small People

In December 1989, a youngster, not dressed appropriately for the winter cold, wondered into the National Guard Armory in Mooresville, N.C. He looked around at the race cars on display in preparation for the first-ever Stocks for Tots. Don Miller, a new resident of the area and the event's organizer, began talking with the boy.

Miller soon discovered the boy's attire didn't misrepresent his living conditions. The boy was poor, but at this time his primary concern was his younger sister. She wanted a doll for Christmas and he thought the event that night at the Armory might provide him with the special gift. Miller took him to the boxes where some new toys were carefully stored and allowed him to select a doll for his sister. The boy left the Armory with his treasure, happy he would be able to provide his sister with the special gift she wanted on Christmas morning.

That was the beginning of Stocks for Tots and my introduction to Don Miller, a man who saw abused children who needed help and believed the racing community should provide it. At that time, there was no NASCAR Foundation and none of the drivers had their own foundations. Those wouldn't occur for another decade. So Miller decided the NASCAR Sprint Cup Series drivers could help SCAN—Stop Child Abuse Now—by signing autographs for a few hours on one night each December. To gain admittance to the event, a fan needed only to bring a new toy or a cash donation.

Within three years, the event had outgrown the Armory and was moved to Lakeside Business Park in Mooresville where many teams' shops were located. Eventually, crew chiefs, NASCAR Nationwide and NASCAR Camping World Truck Series drivers, retired drivers, NHRA competitors and media personalities were added to the signing roster. Recently, the event was moved to The Charles Mack Citizens Center in Mooresville where it continues to grow. Since its creation, the event has raised more than $850,000 and distributed nearly 50,000 toys at Christmas.

Miller, however, didn't stop with this function. The then president of Penske Racing South also worked tirelessly to create the North Carolina Auto Racing Hall of Fame in Mooresville. A non-profit museum, only its operating expenses are taken from the admission price with the rest going to SCAN, an organization whose mission is to continue to help and provide education, counseling and intervention programs for the prevention of child abuse and neglect. It was Miller's civic-minded work that earned him the inaugural NASCAR Home Depot Humanitarian Award in 2007.

Helping abused children became Miller's primary objective after he and his family moved to Mooresville, but his willingness to help others didn't stop there. He became the mentor for many people, including myself, always providing sound advice and a private sanctuary if you just needed to talk with someone trustworthy.

Miller's philanthropy and true friendship are examples for all to follow. However, it is this humble man's attitude toward life that is truly inspirational. A one-time drag racer, Miller suffered life-altering injuries on May 5, 1974 at Talladega, Alabama; injuries that could have left him a bitter man and withdrawn from society.

Miller was helping gas the Roger Penske-owned Matador driven by Gary Bettenhausen when rookie Grant Adcox hit a patch of oil and water on pit road and slammed into the back of Bettenhausen's car. Miller was pinned between the cars and injured. Buddy Parrott, a crewman who later became a winning crew chief, saw the severity of Miller's injury, jumped the pit wall and carried him to safety.

Miller lost his right leg, just below the knee, and suffered severe back and pelvic injuries that would often cause him excruciating pain and would require additional operations later in life. Doctors were not encouraging about his prognosis.

Yet, in true Don Miller fashion, the Chicago native proved them wrong. He went on to set a land speed record at the Bonneville Salt Flats, work on his beloved classic cars, play an instrumental role in Rusty Wallace's and Ryan Newman's NASCAR careers, and spend his life aiding others in an effort to help build a better community in which to live.

~Deb Williams

Interdependence Day

One of the cooler television commercials starring NASCAR drivers features Tony Stewart gazing lovingly at his car—a Corvette, in this case—seemingly oblivious to the rest of the world even as it continues to revolve around him.

Fans use him as a photo op, sort of a living cardboard cutout, unblinking as guys drape their arms across his shoulders and lovely young women ruffle his hair and plant shiny pink Barbie-lipstick kisses on his cheek.

Stewart, though, is unaware of any of these goings-on. He can't take his eyes off that car. For one suspended moment in TV time, nothing exists in his world other than man and machine.

This adoring one-on-one relationship disintegrates, of course, once they hit the race track. Stewart's bright red Chevy may be one of the more distinctive cars and he is surely one of the most popular and recognizable drivers in all of racing, but if they choose to maintain their attitude of exclusivity, neither of them is going anywhere.

Some of the most frustrating NASCAR-related conversations I've had have resulted from comments—not mine—offering up the opinion that stock car racing simply isn't a team sport, but rather just one guy riding around in a car for four or five hundred miles.

Uh-oh. Now they've gone and done it. This attitude is my

kryptonite, my hot button and my Bat signal all rolled into one. Say this to me and you're guaranteed to get my attention, ready or not.

I totally understand that a boy's first love is his car, because I've been there. The occasion was my 16th birthday. The object of my affection was a Chevy Vega, complete with hatchback and metallic finish, the extremely bright blue apple of my eye. I thought it was just the most beautiful thing I had ever seen. It represented my freedom.

With driver's license in hand, so new it was still warm from the DMV laminating machine, I rounded up some willing friends and made plans to celebrate my newfound adulthood the old-fashioned way, by cramming eight or 10 teenagers into my glorious new-to-me rolling palace and going to see a movie.

I was confident that all of the pieces were in place. The mighty Vega was spit-shined, the crew was ready to roll, and we were halfway down the driveway when I realized that my confidence had been misplaced ... along with my cash.

Have you ever tried to wring gas money out of a Vega-load of teenagers? Winged pigs come to mind.

Chastened and reduced to the level of literal begging, I went back into the house and explained the situation to my father. He just looked at me, then took out his wallet and handed me a twenty.

I tried to make a clean and dignified getaway, but alas, it was not to be. As I opened the door to leave, he said, "Happy birthday ... Miss Independent."

Daddy wasn't out there putting on four tires and adjusting the wedge, but it didn't matter. The world loomed limitless and large, but without his help, I couldn't move an inch.

It is all too easy for race fans to fall into the trap of believing that Jeff Gordon, Dale Earnhardt, Jr. and the other top names of the NASCAR Sprint Cup Series are, collectively speaking, "The Man," and in large part this is true. Each of these guys represents the highest and most visible point in his individual orbit, like Seattle's Space Needle or the top floor of Macy's, where they stash all the designer outfits.

After all, how many Super Bowl-winning touchdowns could Joe Montana have thrown without the offensive line out there supporting him? Mr. Montana can tell you that while having control of the football is great, one loose lug nut can cause you to lose it all.

NASCAR offers us a prime example of the principle of interconnectedness. The drivers may indeed be The Man, but without the men (and women) who back them up through ownerships and sponsorships, in the shop and in the pits, they may as well be sitting in the driveway, behind the wheel of an old Vega. Every time their visage grins down at you from a billboard, it is propped up not only by foundations and framework, but also by the catch-can guy and the rear-tire changer.

Throughout our lives and careers we strive to break free of strictures. These include things like our parents, our bosses and the posted speed limit.

But when we spend time in consideration and discussion of things like independence and freedom, it is important to remember that a single man wins neither wars nor races. Rather, the efforts of many focused in a single direction achieve the ultimate goal.

Freedom rings loudest when it has plenty of back-up … and a really fast pit crew.

~Cathy Elliott

That's Racing

Shannon and I had only been dating for a couple of weeks, so when he invited me to ride to the race with his mother, Laura Jean, I couldn't wait to get to know her. Besides, I had never attended a car race before, and the only thing I had to compare it to was horse showing, if you can call that a comparison.

"Are we late? It sounds like they've started." I climbed out of the van and helped Laura Jean unload the cooler.

She smiled. "No, they're still qualifying."

I picked up my end of the cooler and followed her toward the track. When we reached the stands, I spotted several of our friends waving at us. We made our way down the concrete steps, and I scanned the pits.

I was mesmerized by the rows and rows of trucks and trailers that lined the inside of the pits. I set the cooler down and peered through the enormous chain link fence that separated us from the track. One of the cars roared past me, sending a gush of hot air in my face. I sat down and covered my ears. Laura Jean gave my shoulder a squeeze. "You'll get used to it," she said. "I brought some extra ear plugs. Do you want some?"

I nodded and took them from her. I stuffed the squishy cylinders into my ears and watched as, one by one, each car took the track to qualify. Shannon's sister Tonya waved to us from the spotters' section. I waved back, still not understanding the spotter's job. What on earth does she spot? Shannon had tried to explain it to me, but I still didn't get this racing thing.

It was three weeks before our high school graduation. I hadn't planned to fall in love and I sure as heck hadn't planned on spending my summer at the race track. Besides, it was the beginning of horse show season. But instead of riding my three-gaited mare, I found myself baking in 90-degree heat in the middle of a concrete dome.

After the qualifying ended, I noticed a large crowd had gathered around one driver with curly red hair. He was signing autographs near the entrance. "Who is that?" I asked. Laura Jean shielded her eyes from the sun. "Oh, that's Bill Elliott."

Elliott is one of the most popular drivers in NASCAR history. I had never heard of him. I had a lot to learn.

A little while later, I watched a couple of race officials escort a blond woman toward pit road. She wore a short white dress with red high-heeled shoes. Her hair was so big that it looked like her brain had sneezed, and a tiny tiara poked out from the top of her head. She waved to the crowd as she walked by. "That's the track queen, and I think she's dating one of the drivers. She always kisses the winner and poses for a photograph with them after the race," Laura Jean said, scrunching her nose.

For the first time that day, I sort of hoped that Shannon wouldn't win.

A few minutes later, we sang the national anthem. Then I spotted Shannon climbing into his No. 81 Chevy, and watched his crew push the car toward the starting line. Laura Jean grabbed her camcorder, and the announcer instructed the drivers to start their engines. The redolence of racing fuel and horsepower made me dizzy, but in a good way. And as soon as the green flag dropped, my stomach leapt into my throat.

Shannon was the youngest driver in the street stock division. He started racing go-karts when he was 9 years old, with big-time drivers such as Stacey Compton and Ward Burton. He had won the state title a couple of times, and he had also experienced some scary wrecks along the way. But he failed to mention any of that to me. I suppose that's not the sort of thing you tell a girl until after you've dated for a while.

Halfway through the race, he was in third place. But as he rounded Turn 2, the driver running in fourth place slammed into him. Steam rose from underneath the hood and oil oozed onto the track. I gripped Laura Jean's arm.

"Dear God, please let him be all right!" I prayed out loud. But Laura Jean wasn't nervous. She held the camcorder steady and continued recording. "He's OK, Amy. That's just racing," she said with a smile.

I clutched my stomach. "You mean that's legal?"

"Well, no—but that's racing."

That first race was 20 years ago, but Laura Jean's words still echo in my ears. Shannon and I married seven years later and now we have two children of our own. You would think that a boy and girl who are almost five years apart wouldn't care who reaches the front door first, but they do. They even race to see who can finish eating first. For years I've tried countless measures to curtail their behavior, but no matter how many races I've outlawed, they always find another track in one sense or another.

Shannon and I decided it was time to harness those competitive spirits and release them on a real track. So last year we broke ground on our very own go-kart track. If they were determined to race, then we decided we may as well teach them how. While the excavator moved mounds of dirt, I shopped for helmets, gloves and gear. And I had a terrible time keeping the track under wraps, as my neighbors continued to question our landscaping.

At one time, I had hopes of building a horse barn and teaching the children how to ride. But now I know better. Racing is in their blood and they would probably turn our driveway into the Kentucky Derby. I've found that racing is much like showing horses in the fact that once it's in your blood, there's not much you can do to suppress it.

In my 13 years of marriage, I've accepted that racing is part of my life, because it's part of my family. Shannon warns me that the children will experience several bumps along the way, so I instructed the excavator to remove as many trees as possible. Bumping and banging is inevitable and I prepared myself for a little paint swapping, too. I've accepted the fact that it's part of the sport. After all, my mother-in-law, Laura Jean, handed down her words of wisdom to me many years ago when she said, "It's OK, Amy. That's just racing."

And I wouldn't have it any other way.

~Amy Shackleford Tate

In the Presence of a King and a President

*T*wenty-five years ago my family made what had become our annual trek to Daytona Beach, Florida for a family vacation. As was always the case, my dad and I spent just about every possible minute at the Daytona International Speedway watching practice sessions and qualifying in preparation for the Firecracker 400.

Even though we had done this plenty of times before, there was a special feel in the hot, humid air around the 2.5 mile track that year. Richard Petty had won his 199th race just a little over a month earlier in Dover, Delaware. Now, he was poised to score an unprecedented 200th career win at the track where he had experienced so much success throughout his career.

I had grown up a fan of the driver known as "The King." I had little choice. I was named after him, so how could I have cheered for any other driver?

Aside from "The King," there was to be another special guest in attendance that day. President Ronald Reagan would become the first president to attend a major stock car race on that Independence Day morning.

Back then, there were no lights at the Daytona track so the race started at 10 a.m. to keep fans, drivers and crews from baking in the mid-afternoon heat. Even so, it was a sweltering day under the Florida sun.

The president was set to join the proceedings about halfway through the race, so he gave the command of, "Gentlemen, start your engines" in that grandfatherly voice of his from Air Force One while en route.

As the race moved through its initial laps it became obvious Petty would at least have a chance to make history that day. His famous No. 43 Pontiac was clearly one of the stronger machines in the field.

As the laps rolled by, spectators and perhaps even competitors began to look to the sky in anticipation of the arrival of the world's most famous airplane. As if scripted, the Boeing 707, with the seal of its passenger emblazoned on the side, came gliding onto the runway which runs parallel to the speedway's backstretch just as "The King" raced by.

The presidential motorcade eventually made its way out of the airport and toward the track's press box. As luck would have it, my dad and I were seated on the very top row of the grandstand and were able to watch the string of black limousines roll to the point where Reagan would step out and be ushered to the spot where he would watch the race.

What the president got to see was one of NASCAR's greatest shows. Petty and Cale Yarborough distanced themselves from the pack. Petty led while Yarborough stalked just behind in preparation for a slingshot maneuver on the last lap.

As the laps counted down it seemed as though everyone there, no matter who their favorite driver was, began to root for Petty in anticipation of the possible historic moment about to unfold.

As the cars raced toward the signal for two laps to go, a caution suddenly came out for a spin. The first car back to the start/finish line would be the winner. Yarborough pulled off the move everyone knew was coming by passing Petty on the backstretch. I felt my heart sink as I thought that once again I would fail to see my hero win.

But as it turned out, the race was not over. The wily Petty had a trick up his sleeve as well. Yarborough's car drifted high in Turn 3 and Petty shot to the low side. As they raced past the spot where I sat, between Turn 4 and the start/finish line, the two cars looked as if they were glued together at the door.

The track is so big that from where I sat it was impossible to see who crossed the line under the yellow flag first. But the sense of sight was not needed. Even above the sound of racing engines a deafening roar came up from those seated close enough to see what happened. Petty had done it! He had reached the unbelievable milestone of 200 victories!

On that day, more than a quarter century ago, history was made that will never be broken, in the presence of a king, and a president ... and me.

~Richard Allen

The More Things Change

It was Labor Day, 1970. That could only mean one thing in Darlington, South Carolina. The Southern 500, NASCAR's original superspeedway race dating back to 1950, was underway a mile from my house.

I sat beside the window in my room and listened to the roar of the engines as they circled the "Lady in Black." I called the race as only a 4-year-old could—"David Pearson slams the gas as he goes down the frontstretch. Cale Yarborough and Bobby Allison wreck in Turn 1. 'King Richard' Petty takes the lead."

I had no idea what was really happening at the track, but I created my own Southern 500 that day. In my mind, it was as real as if I had been watching from the grandstands.

My dad, Terry Josey, had been a volunteer at Darlington Raceway for several years. He and the legendary promoter/president at the track, Bob Colvin, had been friends for many years and he had persuaded my dad to "help around the office" during races.

This Labor Day was no different. Dad left for the track early that morning, just as he always did.

But later in the day, the front door of our house suddenly opened and there stood Dad. This was unusual, because I could still hear the cars. He looked at me and said, "Let's go and catch the last 50 laps of the race."

I could not believe it. I would finally get to see my first NASCAR race.

As luck would have it, Clarice Lane, Darlington's matriarch for over 50 years, had magically "found" two tickets to what was affectionately known as the "chicken coop."

The chicken coop was one of racing's first suites, if you could call it a suite. It was an open-air structure perched on top of the frontstretch grandstand. It was surrounded by chicken wire to keep spectators from falling on the track, hence the descriptive name.

The only air conditioning was an occasional warm breeze that might pass through on a hot summer day in South Carolina, but I did not care—I was sitting "on top" of Darlington Raceway and could see everything.

By the way, if my mom had seen that structure, she probably would never have allowed us to return.

Down below us, Pearson really was slamming the gas as he went down the frontstretch. "The King" really was racing toward the lead, in hot pursuit of the winged Dodge of Buddy Baker, who eventually won the race. No more pretending—I was really at Darlington Raceway, watching a real race. This had to be greatest day of my life, up to that point.

After that day, I knew that racing would play a part in my life somehow, somewhere. This place known as Darlington Raceway is so special—its history, tradition, and storied past can grab you so quickly. She is, after all, the only track referred to by the media, fans, and competitors as "she," not "it."

That day began a 20-year tradition. My dad and I would attend every race together at Darlington (except one because I had to work at the local Piggly Wiggly). Mom would cook chicken and make ham sandwiches—what more could a dad and son need for a great day together?

But times change, and traditions change with them. I eventually went to work at Darlington Raceway, in the ticket office, fulfilling that instinct from 1970 that NASCAR and, more specifically, Darlington Raceway, would play a major role in my life.

My first race on the job, in 1990, ended my family's 20-year racing tradition. Dad continued on, attending races with friends rather than with me, until 2002, when he passed away.

In 2003, Darlington hosted its final Labor Day weekend race, an idea that would have seemed unimaginable on that hot Labor Day afternoon in 1970. That date moved to Auto Club Speedway in California and later to the Atlanta Motor Speedway.

In 2005, Darlington began hosting only one race annually—an event under the lights on Mother's Day weekend, something that would have also been unimaginable on that same hot summer afternoon a quarter century earlier.

In 2007, my 7-year-old son Stephen attended his first race at Darlington Raceway, not with his dad, but with his mom, Vickie, in tow. Prior to that fateful May evening in 2007, he called his own races—not by the window in his room, but on his wireless microphone. And with the chicken coop long since removed, he sat in the modern Brasington Grandstand.

Yes, traditions painfully end, but new—and hopefully better—ones are born every day. Will this special lady grab Stephen like she grabbed his dad nearly four decades earlier? Will she become a major part of his life?

Check back in 37 years or so and find out what Stephen is doing. Only time will tell.

~Terry Josey

Reconnecting with My Past

In June 2008, Linda's and my friend Joan Laubach won two tickets to the Pocono 500. Neither she nor her family was able to go to the race, so my wife Linda accepted the tickets on my behalf.

In the mid 1960s my friend Bill Miller had introduced me to oval track racing. Owego, New York's Shangri-La Speedway was less than a quarter of a mile from my home, yet I'd never been to a race. I'd heard the annual summer sound of loud engines, squealing tires, and fans cheering every Saturday night since 1952. My nostrils were familiar with the smell of hot rubber that was peculiar to Saturday nights. I'd seen the brightly colored and vastly altered 1930s and 40s chassis with two-foot-high numbers on their doors go by the house. I was familiar with the names of the drivers because the voice of the public address announcer came in loud and clear in my back lawn. Names like Dutch Hoag, Don Diffendorf, Bill Strossal, Benny Stephens and Crazy Eddie Rafferty were an integral part of my vocabulary, but the fact remained I'd never been to a race. I just knew I'd hate it.

Bill was new in town in the fall of 1964. We were both young and single, and both teachers in the Talcott Street elementary school. He was the fourth grade teacher and I was the art teacher.

Over the course of the school year we'd become good friends. Bill was a man of many interests — old-time radio, country music, sports of every kind, motorcycles, go-karts, bicycles, golf, auto racing and just plain just walking up to strangers and within five minutes turning them into lifelong friends. That's how it had happened with us the previous September. Five minutes into that first conversation he said, "I'm going to an Ithaca College football game. How would you like to join me?"

Now it was May and he was going to the race with or without me, so I tagged along. That first race was terrible. I sat in the first turn in fear someone would get hurt.

Following the race Bill wanted to know if I'd caught racing fever. I told him I was terrified and had worried about the safety of the drivers. He laughed and said, "They're going to race whether you watch them or not, so all your fretting won't help any of them." Armed with his common-sense reasoning, he and I returned the following week. He pointed out various track strategies and explained that Shangri-La Speedway and Dutch Hoag were famous among race fans from Maine to Virginia and as far west as Ohio.

That night I caught racing fever. Bill and I traveled across several states taking in small track racing for the rest of that summer and the next.

There was a war going on in those years and when my desire to make a career of teaching art came to an end, my eligibility for the draft became a new reality. With my career decision made I took the only practical option open to me. I joined the Navy to avoid the draft. My parents completely misunderstood the logic I employed to keep myself out of the Army or the Marines. Flawed or not, it kept me out of Southeast Asia.

In February of 1967, I was stationed in Norfolk, Virginia, which just happened to make me close enough to Daytona Beach, Florida that my friend Bob Simpson thought about me when he and several of his friends were buying tickets to the Daytona 500. I joined them under the covered stands at Daytona on race day and experienced the thrill of swollen eardrums. I was hooked on big-time NASCAR racing. Two-foot-high orange, red, green, purple, yellow and blue blurs that had only moments earlier been numbers, passed in front of me at 180 mph. Lap after lap the thunder of un-muffled engines rose and fell as the pack came and went. I couldn't comprehend how a man could control a car at these speeds. Even more, I couldn't understand the mindset of men who walked away from a spectacular crash one day and climbed back into another car the following day, but it fascinated me.

The following two years, the Navy accommodated my taste for racing by giving me ships out of Jacksonville, Florida. I caught the Daytona 500 in both 1968 and 1969, and like my friend Bill I was willing to go alone rather than miss the show. In 1969, I also caught the Permatex 300 NASCAR Late Model Sportsman race the day before the Daytona 500. Dutch Hoag finished half a car length back, to capture second place, to the astonishment of slow, soft southern accents whose voices echoed throughout the entire front straight-away. "Who's the Yankee?"

Time passed, and the Navy took me other places. I came home, met Linda, we got married and raised a family on a marginal income and I never really got back into racing until Joan gave me those tickets to the Pocono 500 in June of 2008.

I took my son, Dan, with me. The guy behind us took a "nap" on my shoulders, and the lady to our left jumped up and blocked our view of the fourth turn every time Carl Edwards came around. My eardrums were swollen and my neck was sunburned. Kasey Kahne graced my return by driving the most perfect race I'd ever witnessed. That Sunday, Jesus Christ remained my king for eternity, but Kahne was king for a day and with great delight I'd witnessed his coronation.

The following week I was again with my much-loved church family, most of whom can't understand how easily I float from our Sunday world of worship to the rowdy Sunday NASCAR world of a parallel universe.

But I felt strangely as if I had come back to the people I had come of age with. I had come home.

~Ed VanDeMark

NASCAR: Bringing Families Together

Mom always said that if she hadn't married Dad, he would have become a penniless stock car driver. She considers herself the influence that kept him from devoting his life to, as she saw it, dirty, dangerous, and costly stock cars.

Dad's non-racing career was teaching business courses at the high school, as well as coaching and officiating sports. For us kids, Dad was the homework checker, the packer of lunch boxes, and the math tutor who made his children safe and warm with bedtime stories and good night hugs. He worked all day—and evening—with other people's kids and came home to his own with time and love to spare.

Dad, by nature, is a helper. As a coach and sports official, his devotion was not to the game but to cultivating the talents of young people.

Dad passed along to me, at a young age, the love of a car. He owned a red 1969 Corvette. The highlight of summer days was climbing in the makeshift backseat without car seats or seat belts, stopping for ice cream, and taking a drive on the open country roads at over 80 mph. Many Sunday afternoons were spent with Dad, a chest of tools, a pan of dirty oil, the Corvette, and an AM radio with Barney Hall calling a NASCAR Winston (now Sprint) Cup race.

One spring, Dad convinced Mom that he was going to take me, at the tender age of 8, to my first NASCAR race; we would travel to the Irish Hills of Michigan to Michigan International Speedway. That first trip was filled with such anticipation. The three-hour drive to our overnight stop in Toledo felt like a week's journey across the Sahara Desert. The next morning when the track came into view I experienced chills of excitement that I had never experienced before. I had to catch my breath as the vast grandstands came into view.

With one exception, I now remember that first day at the speedway only as impressions of sounds and smells and the images I piece together from looking at the collection of 35 mm photos that Dad took that day.

Dad took my hand and we approached a semi-truck trailer. A pleasant man stopped his work, and asked if he could help us. My dad gently pleaded on my behalf (and secretly his own) for a look inside.

The magic of what I saw inside has stuck with me, consistently, since that first day. That view inside the CBS Sports mobile production facility sparked my interest and imagination about all that made the sport possible. Suddenly, NASCAR was bigger than my affection for Awesome Bill Elliott and the No. 9 car. It became more than drivers, crew chiefs, and television personalities. NASCAR became a community of broadcast technicians, mechanics, sponsors, concessionaires, officials, volunteers, front office staff, and sales executives. And this was a community that I wanted to join.

For a few more years my dad would take me back to Michigan in June for our pilgrimage, but eventually other things were getting in the way—sports, boyfriends, and summer jobs. Deep down, I always kept that strong connection with that circle of asphalt in the Irish hills and the people who visited there every summer.

I went to college and studied hard. I chose to play sports and to major in Sports Marketing. I wanted to work for NASCAR, but had no idea how to make it happen. My business school advisor was not impressed with this aspiration and offered little encouragement or assistance.

Late in my time in college, as I was paying my last parking fee at the university, the motherly figure behind the counter commented on my NASCAR-motif personal check. "My son would love these," she said. I replied, "Oh, does your son like racing"? She said with a smile, "Yes, he is the Marketing Director at Michigan International Speedway." I hesitantly asked for his name.

I knew right away the potential for this little moment of serendipity. The first person I called was my father. Dad, in addition to his own unselfishness, also believes in the intrinsic good nature of others. He encouraged me to call and express my genuine interest.

In the next year, I was given the opportunity to interview and was offered an internship. Soon, I was welcomed into the NASCAR family as a corporate sales executive at Michigan International Speedway.

During my first NASCAR event, Dad was ready to come to the race as a spectator. He was thrilled to use my employee tickets in the center grandstand tickets—better than any seat he had ever purchased for himself.

A few days before the race a volunteer service group had to withdraw from helping in the information booths, and our Director of Guest Services was looking for volunteers. I called Dad right away and asked if he would like to help us out. Unable to resist lending a helping hand, he gave up his center grandstand seats to assist other race fans at the guest service tents. He even convinced my skeptical mother to come along. They enjoyed every minute.

Every year since, Dad's role at the speedway has grown. A year later he was a supervisor for a group of guest service tents; a year after that he was in charge of all the guest service tents; later, he was promoted to Assistant Guest Service Supervisor. He takes this part-time job more seriously than many people treat their full-time jobs.

During this time, Mom would spend the week in Michigan and help at the track as needed, but preferred to spend the days at my apartment to make sure Dad and I had clean and ironed clothes, hot food on the table in the evenings, and travel mugs of coffee prepared for our pre-dawn departures.

Later, after six years of working at the speedway, I changed roles in the industry and began work for a major sponsor of a race team based in Kansas City. However, there was no chance of Dad resigning just because I was moving on.

Dad, without a place to stay, purchased a camper and prepared to spend the week living at the speedway. Surprisingly, Mom agreed to go back that first year. In the infield for those three weeks that summer, Mom's appreciation of the event, the culture, and the people grew. And now, Mom is in her sixth year of assisting at the Michigan International Speedway credentials office. They have met some of their dearest friends at the Speedway and rate those weeks there as among their most favorite times of the year.

I view every aspect of my job as helping. Whether it is helping a fan find their seat, helping a sponsor to increase their product recognition, or helping someone set up their hospitality tent, our work is about making everyone's experience enjoyable. It is this goodwill, not the fast cars, which defines the NASCAR experience and community. Every day I thank my father for showing me that helping is a gift.

Now that I am back "at the track" working for Kansas Speedway, I still call my dad up before every race and ask, "Dad, would you like to help us out for the race"? He, as always, still jumps at the chance, eager to help. Mom, once the skeptic, has found a home in NASCAR and now includes herself wholeheartedly in this community.

In the 27 years since my first visit to the speedway, I have found a family in NASCAR. More and more, I find my own family and my NASCAR family are one and the same.

~Jean Ann Bowman

Sisters for Sadler

Five years ago if you had mentioned NASCAR to me, I wouldn't have had anything to say about it. Things have really changed since then. Now I live and breathe NASCAR. I even plan all my vacations around it.

I am a 40-ish wife and mother. My hobbies include gardening, painting, scrapbooking—just the usual things women my age do. Racing was never on my radar. Now it is something my whole family enjoys and it has created a special bond between my sister and me.

How did this come to be? My love of candy played a part in it. I watched a race while visiting my parents and saw a pretty yellow car with M&M's all over it on the television screen. I was captivated by how it stood out on the track. I wanted to know everything about it, including who was driving it.

I started watching the SPEED channel and made NASCAR.com one of my favorite Web sites. I soon learned that NASCAR was not just about the cars, but about the personalities driving the cars. I was so happy to know that my M&M's car was driven by Elliott Sadler, who definitely had southern charm and an infectious personality.

After my sister and I attended a fan event and were able to meet Elliott, we both knew we wanted to join his fan club and show our support. This was how our NASCAR bond started.

Many of the drivers have their own foundations, and Elliott's was for children's autism. We were very proud to support such a fine cause. When the fan club said they were having a "barn party" on the

Sadler property, we knew we had to go. It didn't matter to us that it was at least a 12-hour drive. How often do you get to go to a party on your driver's property?

We dined on bologna burgers (one of Elliott's favorite sandwiches), met his hunting dogs (he now has around 70), had him autograph a few things, took pictures with him (which did not turn out so well since we were too nervous to focus) and then sat in our lawn chairs and listened to Blake Shelton in concert under the stars. The party went on for at least six hours and raised several thousand dollars for children's autism and probably set a new record for the number of bologna burgers consumed in one day.

Oh, did I mention one of the best parts of that day? I had my picture taken with my beloved M&M's car.

Sponsors and teams have changed since then and Elliott no longer drives the M&M's car, but we still support him and his foundation and try to attend every event the fan club offers. Wherever the Sadler fans gather, that is where you will find us, as we are loyal fans. And being sisters, we like to call ourselves "Sisters for Sadler".

Not a day goes by that we don't talk NASCAR, whether it be picking drivers for our fantasy team or just talking about a race, discussing who wrecked whom.

I can't imagine my life without NASCAR thanks to Elliott Sadler … and my sweet tooth.

~Kelley Knepper

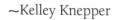

Meet Our
Contributors

Shawn A. Akers is a 15-year journalistic veteran in the NASCAR industry. He is an editor for Anthem Media Group, which produces all souvenir programs for ISC tracks. He has worked as an editor/writer for NASCAR.com and as a PR rep in the former NASCAR Busch Series.

Richard Allen has followed NASCAR racing since his childhood. He writes a weekly column for *The Mountain Press* newspaper in Tennessee and operates two Web sites dedicated to racing coverage, RacingWithRich.com and TennesseeRacer.com. He plans to continue writing columns and has plans for a book about NASCAR. He enjoys spending time with his wife and three children.

Aric Almirola began racing go-karts at the age of 8. He began his NASCAR career in 2004 for Joe Gibbs Racing, moving up to race full-time in the NASCAR Camping World Truck Series in 2006. He moved to the NASCAR Nationwide Series on a regular basis in 2007, and shared the No. 8 Chevrolet with Mark Martin in the NASCAR Sprint Cup Series in 2008. He competed in all three series in 2009. He is a native of Tampa, Florida.

Following a 15-year freelance radio and television on-air talent career, **Fred Armstrong** is the Director of Creative Services for MRN

Radio, and currently responsible for managing the Sprint Vision "Big Screen" programming at NASCAR Sprint Cup Series Events. Living in Concord, N.C. with his wife of 20 years and daughter, Armstrong enjoys spending quality time with his family, writing, music composition and audio/video production.

Elizabeth Atwater developed a great love of reading as a very young child, which led to an even greater love of writing at an early age. She began selling fillers and short stories to romance magazines when she was in her teens. Elizabeth's dream, obviously, is to sell a book.

In 1970, **Buddy Baker** became the first driver to exceed 200 mph on a closed course. He is a member of the International Motorsports Hall of Fame, the National Motorsports Press Association Hall of Fame, the South Carolina Sports Hall of Fame, the Davey Allison Walk of Fame, the North Carolina Racing Hall of Fame, and the Charlotte Motor Speedway Court of Legends. In 1998, he was named one of NASCAR's 50 Greatest Drivers. He worked as a broadcaster with CBS for five years, and with TNN for 12 years. Currently, he is co-host of *Late Shift* on Sirius Satellite Radio.

Roy A. Barnes writes from southeastern Wyoming. He's been fascinated by traveling ever since he rode with his father in a semi-truck as a young boy during school vacation periods. He can be reached via e-mail at travelwriteroy@yahoo.com.

South Carolina Lieutenant Governor **André Bauer** serves as the state's second-highest constitutional officer. Currently, Bauer serves as president of the Senate and assumes the position of governor if the governor is unable to perform the duties of his office. The responsibilities of the Lieutenant Governor were expanded in 2004 when Bauer became the elected official who oversees the Office on Aging. He is a graduate of the University of South Carolina.

Rick Beneteau was a pioneering entrepreneur and is the co-founder of 10 Million Clicks For Peace, a humanitarian organization dedicated to creating world peace through personal empowerment and technology. To learn more visit www.TenMillionClicksForPeace.org.

Jeff Boerger is the President of Kansas Speedway. He oversees day-to-day operations and monitors civic and community responsibilities. Born in Topeka, Kansas, Boerger earned a bachelor's degree in fine arts from the University of Kansas in 1988. To experience the "Best Guest Experience in Motorsports" go to kansasspeedway.com.

Jean Ann Bowman is a 1996 graduate of The University of Toledo with a Bachelor of Science in Sports Marketing. She is a Corporate Sales Executive at Kansas Speedway and resides in Kansas with her husband and son. Jean Ann enjoys playing volleyball, and taking care of her family.

Herbert (Herb) Branham Jr. is Director of Written Communications for NASCAR. He worked for the *Tampa Tribune* for 21 years prior to joining NASCAR, where he won numerous writing awards, including a 1997 award for having one of the nation's top 10 feature stories. Branham has authored four books, most recently a biography of the late Bill France, Jr. He and his wife Catherine reside in Ormond Beach, Florida.

Tammy Brewington began writing 12 years ago at the Middle Tennessee *Racing News*. She is the former public relations coordinator of Nashville Superspeedway, and the public relations manager for the Fairgrounds Speedway in Nashville. Tammy and Rick, her husband of 30 years, live in Lebanon, Tennessee.

Kurt Busch drives the No. 2 Miller Lite Dodge in the NASCAR Sprint Cup Series. A native of Las Vegas, Nevada, he was the NASCAR Auto Zone Elite Division, Southwest Series champion in 1999, the 2000 NASCAR Camping World Truck Series Rookie of the Year, and the 2003 IROC champion. He began his NASCAR Sprint Cup Series career in 2000, at the age of 22, winning the series championship in

2004—the first-ever title determined by the "Chase for the NASCAR Sprint Cup" format. Kurt and his wife, Eva, live in North Carolina.

Jeff Byrd joined Bristol Motor Speedway in 1996. In 2002 Byrd became president of Bristol Motor Speedway and Dragway. Prior to his employment at Bristol Motor Speedway, he was vice president of development for Sports Marketing Enterprises. A 35-year veteran in the sports marketing profession, Byrd has been involved in the development and implementation of a multitude of sports and event marketing programs.

Although her driving record is less than pristine, **Amanda L. Capps** has a better track record as an award-winning writer. Through her company, Amanda Ink, she enjoys helping aspiring writers improve their work and sell it for publication. E-mail her at AmandaCappsInk@gmail.com.

Skip Clayton has been hosting *Racing Wrap*, a weekly one-hour racing show on WBCB Radio in Levittown, Pennsylvania since February 17, 1997. Clayton has covered sports for the ABC Radio Network for over 40 years and has written two books. He resides in Sellersville, Penn. with his wife Joanne.

Best-selling author **Amy Clipston** has been writing for as long as she can remember. Her fiction writing "career" began in elementary school when she and a friend wrote and shared silly stories. Amy lives in North Carolina with her husband, sons, and three spoiled cats. Visit her Web site at www.amyclipston.com.

Tommy Dampier has been the chief motorsports correspondent for the *Lee County Observer* in Bishopville, South Carolina for 32 years. In addition, he is the publication's primary motorsports photographer. He has covered all series of motorsports, with NASCAR being his primary assignment. Tommy continues to provide motorsports coverage for the *Observer* and is a contributing correspondent for americanmotorjournal.com. He is a native of Bishopville, and now resides in Charleston, South Carolina.

Brad Daugherty hails from Black Mountain, N.C. He entered the University of North Carolina at the age of 16 and was a two-time All ACC first team selection and a first team All American while playing basketball for the Tarheels under legendary coach Dean Smith. He was the first overall pick in the 1986 NBA draft, and a five-time NBA All Star for the Cleveland Cavaliers. Daugherty joined ESPN's return to NASCAR racing telecasts in 2007. He is currently an analyst on *NASCAR Countdown*, ESPN's pre-race show, and on *NASCAR Now*, a nightly newscast on the sport. He is also part owner of JTG Daugherty Racing and Tony Kostelnak Racing.

Dwight Drum, a member of the National Motorsports Press Association, has served as a photojournalist, writer, and editor with Stripbike.com since 1998. He is also the creator of Zoomster.com (1999) and Racetake.com (2007). He has interviewed almost every big name in NASCAR, NHRA and Indycar and is a regular contributor for Examiner.com and Myfoxorlando.com. He also has experience covering the Tampa Bay Buccaneers. Send Dwight an e-mail at Zoomguys@aol.com and follow Dwight on Twitter.com/racetake.

Greg Engle is a Florida resident and lifelong NASCAR fan who raced late models in the late 1970s and early 1980s and began covering NASCAR in the mid-90's. He has worked full-time as a NASCAR reporter for the *Sporting News* and is a National Motorsports Press Association award-winning columnist.

Joanne Faries, originally from the Philadelphia area, lives in Texas with her husband Ray. Published in *Doorknobs & Bodypaint*, she has stories and poems in *Shine* magazine, and *Freckles to Wrinkles*. Joanne is the film critic for the *Little Paper of San Saba*. Check out her blog: http://wordsplash-joannefaries.blogspot.com.

Currently the Editor of *Circle Track Magazine*, **Rob Fisher** has spent 20 years in the racing industry. He has won a number of national writing awards and has been continuously published since the age of

21. In his spare time, Rob enjoys time with his family, cooking and racing bicycles.

Brian France, a member of the NASCAR-founding France family, is the chairman of the board and CEO of NASCAR. His extensive racing background includes helping to develop and manage the Weekly and Touring Series divisions and launching the Craftsman Truck Series. Widely considered a visionary, he took over NASCAR's marketing responsibilities in 1994, and was *The Sports Business Daily's* Industrialist of the Year in 1999. He resides in Daytona Beach, Florida.

Lewis Franck has covered motorsports as a photographer for *Sport Magazine* and magazines in Europe. Subsequently switching to writing Franck had a monthly column in *Inside Sports* and later worked regularly for *Sports Illustrated* and SI.com. Currently he contributes to *ESPN The Magazine* and *Reuters*.

A native Virginian, **Doug Fritz** is a Virginia Tech graduate. He spent 10 years in Daytona as NASCAR's Senior Director of Marketing and Business Development. In the spring of 1999, Doug joined International Speedway Corporation as Director of Corporate Administration and became President of Richmond International Raceway on December 1, 1999.

Andrew Giangola, author of *The Weekend Starts on Wednesday: True Stories of Remarkable NASCAR Fans*, is NASCAR's Director of Business Communications. He previously held senior PR positions at McKinsey, Simon & Schuster and Pepsi-Cola. Andrew graduated from Fordham University and lives in Manhattan with his wife, Viviane, and scary-smart daughter Gaby.

Becca Gladden is a freelance writer specializing in NASCAR and also works in motorsports marketing, public relations, and social media. Becca has been published in numerous newspapers and magazines on non-NASCAR topics as well. Becca has two sons and lives in Arizona. Please e-mail her at nscrwriter@aol.com.

Andrew Gurtis has worked in various capacities for International Speedway Corporation for 18-plus years. Born in Winter Park, Florida, the seventh of eight children, he received a B.A. from the University of Notre Dame in 1988. He is married with three children and enjoys family time, travel and surfing.

Sarah Gurtis was raised in Florida with her seven siblings. She enjoyed successful careers in Banking and Motorsports before following her heart to Camp Boggy Creek where she volunteered for years. She loves to travel and spend time with her 32 nieces and nephews. You can contact her at www.BoggyCreek.org.

Betty Hanks is a graduate of Sam Houston State University with a Bachelor of Arts. She tried many jobs before pursuing a career in writing. Betty's passion is helping women who have survived childhood abuse. Betty and her husband and two teenage children live in North Texas. Please contact her via e-mail at bhanks@realizingtruehope.com.

J. Todd Hardee was born and raised in the shadow of Darlington Raceway, which he calls the "Taj Mahal of auto racing." Todd owns and operates Kistler-Hardee Funeral Home and is the Darlington County Coroner. He and his wife Jenny and their two sons Templin and Sandy live — where else? — in Darlington.

Mike Harris recently retired after 40 years with The Associated Press, the last 30 as the AP's Auto Racing Writer. He stays busy writing part-time for Racintoday.com. A graduate of the University of Wisconsin, Harris is enjoying retirement with Judy, his wife of 41 years. Please email him at mharris@racintoday.com.

Cathryn Hasek is a freelance writer from North Ridgeville, Ohio. She enjoys writing inspirational material for the Christian marketplace and has been published therein. Cathy enjoys reading, sports, music and volunteering for her church, public library and local Hospice organization.

Rhonda Hensley received her Bachelor of Arts in Christian Studies and a minor in Youth Ministry, with honors from N. Greenville University. She is a graduate of CLASSeminar for Christian Writers and Speakers. She works as a freelance writer, inspirational speaker and Bible Teacher. E-mail her at frstldy@bellsouth.net.

Marty Hough has worked in the radio industry since 1987 and was hired at MRN Radio in 2000. In 2008 he won the National Motorsports Press Association Broadcaster of the Year award. Marty is found on most social networking sites and via e-mail at mhough11@carolina. rr.com. He continues to work on more inspirational material.

Jim Hunter was a two-sport letterman (baseball, football) at the University of South Carolina. He is currently Vice President of Corporate Communications at NASCAR. He has produced numerous magazine articles over the years and has written several sports books. Hunter is currently working on a co-authored novel with bestselling author Janet Evanovich.

Jimmie Johnson, driver of the No. 48 Lowe's Chevrolet for Hendrick Motorsports, is the only driver in history to win four consecutive NASCAR Sprint Cup Series championships, in 2006 through 2009. A native of El Cajon, California, he was the 1998 ASA Rookie of the Year, and the 2006 Daytona 500 champion. Founded in 2006, the Jimmie Johnson Foundation is dedicated to assisting children, families and communities in need throughout the United States. Jimmie and his wife, Chandra, were married in December 2004.

Paul (PJ) Johnson is an award winning anchor/reporter from WEMT-TV in Bristol, Virginia. He has covered NASCAR since 1980. In 2005 he won the Russ Catlin award, NASCAR's highest journalism honor. PJ plays a lot of golf and lives in Bristol, with his daughter Morgan and dog Moose.

Terry Josey, a native of Darlington, S.C., is the vice president and general manager of Darlington Raceway. He holds a bachelor's degree in political science from Francis Marion University in Florence, S.C. and an MBA from Columbia University in New York, N.Y. He and his wife Vickie and their son Stephen live in Darlington.

Godwin Kelly has been Motorsports Editor at the *Daytona Beach (FL) News-Journal* since 1982 and won several national awards for his coverage of racing. In addition Godwin has published four books about stock car racing. Godwin grew up in Daytona Beach and he has lived in that area of Florida most of his life.

Kelley Knepper is a graduate of Huntington University in Huntington, Indiana. She works part-time doing accounting for an insurance office. Kelley likes scrapbooking, painting, crafts, and spending time with her family and friends. This is Kelley's first story and she hopes you enjoy it.

Texas native **Bobby Labonte** was the 1999 NASCAR Busch (now Nationwide) Series champion, the 2001 IROC champion and the 2000 Winston (now NASCAR Sprint) Cup Series champion. He and his brother Terry are the only brothers to have both won the championship in NASCAR's top series. Bobby and his wife Donna and their two children live in Trinity, N.C.

Claire B. Lang is a veteran and well-respected NASCAR broadcast and print journalist. Her popular *Dialed In with Claire B. Lang* show airs on SIRIUS NASCAR Radio and she anchors event coverage from the garage and media center for SIRIUS NASCAR Radio. Claire travels the NASCAR circuit, taking listeners and readers along for the ride.

Jonathan Lintner is a journalism student at Western Kentucky

University. He currently works the football and basketball beats for the student paper, the *College Heights Herald*, and has contributed to FoxSports.com and CBSSports.com. Jonathan plans to graduate in 2012, knowing his dream job is one as a full-time NASCAR writer.

Joey Logano made history in 2008 by becoming the youngest driver ever to win a NASCAR Nationwide Series race, at Kentucky Speedway. He topped that feat in 2009, becoming the youngest NASCAR Sprint Cup Series winner in history, at New Hampshire Motor Speedway. The driver of the No. 20 Home Depot Toyota for Joe Gibbs Racing was also named the 2009 NASCAR Sprint Cup Series Raybestos Rookie of the Year.

Sammie Lukaskiewicz is the Director of Communications at Michigan International Speedway. A native of Texas, she's a former newspaper reporter who's lived all over the world and enjoys all forms of motorsports. She has a B.A. in journalism and an M.A. in management. Feel free to contact her via e-mail at slukaskiewicz@ MISpeedway.com.

Dr. Joseph Mattioli, Pocono Raceway C.E.O. and Chairman of the Board, is the driving force behind the dramatic growth of Pocono International Raceway. From the Raceway's inception in the mid-1960's, Pocono Raceway has grown to the level that the Raceway's two NASCAR Sprint Cup Series events are now the two largest single-day spectator sporting events in the state of Pennsylvania.

Ryan McGee is a senior writer with *ESPN The Magazine* and author of two books, *The Road To Omaha: Hits, Hopes, and History at the College World Series* and *ESPN Ultimate NASCAR: 100 Defining Moments in Stock Car Racing History*. He lives in North Carolina with his family.

Jim McLaurin is a former sportswriter for *The State* (Columbia, S.C.) newspaper who covered motorsports for over 25 years. He is a past president of the National Motorsports Press Association, and has won that organization's Writer of the Year award twice. You may e-mail him at JMHimmymac@aol.com.

Casey Mears, nephew of four-time Indianapolis 500 winner Rick Mears and son of Indy and off-road veteran Roger Mears, veered slightly from family tradition and pursued a career in NASCAR. He was the overall co-winner of the 24 Hours of Daytona in 2006. In NASCAR, his first win came at Charlotte in the 2007 Coca-Cola 600. The Bakersfield, California native enjoys wakeboarding and snow-boarding in his free time.

Joe Moore has worked for MRN Radio for 28 seasons, first as a turn announcer and for the last 10 years as co-anchor. He is also the creator and host of *Raceline*, a weekly, nationally-syndicated TV show covering NASCAR Racing. Joe lives in Chesapeake, Virginia and is married to Tiffany.

Brandon W. Mudd has been involved in motorsports for nearly 10 years as a writer, broadcaster, and team/track public relations. He is a veteran of the U.S. Navy and is working on his first book. Please e-mail him at bwmudd@yahoo.com.

Ryan Newman drives the No. 39 U.S. Army/Haas Automation Chevrolet Impala for Stewart Haas Racing in the NASCAR Sprint Cup Series. A 2001 graduate of Purdue University with a B.S. in vehicle structure engineering, he is the only active NASCAR driver to have a college degree. Newman won the Daytona 500 in 2008 and was the 2002 Raybestos Rookie of the Year, setting the rookie record for most poles in a season with six. He was a Chase for the NASCAR Sprint Cup contender in 2009, finishing ninth in the driver standings. He and his wife Krissie live in Sherrill's Ford, N.C.

Tim Packman started his motorsports career at short tracks around his native Buffalo, NY. He has more than a decade of NASCAR experience as a six-time award winning writer/broadcaster, published author, two Daytona 500 wins and now does public relations. He lives in Mooresville, N.C. with his wife, Dawn.

Gloria Panzera received her BA from the University of Miami in 2006 and is currently working on a Masters of Fine Arts at Florida Atlantic University in creative writing. She teaches English Composition to incoming freshman. Gloria enjoys writing, reading, cooking, traveling, and dancing. After her graduation from FAU she plans to teach and write. Please e-mail her at g.m.panzera@gmail.com.

Steve Post from Hallstead, Pa., grew up attending short tracks in Pennsylvania and New York. After working as a track announcer and publicist in the Northeast and in the NASCAR industry, he moved to broadcasting where he continues working for MRN Radio, SIRIUS NASCAR Radio and *Raceline*; he also co-owns www.AroundTheTrackOnline.com.

Ramsey Poston is managing director of NASCAR Corporate Communications. Poston is responsible for all day to day communications including racing competition, business and lifestyle. He joined NASCAR in May 2004 after serving as a consultant as Senior Vice President at Powell Tate in Washington D.C. There he provided strategic communications counsel to NASCAR dating back to 2001. Poston holds a bachelor's degree in political studies from Roger Williams University.

Born and raised in Louisville, Kentucky, **John Potts** got involved in motorsports selling race papers in grandstands at 9 and writing race reports at 13. He worked as an editor of weekly newspapers in southern Indiana and part-time as a race official. John was an ASA Chief Starter from 1972 to 1984 and News Director at Indianapolis Raceway Park from 1985 until 2000. John is now semi-retired and living in London, Kentucky assisting with the operation of Corbin Speedway in Corbin, Kentucky as Director of News and Administrative Services.

Chris Powell is president of Las Vegas Motor Speedway, having moved to Nevada in 1998 after spending 11 years in various public relations roles in the sports marketing department at R.J. Reynolds Tobacco Co. A native of Ahoskie, N.C., he is a graduate of the University of North Carolina with a degree in journalism. He and his wife, Missy, are the parents of five children, all boys.

Kay Presto is an award-winning book author, photographer, and former television talk show host. She is an international professional speaker, and has been a motorsports reporter on CNN Television and Mutual Radio. Honors for her writing include the 2005 Woman of Achievement Award from the National Association of Female Executives (NAFE) in New York. She also honors seniors at www.shirts4seniors.com. Kay can be reached via e-mail at prestoprod6@yahoo.com.

Rusty Ray received his Bachelor of Arts in broadcast journalism from the Philip Merrill College of Journalism at the University of Maryland in 2002. Shortly after that, he became a reporter at WBTW-TV in the Eastern Carolinas. He's remained with the station in a variety of roles since then, and is now a morning news anchor. He and his wife, Sarah, live in Myrtle Beach, S.C. and still watch NASCAR, together, almost every weekend.

R. Stephen Repsys received his Bachelor of Arts, with honors, from Stonehill College, and his master of education from Springfield College. He works in higher education in Illinois. Stephen enjoys reading, playing fantasy sports, and spending time with his two daughters, Erin and Elizabeth. He can be reached via e-mail at repsys@hotmail.com.

Robyn Schroder is currently a senior at Sonoma State University pursuing her Bachelor of Arts in English. She enjoys reading, writing, traveling, and hanging out with friends. This is her second contribution to the *Chicken Soup for the Soul* series.

Ellen Slothour Siska considers her greatest accomplishment to be surviving the death of her son, Edward, to SIDS in 1991. Raising a son with Asperger Syndrome, a deaf daughter, and another son, as a single mother, introduced Ellen to the power of Internet support groups. A member of the National Motorsports Press Association, Ellen has written a weekly NASCAR column for *The York (Pa.) Dispatch* since 2006 and is a contributor to ESPN.com.

ESPN NASCAR reporter **Marty Smith** likes real people, well-written prose, Jack Daniel's whiskey and Virginia Tech football. He loves Jesus, and he loves his family. Smith, 33, resides in Huntersville, NC with his wife, Lainie, and their two young children, Cambron and Mia. E-mail him at ESPNSider@aol.com.

Mary Z. Smith has written for four other *Chicken Soup for the Soul* books as well as *Guidepost* and *Angels in Earth* magazines. She resides in Richmond, Virginia with her husband Barry and her mother-in-law Flora and Rat Terrier Frankie.

Melissa Sorensen owns a professional organizing company in Woodbridge, Virginia. She and Scott were married in 1993 and moved to Virginia in 1999. Melissa continues to check items off Scott's list.

Scott Speed won championship titles in Formula Renault 2000 Eurocup and German Formula Renault in 2004. In 2005 at the Canadian Grand Prix, he became the first American driver to participate in a Formula One event since Michael Andretti in 1993. His first NASCAR win came in a Camping World Truck Series race, in only his sixth start. 2009 was his first full-time season of racing in the NASCAR Sprint Cup Series, where he drives the No. 82 Toyota for the Red Bull Racing Team.

Tony Stewart has won titles in Indy cars and stock cars, as well as midget, sprint and USAC Silver Crown cars. He was the 2006 IROC XXX champion. He currently owns and drives the No. 14 Office

Depot/Old Spice/Burger King Chevrolet Impala SS in the NASCAR Sprint Cup Series for his own team, Stewart Haas Racing. Stewart is the only driver to win both the Winston Cup under the old points system, and the Sprint Cup under the chase playoff format, winning those championships in 2002 and 2005 respectively. He lives in Columbus, Indiana.

Amy Tate, a member of SCBWI and American Christian Fiction Writers, has written for children's magazines and regional publications. A resident of Boones Mill, Virginia, Amy currently writes middle-grade novels. She enjoys blogging (thevirginiascribe.blogspot.com) and spending time with her family.

Martin Truex, Jr. won the NASCAR Nationwide Series championship in 2004 and 2005. The Mayetta, N.J. native posted his first career NASCAR Sprint Cup Series victory in 2007, at his "home track," Dover International Speedway. He is a fishing and hunting enthusiast and a fan of all Philadelphia pro sports franchises, who lives in Mooresville, N.C.

Ed VanDeMark is a retired Tioga County NY employee. Husband of Linda, father of Tony, Lisa (Mosher) and Dan, Ed has eight grandchildren plus one on the way. He enjoys writing, cartooning, sports, lawn work, and is active in the Owego United Methodist Church.

Brian Vickers drives the No. 83 Red Bull Toyota Camry for the Red Bull Racing Team. Vickers was the 2003 NASCAR Nationwide Series champion, and at age 20, the youngest champion in any of NASCAR's three top-tier series. He earned his first NASCAR Sprint Cup Series career win in 2006 at Talladega Superspeedway, and in 2009, qualified for the Chase for the NASCAR Sprint Cup for the first time, finishing 12th. He lives in Charlotte, N.C.

Steve Waid is a vice president at Street & Smith's Sports Group, publishers of *NASCAR Scene* and *NASCAR Illustrated*. As a journalist he has covered NASCAR for more than 30 years and has won numerous awards. He is also a regular contributor to the publication's Web site, www.scenedaily.com. He can be reached via e-mail at swaid@ streetandsmiths.com.

Darrell Waltrip is a three-time former NASCAR Sprint Cup Series champion, winner of the 1989 Daytona 500 winner, current television race commentator serving as lead analyst with Fox Broadcasting Company and columnist at Foxsports.com. One of NASCAR's all-time most popular drivers, he is an inductee of both the International Motorsports Hall of the Fame and the Motorsports Hall of Fame of America and a recipient of the Bill France Award of Excellence. His 84 wins in the Cup Series are tied for third place in NASCAR history. In 1998, he was named as one of NASCAR's 50 Greatest Drivers.

Michael Waltrip is a two-time winner of the Daytona 500 and co-owner of Michael Waltrip Racing. He was the 1993 NASCAR Dash Series champion. One of the most popular and engaging figures in NASCAR, he is also a part-time commentator for SPEED TV's coverage of the NASCAR Camping World Truck Series and is a member of the "expert panel" on SPEED Channel's *This Week in NASCAR* program. He currently lives in Sherrills Ford, North Carolina.

Lee Warren is an author and freelance writer with five books and hundreds of articles in print. He writes for *Baptist Press Sports* and the *Heartland Gatekeeper* newspaper. He also co-owns A Write Start Communications—a company dedicated to helping writers. You can visit his Web site at www.leewarren.info.

Rick Weber graduated from Penn State with a B.A. in Journalism. He has won the Casey Medal for Meritorious Journalism and been honored twice by the Associated Press Sports Editors and numerous times by the Florida Sportswriters Association. His first book, *Pink Lips and Fingertips*, was published in 2009 and he also contributed to

Chicken Soup for the Soul: The Golf Book. He lives in Katy, Texas, with his son, Austin.

Bill Wetterman managed and trained some of the finest professional search consultants in the country before retiring from Wolters Search Group. He is a member of several professional writers' organizations. Bill writes both non-fiction and fiction short stories and novels. You can reach Bill via e-mail at bwetterman@cox.net.

Libby Swope Wiersema is a freelance writer and editor living in Florence, S.C. She attended Francis Marion University and the University of Alabama. Please e-mail her at libmich@bellsouth.net.

A veteran motorsports journalist, **Deb Williams'** honors include National Motorsports Press Association Writer of the Year, the Russ Catlin Award, and the Henry T. McLemore Award. The Canton, North Carolina, native had a book published on NASCAR driver Ryan Newman in 2004 and one on former NASCAR team owner Ray Evernham in 2002.

Kim Wilson is a freelance writer and the co-author/co-editor of *Living Miracles: Stories of Hope from Parents of Premature Babies*. She's the mother of two sons, Dustin and Dakota, and is married to MSG George Wilson. From February through November Kim lives for the Sprint Cup races. For more information please visit her Web site at www.kimwilsononline.com.

Gillian Zucker became the fourth president of the Auto Club Speedway on June 23, 2005. She is the first female president of a track that hosts auto racing's most popular event, the NASCAR Sprint Cup Series. Prior to her appointment at the Auto Club Speedway, Zucker served as Daytona International Speedway's vice president of business operations and development. She graduated from Hamilton College, where she received her Bachelor of Arts degree in creative writing. She resides in Los Angeles.

Meet Our Authors

Jack Canfield is the co-creator of the *Chicken Soup for the Soul* series, which *Time* magazine has called "the publishing phenomenon of the decade." Jack is also the co-author of many other bestselling books.

Jack is the CEO of the Canfield Training Group in Santa Barbara, California, and founder of the Foundation for Self-Esteem in Culver City, California. He has conducted intensive personal and professional development seminars on the principles of success for more than a million people in twenty-three countries, has spoken to hundreds of thousands of people at more than 1,000 corporations, universities, professional conferences and conventions, and has been seen by millions more on national television shows.

Jack has received many awards and honors, including three honorary doctorates and a Guinness World Records Certificate for having seven books from the *Chicken Soup for the Soul* series appearing on the New York Times bestseller list on May 24, 1998.

You can reach Jack at www.jackcanfield.com.

Mark Victor Hansen is the co-founder of Chicken Soup for the Soul, along with Jack Canfield. He is a sought-after keynote speaker, bestselling author, and marketing maven. Mark's powerful messages of possibility, opportunity, and action have created powerful change in thousands of organizations and millions of individuals worldwide.

Mark is a prolific writer with many bestselling books in addition to the *Chicken Soup for the Soul* series. Mark has had a profound influence in the field of human potential through his library of audios, videos, and articles in the areas of big thinking, sales achievement, wealth building, publishing success, and personal and professional development. He is also the founder of the MEGA Seminar Series.

Mark has received numerous awards that honor his entrepreneurial spirit, philanthropic heart, and business acumen. He is a lifetime member of the Horatio Alger Association of Distinguished Americans.

You can reach Mark at www.markvictorhansen.com.

A native of North Carolina's Outer Banks, **Cathy Elliott** has lived in the Darlington, South Carolina area since 1993.

Cathy began her journalism career in 1994 as a columnist for Darlington's weekly newspaper, the *News and Press*, and was named that publication's first female editor in 1995. In 1996, she co-founded the arts and entertainment weekly magazine *Five O'clock Friday*. In 2000, she made the move to NASCAR, serving as director of public relations at Darlington Raceway for seven years. Her weekly opinion column, *On NASCAR*, is syndicated nationally through the NASCAR Public Relations department's media Web site.

Cathy is a member of the National Motorsports Press Association and the South Carolina Press Association, where she has received numerous awards for excellence in journalism. In addition to stock car racing, she loves beagles, the beach, and the UNC Tarheels, not necessarily in that order.

Cathy returned to the *News and Press* in 2007, where she currently serves as both editor and publisher.

Thank You!

Anyone who works in the wonderful world of NASCAR will attest to the fact that the sport isn't the only thing that is fast-paced — so is the lifestyle. Every second is valuable. Many thanks to the drivers, broadcasters, writers, industry professionals and fans who took the time to share their love of NASCAR through the stories in this book. When we say NASCAR is a family, we really mean it. Having the opportunity to work with all of you for nearly a decade still seems slightly surreal to me.

Thanks to NASCAR CEO Brian France for your support of this project. Your family is the reason we are all able to do what we do. I can't wait to see your vision of NASCAR's future play out in years to come. If the past is any indication, it will be spectacular.

To my publisher Amy Newmark, editor Kristiana Glavin, assistant publisher D'ette Corona and everyone at Chicken Soup for the Soul, well, let's just say I hope one day to have your patience. In NASCAR, rookies have stripes on the bumpers of their cars so the professionals around them can adjust to the fact that they're dealing with someone less experienced. Fortunately stripes are fashionable right now, since I have been sporting one on my own bumper for the past year. Thanks for bearing with me.

I owe a huge debt of gratitude to everyone at NASCAR Public Relations, particularly my editor and friend Herb Branham. In addition to attempting to keep me on the straight and narrow, Herb has been my go-between on more than one occasion when people questioned the wisdom of publishing a NASCAR column that compared drivers to dog breeds, or race tracks to college mascots. I guess it has all worked out OK.

Thanks to Catherine McNeil and John Farrell of NASCAR Publishing for their careful and concise editing of the manuscript. Your attention to detail is a credit to NASCAR.

When Chicken Soup for the Soul President Bob Jacobs first approached me about this project, I thought I was the victim of a practical joke. I will be forever grateful that Bob and CSS CEO Bill Rouhana actually took me seriously.

Finally, much love to my wonderful family and friends and my tolerant co-workers at the *News and Press*. No one can quite figure out how I came from a tiny fishing village in eastern North Carolina to the huge phenomenon of NASCAR, but we all think it's a pretty cool place to be. How did I get so lucky?

~Cathy Elliott

Improving Your Life
Every Day

Real people sharing real stories—for fifteen years. Now, Chicken Soup for the Soul has gone beyond the bookstore to become a world leader in life improvement. Through books, movies, DVDs, online resources and other partnerships, we bring hope, courage, inspiration and love to hundreds of millions of people around the world. Chicken Soup for the Soul's writers and readers belong to a one-of-a-kind global community, sharing advice, support, guidance, comfort, and knowledge.

Chicken Soup for the Soul stories have been translated into more than forty languages and can be found in more than one hundred countries. Every day, millions of people experience a Chicken Soup for the Soul story in a book, magazine, newspaper or online. As we share our life experiences through these stories, we offer hope, comfort and inspiration to one another. The stories travel from person to person, and from country to country, helping to improve lives everywhere.

Share with Us

We all have had Chicken Soup for the Soul moments in our lives. If you would like to share your story or poem with millions of people around the world, go to chickensoup.com and click on "Submit Your Story." You may be able to help another reader, and become a published author at the same time. Some of our past contributors have launched writing and speaking careers from the publication of their stories in our books!

Our submission volume has been increasing steadily—the quality and quantity of your submissions has been fabulous. We only accept story submissions via our website. They are no longer accepted via mail or fax.

To contact us regarding other matters, please send us an e-mail through webmaster@chickensoupforthesoul.com, or fax or write us at:

Chicken Soup for the Soul
P.O. Box 700
Cos Cob, CT 06807-0700
Fax: 203-861-7194

One more note from your friends at Chicken Soup for the Soul: Occasionally, we receive an unsolicited book manuscript from one of our readers, and we would like to respectfully inform you that we do not accept unsolicited manuscripts and we must discard the ones that appear.

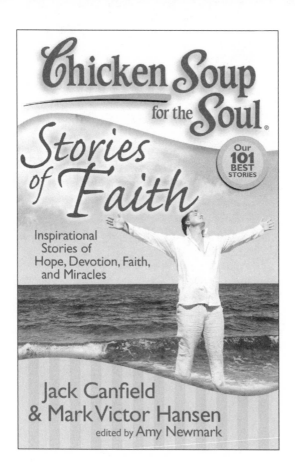

Everyone needs some faith and hope! This book is just the ticket, with a collection of 101 of the best stories from Chicken Soup for the Soul's past on faith, hope, miracles, and devotion. These true stories, written by regular people, tell of prayers answered miraculously, amazing coincidences, rediscovered faith, and the serenity that comes from believing in a greater power, appealing to Christians and those of other faiths—anyone who seeks inspiration.

978-1-935096-14-6

More great stories for NASCAR fans!

Chicken Soup for the Soul
for the **Soul**®

Count Your Blessings

101 Stories of Gratitude, Fortitude, and Silver Linings

Jack Canfield,
Mark Victor Hansen, Amy Newmark,
Laura Robinson & Elizabeth Bryan

This uplifting book reminds readers of the blessings in their lives, despite financial stress, natural disasters, health scares and illnesses, housing challenges and family worries. This feel-good book is a great gift for New Year's or Easter, for someone going through a difficult time, or for Christmas. These stories of optimism, faith, and strength remind us of the simple pleasures of family, home, health, and inexpensive good times.

978-1-935096-42-9

More great stories for NASCAR fans!

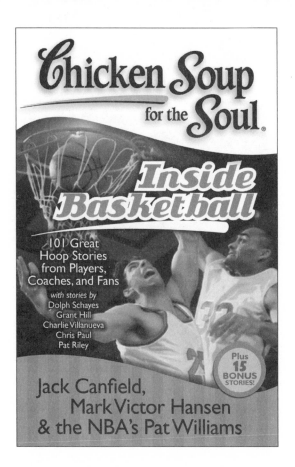

Chicken Soup for the Soul
for the Soul.

Inside Basketball

101 Great Hoop Stories from Players, Coaches, and Fans

with stories by
Dolph Schayes
Grant Hill
Charlie Villanueva
Chris Paul
Pat Riley

Plus 15 BONUS STORIES!

Jack Canfield,
Mark Victor Hansen
& the NBA's Pat Williams

The Orlando Magic's Pat Williams, well-known author and motivational speaker, compiled great stories from on and off the basketball court. With inside stories from well-known coaches and players, fascinating behind-the-scene looks, and anecdotes from celebrities in the sports world. Words of wisdom and motivation from Pat are included, along with 15 bonus stories, including one about President Obama's favorite pickup game on the campaign trail.

978-1-935096-29-0

More great stories for NASCAR fans!